A Toolbook for Quality Improvement and Problem Solving

A Toolbook for Quality Improvement and Problem Solving

David Straker

Prentice Hall

London   New York   Toronto   Sydney   Tokyo   Singapore
Madrid   Mexico City   Munich

First published 1995 by
Prentice Hall International (UK) Limited
Campus 400, Maylands Avenue
Hemel Hempstead
Hertfordshire, HP2 7EZ
A division of
Simon & Schuster International Group

Printed and bound in Great Britain at the University Press, Cambridge

Library of Congress Cataloging in Publication Data

A catalogue record for this book is available from
the publisher

British Library Cataloguing in Publication Data

A catalogue record for this book is available from
the British Library

ISBN 0-13-746892-X

1 2 3 4 5   99 98 97 96 95

Contents

Preface

The original idea for this book came about after I had become involved in working with quality improvement teams, helping them to work through a problem solving process to make their work processes more efficient and effective.

In preparation for this work, I found that I wanted three distinct types of information:

(a) I wanted to know what tools were available and to be able to understand them in sufficient detail to be able to know which to recommend for which situation, and then to be able to help individuals and teams make effective use of them.

I wanted to know about a broad range of tools as this would help to sharpen my choice of a basic toolkit whilst giving me a deep toolbox of specialized tools for specific situations.

(b) I wanted information about tools that I could give to the people who were using or intending to use them. This information was needed as a practical reference for those who had been trained in using these tools, and as basic learning material for those who did not have the opportunity for such a gentle introduction to their use.

(c) I also wanted people who were not directly involved in the work of these teams to be able to understand the results of team activities. This included managers and others who had to authorize or participate in the changes identified. These people did not have to understand the mechanics of using the tools, but they did have to understand the output from their use and to have confidence in these results.

In looking for material to satisfy the above needs, I found a number of excellent books and articles, but no single source. Most books tended to fall into one of two categories, being either too technical or containing too brief details for the above purposes. Others contained useful detail, but focused on only a few tools.

The detailed books were clearly aiming at quality professionals and often delved into significant levels of mathematics and statistics. Although these were helpful to me, it was often heavy going, and impractical to expect other people to use them. The less detailed books and articles were useful for giving an overview of tools, but seldom contained enough meat to enable the tools to be confidently used in practice.

Most noticeably, there were very few books in the middle ground, giving sufficient detail for the tools to be clearly understood and used, but without the level of theory that might dissuade ordinary people from reading them.

Overall, I learned from books, articles, training courses, colleagues and from experience in teaching, facilitating and applying many tools in quality improvement and problem solving situations. This book is a result of that learning, and is, to some extent, the book I originally wanted, describing a broad set of tools in sufficient detail so that they can be both understood and used.

Although quality professionals may find it useful, the main group of people it is aimed at are those who will use or be affected by the use of tools in quality improvement or problem solving activities. I have assumed that these people are intelligent, but are neither mathematicians nor interested in theory beyond that needed to understand the application and results of using the tool.

The tools described come from a number of different origins. The most well-known set of tools is sometimes known as the 'first seven QC tools'. There is also a second set of seven tools, somtimes called the 'seven new QC tools' or the 'seven tools for management and planning' or just 'seven MP tools'. For simplicity, they are referred to here as 'the first seven tools' and 'the second seven tools'. To make matters more complex, there are differences of opinion about which tools make up each seven. All variations are described in this book.

There are also a number of other useful sources of tools which have been tapped. General quality assurance gives additional tools for use in various situations. Method Study, a forerunner of modern quality assurance, gives tools for investigating the detailed actions within a process. Computer systems analysis and design give graphical ways of describing different aspects of processes. There are also some general business tools that can be used, for example those that help with decision making.

Another complication is that there are often several available names for one tool, some of which can sound quite impressive but can also be off-putting. To counteract this, I have generally used the simplest and most descriptive names. For example, I use 'Relations Diagram' [Mizuno 88] rather than 'Interrelationship Digraph' [Brassard 89], and 'Tree Diagram' [Brassard 89] rather than 'Systematic Diagram' [Mizuno 88]. Where alternative names exist, these are mentioned and can also be found in the index.

The book is structured as follows. Chapter 1 describes a framework for process improvement and problem solving projects, in which the tools may be used or their application understood. You may or may not wish to use this framework, or may already use something similar. Chapter 2 discusses common themes in tools and shows that, although there are a large number of tools, they are largely based on a limited set of principles. Chapter 3 looks at the practical aspects of turning dry descriptions into active and useful tools. An important point discussed here is that, although there are large number of tools described in the book, in practice most work is done best with a selected small subset. Chapters 4 to 7 describe some general concepts of process improvement which are salient to understanding broad sets of tools.

The rest of the book is taken up with one chapter per tool. Each chapter uses a standard format, with the following sections:

What it's for
This is a one-line description of the basic purpose of the tool.

When to use it
This describes basic situations in which the tool may best be used. It also indicates where the tool may be used in the project framework described in Chapter 1.

How to understand it
This section helps the use of the tool to be understood, without necessarily knowing the detail of how it is applied. This will help people who will be affected by the use of the tool to have confidence in its use and to interpret the results.

Example
This gives a complete example of the tool being used, plus descriptions of several other situations where it might be used.

In the examples used in the book, I have opted to randomly use 'he' and 'she', rather than the more cumbersome 'he/she' or trying to massage sentences into some kind of neutral form.

How to do it
This gives step-by-step numbered instructions on how to apply the tool in practice.

Practical variations
In practice, there are often many different ways that tools can be used and this section briefly describes a number of these. Thus, as you become experienced in the use of the tool, the ideas here may help you to customize it to suit individual situations. This section may also describe related or similar tools.

Notes
Any points that did not fit into the preceding sections are given here, for example notes on the source of the tool and any alternative names that it may be called.

See also
This gives references to other tools in the book and to other outside sources of information.

To help you find the tool you want, tools that may be used in a range of situations are described in a 'tool finder' section at the back of the book.

In the end, however, the success of using the tools lies in your hands. A tool will not solve problems by itself, but it can make your task easier and more enjoyable.

David Straker, August 1994

Acknowledgements

As with most books, the help with ideas, learning and application has come from many sources, and I am indebted to many people, a few of whom are mentioned below.

Thank you to colleagues in Hewlett Packard for their encouragement, reviews and ideas, including Yin Wong and Dave Whittall. Also to all those people with whom I have worked with in problem solving and quality improvement activities. Thanks also to friends in the IQA, including Neal Esslemont, Alex McKie, Peter Dack and Ted Beckett.

I am also grateful to all the authors in the bibliography, each of whom has helped me to learn something more about both the theory and practice of various tools.

Publishers also do their share of helping, not the least in having the confidence to publish the book! Thus thanks are due to all at Prentice Hall, especially Susan Richards, John Yates and Ann Greenwood.

Man does not write by word processor alone, and my essential cups of tea, along with endless patience, grammatical reviews and many other forms of assistance came from my wife, Eleri. My two children, Heledd and Geraint, make it all worthwhile, and our retrievers, Gwen and Bella, also give their share of affection.

Dedication

This book is dedicated to my sister, Margaret, for the strength and quality of her spirit.

Part 1 : Application

Before tools can be used, consideration needs to be given to where and how they may be applied. Part 1 takes this step by first identifying a framework that may be used in quality improvement or problem-solving projects (Chapter 1), then linking this to actual tools through the identification of common themes where tools may be applied (Chapter 2). Chapter 3 discusses some of the practicalities of using tools and the considerations taken into account that can help to make their use successful.

1 Applications For Tools

Objective of chapter
To identify the situations where there is a need for tools.

Tools have no value until they are used, so in order to identify those that may be useful in quality improvement and problem solving, the applications where they might be used must first be recognized and understood.

This chapter describes a general framework that can be used for both quality improvement and problem solving, and from this identifies applications where the tools described in this book may be used.

Quality improvement and problem solving

Quality improvement and general problem solving both address similar situations where what is (or is not) happening is less than desirable. In either case, the aim is to rectify the situation.

A major difference between the approaches taken is that quality improvement activities tend to be organized and part of a larger program, whilst problem solving is usually more reactive and unplanned.

Despite these differences, the similarity in aim means that a similar approach can be taken to both situations, although in practice the immediacy of general problem solving may mean that a more abbreviated (and consequently less certain) approach may be taken. Nevertheless, if available tools are understood, then situations where they can be usefully applied may be identified.

Process improvement

A way of viewing any problem is to consider everything that is done as a *process*, and that quality improvement or problem solving is simply a matter of identifying and improving the (formal or informal) processes in question (Chapter 4 discusses processes in greater detail).

Quality improvement and problem solving can thus both be treated as *process improvement* activities, and a common approach can be used for either activity.

Individual process improvement activities may be carried out as projects, using a structured approach to achieve specific objectives. This approach is typically embodied in a framework which provides guidelines for repeatable and reliable projects.

A framework for process improvement projects

There are probably as many process improvement frameworks as there are companies with improvement programs, although many tend to be very similar. The process improvement framework described here is not intended to replace your framework; its main aim is to provide a general context in which the applications for tools may be identified.

The basic stages of the framework are:

1. Identify   Identification and selection of the process to be improved.
2. Define   Resourcing project, setting objectives and planning future stages.
3. Problem   Gaining a detailed understanding of the process and identifying specific problems to be addressed.
4. Cause   Identification and verification of key causes of specific problems.
5. Solution   Identification and verification of alternative solutions to key causes.
6. Implement   Implementation of identified solution.
7. Review   Checking on success of project.
8. Follow-up   Action on findings of review, including standardization of successes, following up on failures and identifying further improvements.

There are several situations where stages of the framework may need to be repeated, either within a stage where an assumption is proved to be incorrect, or as a follow-up action, as shown in Fig. 1.1.

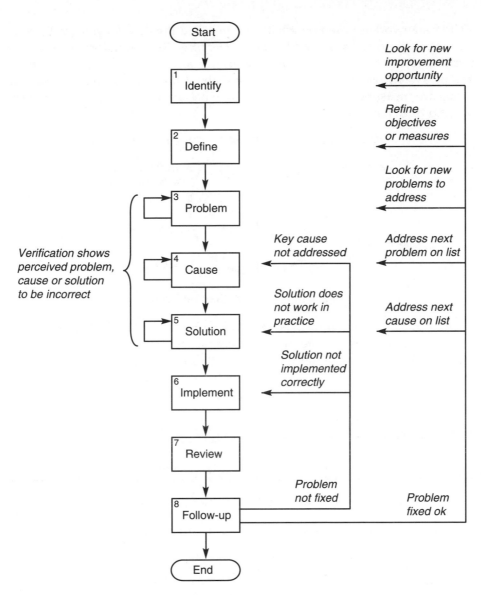

Fig. 1.1 Loops within the project framework

The project may also have a widely varying size and scope, ranging from a one-person, one-hour project to a project with a multi-departmental team working for several months (or even years) on a significant problem. In each case, the framework can be used at the appropriate level.

The framework is based on what is often called the *PDCA cycle* (or *Deming cycle* after its popularizer or *Shewart cycle*, after its originator). This uses a repeating cycle of Plan, Do, Check and Act as a simple framework for a learning system, as in Fig. 1.2. A key point about this cycle is that incremental actions are measured and compared with expectations in order to learn what does and does not work.

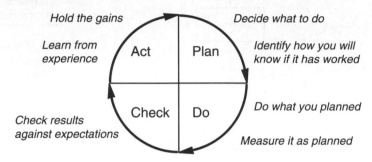

Fig. 1.2 The PDCA Deming cycle

PDCA in the process improvement project framework is shown in Fig. 1.3. The 'plan' stage takes a large portion, because it is focused on reducing the chance of the implementation failing. In addition, each individual stage may follow a PDCA cycle. For example, potential causes are identified and then checked as valid before solutions are sought.

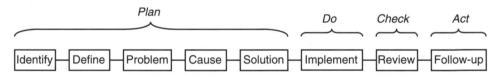

Fig. 1.3 PDCA in process improvement project framework

The stages of the framework are described in greater detail in the following sections.

1. Identify

The first step in a process improvement project is to identify the process which is to be improved. This may be obvious or a given situation, for example when dealing with a known problem or where measurement of an existing process indicates a need for further attention. However, there may be a number of known potential improvement projects, and the problem is now to select which project to do first.

Activities in this stage may thus include:
- Reviewing existing measurements, looking for poorly performing processes.
- Identifying customers, their needs, expectations and satisfaction with current processes.
- Defining criteria for selecting candidate projects.
- Describing candidate projects in a format that will ease selection.
- Selecting a process to be improved.

When starting a quality improvement program, it is important to select early projects that will lend credibility to it. They should be reasonably easy to do (but not too easy!) and should give significant results. Similar care should be used when selecting subsequent projects, balancing the cost, potential benefit and chance of success.

2. Define

Once the project is selected, it must be given the best chance of success. This includes ensuring that the right people with the right skills are working on it, it is clear what 'success' means and the way forward to achieving this is clear.

Activities in this stage may include:
- Identifying resources needed, such as team members, expertise, training and facilitation.
- Gaining commitment from management to support project.
- Recruiting and training the project team.
- Gaining a basic understanding of the problem to be addressed.
- Understanding the context and purpose of the process to be improved.
- Defining specific objectives for the project.
- Identifying measures to determine how well the objectives are met.
- Deciding what data to collect and how it will be collected.
- Making initial plans for future stages.

In practice, the most difficult part of this stage can be in gaining the real commitment of resource, particularly where it requires people to be taken away from other high -priority jobs. It can also be a difficult period where the real problem is as yet unknown (in which case, the decisions made here may be revisited during the next stage).

3. Problem

In order to identify specific problems to address, the current performance of the process needs to be grasped in sufficient detail to enable the identification of those parts which are in need of attention. This usually requires more detailed information than is available when the project is first selected.

Activities in this stage may include:
- Mapping out the process or problem to understand it in detail and identify potential problem areas.
- Measuring the process to identify and verify problems.
- Prioritization and selection of specific problems to be addressed.
- Revising plans to reflect new knowledge.

When identifying problems to address, it is usually better to select only a few (or even one) at any one time, as multiple changes to the process can make it difficult afterwards to determine the effectiveness of each change. This is also true of the Cause and Solution stages. A common characteristic of this framework is illustrated in Fig. 1.4, where a broad set of possible items are first identified, then one or two are selected to be carried forward for further action. This pair of activities also occurs for Problem, Cause and Solution stages and is sometimes called *divergent thinking* and *convergent thinking* (or simply *divergence* and *convergence*).

4. Cause

Once the process or problem is better understood, steps may be taken to identify the key causes of the selected problem, thus ensuring that the problem will be removed or reduced, rather than just having its symptoms treated.

Activities in this stage may include:
- Identifying possible causes of the problem.
- Selection of key causes to address.
- Determining measures to verify identified key causes.
- Designing experiments to verify key causes.
- Measuring the process to verify that causes are key, as suspected.

In practice, there may be a temptation to skip this stage and go direct to an 'obvious' solution. Although this may work, it can also result in a solution that addresses symptoms or minor causes, rather than the key cause, and should thus be resisted.

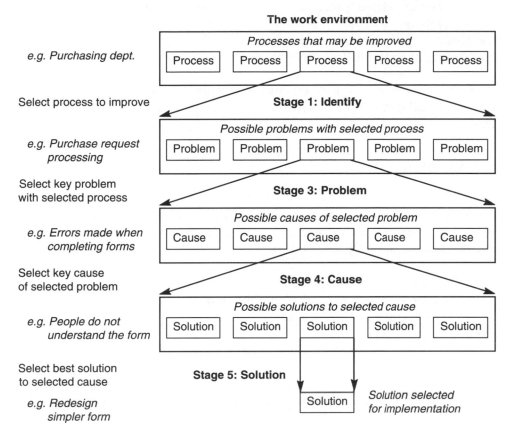

The work environment

e.g. Purchasing dept.	Processes that may be improved
	Process Process Process Process Process

Select process to improve — **Stage 1: Identify**

e.g. Purchase request processing	Possible problems with selected process
	Problem Problem Problem Problem Problem

Select key problem with selected process — **Stage 3: Problem**

e.g. Errors made when completing forms	Possible causes of selected problem
	Cause Cause Cause Cause Cause

Select key cause of selected problem — **Stage 4: Cause**

e.g. People do not understand the form	Possible solutions to selected cause
	Solution Solution Solution Solution Solution

Select best solution to selected cause — **Stage 5: Solution**

e.g. Redesign simpler form

Solution — *Solution selected for implementation*

Fig. 1.4 Successive divergence and convergence

5. Solution

When the key causes are identified and verified, then potential solutions can similarly be identified, narrowed down and checked. The checking should also ensure that, although the solution may fix the key causes, it does not result in other problems outside the immediate problem area, for example in related processes (this is often called *sub-optimization*).

Activities in this stage may include:
- Identifying a number of possible solutions to fix the identified key causes.
- Selection of a subset of possible solutions.

- Identifying feasibility, cost and benefit of selected solutions.
- Examining related processes, to ensure the solution will not adversely affect them.
- Designing experiments to verify selected solutions.
- Testing of final solution, preferably using measures identified in stage 2.

In practice, there may be a clear solution to a given cause, which can simplify this stage, although there is sometimes the danger of the 'obvious' obscuring the ideal.

6. Implement

Once the solution to fix the key causes of the identified problems is selected, it can then be put into effect. Note that the solution is still on trial until it is proven to work in practice, and in higher risk situations the implementation may be done in carefully reviewed stages.

Activities in this stage may include:
- Obtaining authority to implement the solution.
- Training people on the changes made.
- Changing documentation.
- Ensuring that the solution implemented is as planned.
- Using measurements (as identified in stage 2) to identify the real improvements.
- Measuring related processes, to ensure that they are not adversely affected.

It may seem unnecessary to recheck the solution, but in practice it is not uncommon for changes that work well under artificial test conditions to cause problems when put into more general use. This measurement also gives the real proof that the solution really works and enables the actual benefits gained to be identified.

7. Review

This stage is used to determine the real success of the project, both in the short-term gains of the most recent implementation activity and in the overall success of the tools and processes used. The results are then used in the following stage to determine subsequent actions.

Activities at this stage may include:
- Reviewing measures made, to determine the actual improvement in the process against goals or expectations.
- Determining why improvements did not occur as expected.
- Reviewing the use of the tools and framework, to find how well they were applied and how their use may be improved.
- Deciding whether to continue the project, by looping back to previous stages for further process improvement, or to draw it to a close.
- Holding a general project review of the success of the overall project to determine 'best practices' and other learning points.

In practice, this can be a difficult stage when improvements have not occurred as expected, and it can be tempting to blame the tools. If that can be overcome, then it can be a real learning opportunity, especially when things have gone wrong.

8. Follow-up

Depending on the results of the review, there may be three different classes of follow-up action:

If the implementation was successful:
- Standardizing the solution, writing it up as a normal operating procedure and spreading it to other areas.
- Looping back to previous stages for further improvements.
- Closing down the project, as below.

If the implementation was unsuccessful:
- Addressing the cause of the lack of success, to prevent it recurring.
- Looping back to previous stages, to correct and repeat actions.

If the project is being closed down:
- Writing up the project as a 'success story'.
- Identifying additional improvements that may be made in the future.
- Presenting results to managers and other groups.
- Using the lessons learned to improve the improvement process itself.
- Celebrating the success.
- Planning for future projects.

A difficult part of this stage, particularly if the implementation was unsuccessful, is in maintaining enthusiasm and keeping the project alive.

Applications in process improvement projects

Within this process improvement framework, the broad activities of collecting, organizing and interpreting information in various forms appear regularly, reflecting the general approach of basing decisions and actions on a good understanding of the best available data. These three areas are expanded in a Tree Diagram in Fig. 1.5 and discussed further in the sections below in order to identify activities which may be addressed with specific tools.

Collecting information

The first step in information-based decision making is to collect the best data available, whether numeric (quantitative) or textual (qualitative). If this data is made up of verifiable facts, then this will enable confident decisions to be made with it. Unfortunately, this certainty is not available in many problem situations where unverifiable information may be classified as 'opinion'.

Typically, opinions come from people who have a good working knowledge of the situation and they often give very useful and credible data. Sometimes, however, opinions may be affected by personal prejudice or pet theories and the vehemence with which opinions are voiced should not affect the impartiality of anyone using them.

A third situation exists where the opinions are deliberately creative, such as where possible solutions to a known problem cause are being devised.

The tools used to collect data must thus be able to cope with demands for different levels of certainty and assist in creating an appropriate environment for that collection.

Structuring information

The effort required for collecting information varies greatly between different situations; some projects start with much available information whilst others require laborious data collection processes. Whichever way the information is acquired, it still must be organized into a format which enables appropriate decisions and actions to be identified.

The structuring of information is largely divided by the type of information being organized. Traditional quality control information is numeric, reflecting accurate measurement and enabling certain decisions to be made. In many other problem situations, the information is more qualitative and the working unit is typically a sentence or phrase describing some aspect of the problem. In this case, these chunks of information must be organized into a form which sheds further light on the problem.

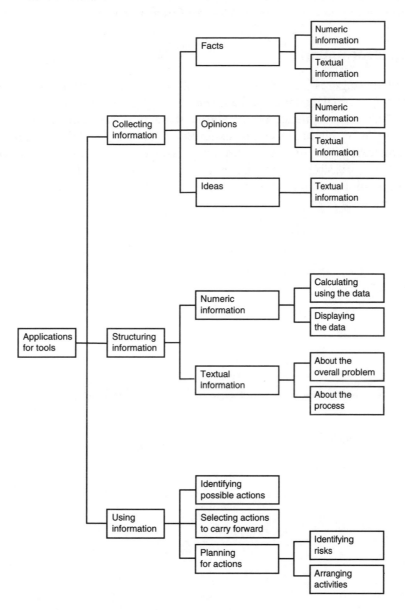

Fig. 1.5 Application areas within process improvement project framework

The tools for organizing information thus need to convert what is often a mass of unintelligible data into a format where key decision points are easily identified and good decisions may be confidently made.

Using information

The third stage is *using* the information found through collection and structuring, to make confident decisions.

The first stage of usage is to identify the actual decision points, and tools may help to highlight these. For example, a tool might highlight that several problems exist. This may be followed by selection of items to carry forward, from a list of possibilities. Finally, in order to ensure these happen as required, the implementation may be carefully planned, including identification and management of risks.

2 Tools For Applications

Objective of chapter
To identify tools that satisfy the needs of applications.

For tools to add value in any situation, they must help satisfy specific needs. This chapter identifies key needs in these areas and identifies characteristics of tools that are required to address these needs. These are then used to classify and identify types of tools. Finally, tools in this book are related back to the applications that were identified in Chapter 1.

Key needs

There are two key needs that can be identified for quality improvement and problem-solving tools:

1. Ease of use   Enabling anyone to make good use of the tools.
2. Reliability   To give confident, repeatable results.

Ease of use
Quality improvement and problem-solving tools need to be usable by anyone in their normal working environment, and not just highly trained experts. Although it can be useful to know why the tool works, it is most important that people who use the tools know how to apply them and interpret the results. In practice, the usability of a tool is likely to be as great an influence on the decision to use it as the reliability of the results that may be achieved.

Another important factor in usability is the ease with which people can learn to use the tools. If this hurdle cannot be surmounted, then again the tool is not likely to be used, even if its eventual application is easy and its results are of significant value.

The reliability of the results gained from using a tool is also related to its ease of use. This is because easy tools give less scope for misunderstanding or misuse.

Many problem-solving situations require that people work as a team, either because of the amount of work to be done, or because individuals have specific skills or knowledge that is required. In such circumstances, tools should help people to work together towards the solution (Chapter 7 discusses teamwork in more detail).

Reliability of results

Ad hoc problem solving, such as 'how to open a stuck door', can produce good results and is appropriate in many situations. However, in many other situations there is a need for greater confidence that an effective solution will be found. A key reason for using tools is to provide this confidence.

There are two related areas of reliability in the use of tools. Firstly, their application needs to be predicable and controllable, so different people using the tools under different circumstances may get comparable results. Secondly, the tools should give results which can be confidently interpreted, enabling good decisions to be made.

To some extent, the need for reliability can work against the need for ease of use, such as when a good measurement is required quickly. In such cases the degree of reliability that is required must be understood and an appropriate tool selected.

Tool characteristics

Two very evident characteristics of tools are the use of visual techniques and the separate handling of numerical and textual information. A third characteristic is that tools tend to bring a degree of structure to their use.

Pictorial tools

Much of the way people understand and communicate is through the visual sense, as this allows us to rapidly absorb and process large quantities of information. Many tools take advantage of this, using some form of visual display to make them easier to use.

This visual component is particularly helpful when interpreting information, as the first impression of a visual display is as a whole, with the overall shape of the information helping to give an immediate understanding of the 'big picture'. From this, attention may be focused on specific decision points and other areas of interest.

Pictures can also be easier to build, and some tools make use of this, transforming what might otherwise be a dry reporting process into an interesting and productive activity of piecing together the jigsaw puzzle of the problem.

Some situations suit visual methods very well, whilst others are less graphic, and tools range from highly pictorial ones through those that provide some visual organization to those that are not at all graphic.

Numeric and non-numeric tools

Numeric information is usually more desirable when making decisions than non-numeric information, as it shows the relative size of measured items, enabling clear decisions to be made.

Unfortunately, not all information is numeric and, as indicated in the applications identified in Chapter 1, there is a need for tools that can be used with less structured information such as human opinions or named activities.

Several tools introduce the benefit of numeric aspects to situations which are initially non-numeric, although the accuracy of the figures may well vary according to the rigour with which they are derived.

Structure in tools

All tools are structured in some way, in that they contain rules for their own use. They also often help to structure information in a way that enables it to be interpreted and key decisions to be made.

Structure in tools helps the key need for reliability, as a defined structure results in a repeatable process. Assuming the structure is correct, this will also lead to optimum results. Structure also helps usability, as it provides a framework for action which answers the question 'How?' and enable the people to get quickly down to the more immediate 'What?' of the situation.

The degree of structure in a tool may reflect the confidence that can be placed in its results, and tools may be selected on this basis. Some tools, such as Brainstorming, need to break down barriers and minimize structure, leaving only enough control to make the session work.

Specific tool types

These broad groupings of pictorial and numeric tools can be combined to describe specific types of tool and to identify actual examples of these. Figure 2.1 lists the tools described in this book and shows their basic pictorial and numeric type.

This is a useful way of dividing up the tools, as it shows how many different tools actually use similar principles for displaying different aspects of problems.

Relationship: ◎ = strong, ○ = partial, △ = weak Tool	Pictorial		Non-pictorial	
	Numeric	Non-numeric	Numeric	Non-numeric
Activity Network	△	◎	○	
Affinity Diagram		◎		
Bar Chart	◎			
Brainstorming				◎
Cause-Effect Diagram		◎		
Check Sheet	○	○	◎	
Control Chart	◎		○	
Decision Tree	○	○		
Design of Experiments	○	○	○	○
Fault Tree Analysis		◎		
Failure Mode and Effects Analysis	△		◎	◎
Flowchart		◎		
Flow Process Chart		◎		
Force-Field Diagram		◎	△	
Gantt Chart	○	◎		
Histogram	◎			
IDEF0		◎		
Line Chart	◎			
Matrix Diagram	○	◎		
Matrix Data Analysis Chart	◎		◎	
Nominal Group Technique				◎
Pareto Diagram	◎			
Prioritization Matrix	△	◎	○	
Process Capability			◎	
Process Decision Program Chart		◎		
Relations Diagram		◎		
Scatter Diagram	◎		○	
String Diagram		◎	△	
Surveys			○	◎
Tables			○	◎
Tree Diagram		◎		
Value Analysis			○	◎
Voting			◎	○

Fig. 2.1 Tools and types

Non-numeric pictorial tools

Non-numeric information often arrives in, or can be broken down into, discrete and relatively independent chunks. Visual tools help to discover and organize these chunks, showing the various types of relationships between them.

Hierarchies

Hierarchies are used in several tools, where they are used to either break down information into component parts or to build up detailed data into an organized structure. Hierarchies are often called *trees* and are characterized by their parent-child organization, as shown in Fig. 2.2. A *parent* item has any number of children, whilst a *child* has only one parent. At the top of the hierarchy is the *root*, or one parent with no parents of its own, whilst at the bottom of the hierarchy are *leaves*, or individual items with no children of their own.

 Examples: Tree Diagram, Cause-Effect Diagram, Fault Tree Analysis

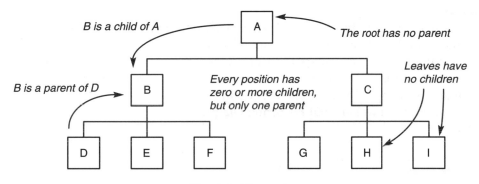

Fig. 2.2 Hierarchy

Networks

Networks provide pictures of actual or conceptual systems, and are characterized by the way they show the *relationship* between individual elements of that system, as in Fig. 2.3. They also effectively appear where hierarchies become complex, with cross-links between individual elements.

 The relationship between network elements varies with the tool. For example, an Activity Network shows sequential relationship, whilst a Relations Diagram may show causal relationship.

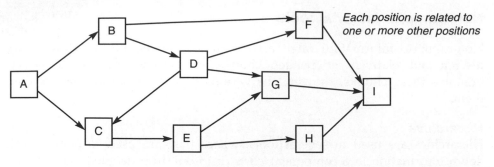

Each position is related to one or more other positions

Fig. 2.3 Network

Networks usually show their elements within boxes, which may be shaped to indicate the element type. The box clearly delimits the element, visually separating it from other elements. The boxes are then connected with lines. If there is directionality in the relationship, then this is commonly shown with arrowheads or other symbols on the lines.

Examples: Relations Diagram, Activity Network

Maps

Maps may be thought of as a subset of networks which are used to show the elements and relationships within actual systems, as in Fig. 2.4.

A common use of a map is to break down a process into its individual actions. This may be repeated in a hierarchical fashion, resulting in a sequence of maps showing increasing levels of detail.

Examples: Flowchart, IDEF0, String Diagram

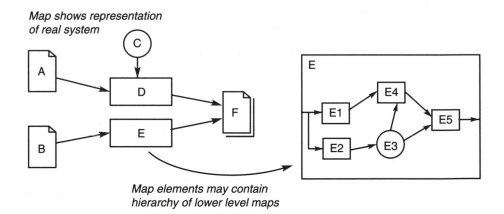

Map shows representation of real system

Map elements may contain hierarchy of lower level maps

Fig. 2.4 Map

Numeric pictorial tools

Numeric information lends itself well to visual representation in graphs and chart. These convert what can be a mass of unintelligible numbers into a form which clearly conveys important attributes of the problem.

Block charts

A block is a pictorial way of representing a discrete quantity, where the physical area or size of the block is proportional to the measured quantity, as in Fig. 2.5.

Block charts typically show the quantity of an item within a defined range, for example the number of loaves of bread bought in a town during the first week of January. Multiple blocks may then be used to compare similar measures. Decision points may be identified by the actual or relative size of blocks.

Examples: Bar Chart, Pareto Chart, Histogram

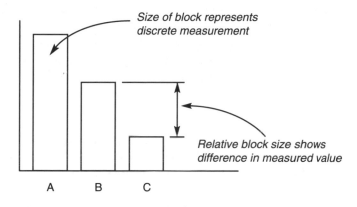

Fig. 2.5 Block chart

Point graphs

Point graphs generally plot pairs of measurements in a two-dimensional 'traditional' x-y format, as in Fig. 2.6. Lines may be added to show the sequence of measurement, overall trends or significant boundaries.

Decision areas are typically highlighted by the way points form groups, change across a sequence of measurements, or cross significant boundaries.

Example: Control Chart, Line Graph, Scatter Diagram

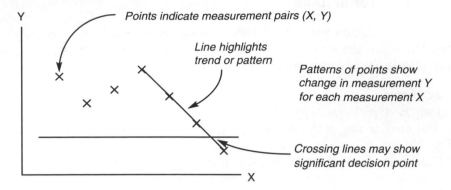

Fig. 2.6 Point graph

Numeric non-pictorial tools

Tools that are numeric and pictorial are usually limited by the complexity of the data that they can display. For example, a complex graph containing a dozen different lines can be extremely difficult to interpret. This type of data may be better shown in a numeric, non-graphical format. These have the advantage of showing exact numbers, but lose the impact and ability to highlight decision points of more graphical displays.

Matrices

A matrix shows a set of data in a rectangular format where each of the two dimensions either represents a simple variable or a set of related items, as in Fig. 2.7. They can often be considered as a form of point graph, where a point is replaced with a cell containing a value rather than a simple mark.

Matrices may also be used for non-numeric situations, where cells contain symbols or text rather than numbers.

Examples: Matrix Diagram, Prioritization Matrix

Group B / Group A	B1	B2	B3	B4	Tot.
Item A1	1	2	3	4	10
Item A2	2	1	1	5	9
Item A3	2	2	3	1	8

Fig. 2.7 Matrix

Calculations

Some tools involve calculation, but of too few numbers to be displayed in a matrix. Where these result in a single number, then there is usually no alternative way of displaying it, other than writing it large, although if this calculation changes across time, then it may be shown in a line graph.

Where there are a simple set of calculations, then they may be displayed in a table.

Examples: Process Capability, Activity Network

Non-numeric non-graphical tools

There are applications where information is not numeric and where a pictorial display is either inappropriate or impossible.

Group tools

Probably the largest non-numeric, non-graphical group of tools have a sociological nature, in that they have a focus in helping groups work together. Thus, for example, Brainstorming has deliberate rules about not criticizing other people, as this can cause them to be less creative.

These tools do not have the dramatic display value of other tools, but they are important in the many situations where numeric methods are not available, and are often integrated with the use of other tools that add structure to their output.

Examples: Brainstorming, Surveys

Tables

Tables give a flexible approach to structuring various types of information, and may be viewed as a form of matrix. They typically contain text, symbols or numbers, arranged in rows and columns, as in Fig. 2.8.

Examples: Failure Mode and Effects Analysis, Tables

	Attributes A		Attributes B	
	Group a	Group b	Group a	Group b
Item 1	High	Medium	V. High	Medium
Item 2	V. Low	Medium	High	Low
Item 3	Medium	High	Medium	V. Low
Item 4	V. High	Medium	Medium	Low

Fig. 2.8 Table

Relating tools and applications

Figure 2.9 uses a Matrix Diagram to show the relationship between the tools described in this book and the applications identified in Chapter 1. In this diagram, it can be seen that there is at least one tool that has a strong focus in each application area, although the greatest number of tools appear around the numeric and textual organization of problem information. This is probably because this is often a difficult area of problem solving, where you have a large amount of data, and simply want to arrange it in some order that will enable you to identify important elements of the problem which must be addressed.

Many tools have some relation to collection, at least in that they require the collection of specific information. There are fewer tools whose prime objective is the collection process, although these are still important.

Most tools also aim to help with the identification of areas for further decision making, as enabling effective decisions is a key reason for using tools. This decision may simply indicate areas for further investigation or may be a more focused selection from a number of different possible courses of action.

Fewer tools are aimed at planning, although these tend to have a particular focus in this, more specialised, area.

Relationship: ◎ = strong, ○ = partial, △ = weak

Tool	Collecting: Facts — Number	Facts — Text	Opinions — Number	Opinions — Text	Ideas — Text	Structuring and understanding: Number — Calculation	Number — Display	Text — Problem	Text — Process	Using: Identification	Selection	Plans — Risks	Plans — Activities
Activity Network	△	△	○	○		◎	○		△				◎
Affinity Diagram		△		○	△			◎		○			
Bar Chart							◎			○	△		
Brainstorming				○	◎								
Cause-Effect Diagram		○		◎	△			◎		○	△		
Check Sheet	◎	○					○						
Control Chart						○	◎			◎			
Decision Tree	△	△	△	△							◎	◎	○
Design of Experiments	◎					○	○			◎			
Fault Tree Analysis		○		◎	△				○	○		◎	△
Failure Mode and Effects Analysis	○	○	△	△		○			○	◎	○	◎	
Flowchart		○		△					◎	△			
Flow Process Chart	△	○							◎	△			
Force-Field Diagram		△	△	○			○			○	◎		
Gantt Chart	△	△	○	○									◎
Histogram	△						◎			△			
IDEF0		◎		○					◎	△			
Line Chart	△						◎			○			
Matrix Diagram	△	○	○	○			△	◎		○			
Matrix Data Analysis Chart	○					○	◎			○			
Nominal Group Technique				◎	○					○	○		
Pareto Diagram							◎			○	◎		
Prioritization Matrix			△	○						○	◎		
Process Capability	◎					◎				○			
Process Decision Program Chart				○						△	△	◎	
Relations Diagram		○		○	△			◎					
Scatter Diagram	△					△	◎			○			
String Diagram	○	○				△			◎	○			
Surveys		○		◎	△					○			
Tables	△	△	△	△				○	◎				
Tree Diagram		△		△					◎	△			
Value Analysis	△	○	○	○		○	○	○		○			
Voting		△		◎	△						◎		

Fig. 2.9　Tools and applications

3 Making Tools Work

Objective of chapter
To give practical suggestions for choosing and using tools.

The skill of a craftsperson is not only in using their tools, but also in selecting the right tool for each job. For any one task, there is usually a large number of possible tools that could be used. For example, to remove a small amount of wood from a chair leg, a carpenter might select a piece of medium sandpaper from a large set of tools, many of which could reasonably be used do the job.

There are a large number of possible tools that a carpenter could have in his toolbox, although he typically carries around only a small set of the most commonly used tools, keeping a larger set of more specialist tools at his workbench. Even then, there are many tools that he does not have, and an occasional trip to the hardware store is needed for special jobs.

In order to stock his toolbox and workbench, the carpenter must first find out what tools are available and which of these are appropriate for the carpentry jobs that he does. He must then learn how to use them, understanding the applications, the 'tricks of the trade' and the limitations of each one.

This chapter looks at how an understanding of both applications and tools can help in the selection of a tool to fit the job. It also discusses other practical aspects of making tools useful.

Understanding the application

In order to choose the right tool for a task, the context of its use must first be understood. Determining the real objectives can help to find the actual constraints and benefits of solving a problem, and thus guide the tool resource to be used.

Finding the real objectives

In the same way that finding root causes can help to solve a problem, finding the real 'root objectives' can help in the understanding of a task. For example, a task which on the surface is to 'improve the way invoices are sent' may turn out to have a root objective of 'increase customer satisfaction' or 'reduce the time it takes to get payment from customers'. Taking time to discover these 'real objectives', for example by repeatedly asking 'Why?', can give clear directions for selecting and using an appropriate tool.

Identifying the benefit to be gained

If solving a problem can result in significant savings or gains, then it will be worth putting a lot of time and effort into it. On the other hand, it is not worth using a tool that requires much painstaking work, when the potential benefit does not merit this effort.

Understanding the constraints

The right quality improvement tool to use in any situation depends not only on the task to be completed, but also upon the constraints of the situation. These can be multiple and are not always obvious. They can fall into broad areas, often to do with time and resource.

Time constraints typically limit the overall time available to work on a problem. For example, if a problem must be solved within a one hour meeting, then there is no point in using a tool that will take several hours.

Resource constraints are often to do with the ability or availability of people. If people with particular knowledge or authority must be involved with the use of the selected tool, then they need to understand it. Resource also includes machines and other costs; for example, some tools are best applied through the use of a computer.

Choosing the right tool

Tools are used because they serve a purpose in completing a task. This use may be essential, as the task can only be completed by using the tool, although tools are often used simply to make the job easier. Another key reason for choosing a tool is to increase confidence in the reliability of the result.

To choose the tool for a given application requires a knowledge of both the principles and practicalities of use. To make effective use of a tool, it must be applied correctly and the people interfacing with it must be able to interpret the results.

Knowing the principles

Each tool has a basic purpose which can usually be stated quite simply. For example, a screwdriver is for inserting and removing screws. If, however, a deeper understanding of the fundamental principles of how the tool works can be gained, then it can also be used in any appropriate circumstance.

An approach to this it to identify the 'root purpose' of the tool and then to use this knowledge to extend the tool's application. For example, the 'root purpose' of a screwdriver may be defined as 'applying leverage' and additional uses derived from this, such as opening tins of paint.

Thus a detailed understanding of tools can help not only in appropriate usage, but also in maintaining a relatively small but flexible toolkit.

Knowing the practicalities

Knowing when a tool should and should not be used is often more than knowing its basic purpose. This usually requires a more detailed knowledge of its limits and constraints.

There are usually various limitations on the use of tools. For example, an ordinary screwdriver may give insufficient grip to remove a corroded screw. Tools may also have circumstances where they can be used in combination, for example where a drill is used to tap a hole for a screw.

Although many tools can be successfully used for more than their basic purpose, the hazards should be understood before they are used outside their normal domain. For example, a flat-bladed screwdriver can usually be pressed into screwing in a cross-point screw, but the risk of slipping and damaging the screw head or the surroundings makes it an unwise choice for visible screws around decorative surfaces.

Using the tool effectively

To be effective, a tool must be applied skilfully and the results interpreted to ensure the desired outcome.

Skilful application

When a tool has been selected, it requires skill in applying it to achieve the desired results. This skill comes first from the knowledge of what to do, then from experience of actually doing it. This is where books such as this are limited, as they can give you knowledge, but not experience.

The first time a tool is used, it is unlikely to be as effective as when it is used for the fiftieth time, as indicated in Fig. 3.1. This learning period can be shortened by ensuring that good knowledge of the tool is gained beforehand and by practising its use in a 'safe' environment before using it in critical real-world applications.

Sometimes this practice is not possible, for example with tools which are applied at an organizational level. In such cases, the risks should be recognized and progress with the tool should be slow and careful, stopping often to check. These risks can be significantly reduced by employing an expert to help with the early implementation.

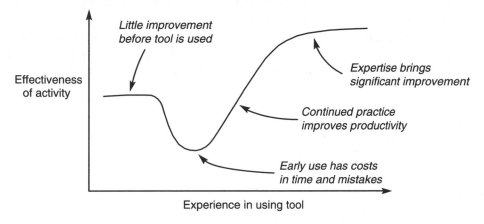

Fig. 3.1 The J-curve of learning

Understanding the results

It is possible to select and use a tool quite intelligently, but this is of no use if no-one understands the results. Interpretation of the results of using a tool is often more skilful that applying the tool to generate those results, as this requires both an understanding of circumstances surrounding the use of the tool and an appreciation of the theory behind the tool.

Quality improvement and problem solving tools are often aimed at helping to analyze a situation and give indications of points where decisions need to be made about possible action.

Stocking the toolkit

When starting out, it is a good idea to have a basic toolkit, and then to add tools as applications occur. A very common basic toolkit is the 'first seven tools':

1. Cause-Effect Diagram (Chapter 12)
2. Pareto Chart (Chapter 29)
3. Check Sheet (Chapter 13)

4. Scatter Chart (Chapter 34)
5. Bar Chart and other graphs (Chapters 10 and 25)
6. Histogram (Chapter 23)
7. Control Chart (Chapter 14).

These are mostly easy to use and understand, although control charts usually take more effort (which is worth it). It has been said that 90% of all problems can be solved with these tools.

The first seven tools originated in manufacturing industries, and are most suited to problems where quantitative measurement is possible. When dealing with more uncertain and qualitative situations, selections from the 'second seven tools' can often be very useful:

1. Relations Diagram (Chapter 33)
2. Affinity Diagram (Chapter 9)
3. Tree Diagram (Chapter 38)
4. Matrix Diagram (Chapter 27)
5. Matrix Data Analysis Chart (Chapter 26)
6. Process Decision Program Chart (Chapter 32)
7. Activity Network (Chapter 8).

Of these tools the Affinity Diagram, Relations Diagram and Tree Diagram are most common, and the Matrix Data Analysis Chart is so complex that some descriptions of the seven tools replace it with other tools, such as the Prioritization Matrix.

Other tools which are often useful early choices include Flowcharts or other ways of mapping processes, Prioritization Matrices or Voting for choosing what to do, and Brainstorming or Nominal Group Technique for divergent identification of new items.

As discussed above, it helps if you can get help and practise the use of the tool in a 'safe' environment before using it in real situations. Even then, be prepared for a few false starts.

Useful resources

When working with improvement tools, particularly in groups, there are a number of resources that can be used to make their application easier and more effective. These may include:

- Comfortable meeting rooms provide an atmosphere more conducive to concentrated group work than an informal cluster around an office desk.
- Large vertically mounted sheets of paper and appropriate marker pens can be used to make writing visible to a group of people. These are

commonly known as *flipcharts, easelcharts* or *butcher paper*.

- Blackboards or whiteboards are like flipcharts, with the added advantage of being erasable. A problem with these is that they cannot be removed and must be erased when full. Whiteboards with built-in photocopiers help to get around this limitation.
- 3" x 5" cards add another dimension of flexibility, allowing individual 'chunks' of information to be moved around relative to others or some underlying structure. Pinboards can be used to hold cards in one position.
- Adhesive memo notes, such as 3M's Post-its, are a less durable alternative to 3" x 5" cards, but do not need a pinboard to keep them in one place.

Four keys to successful projects

When working in a quality improvement or problem-solving project, there are four fundamental principles that can be applied to significantly improve the chance of a successful outcome:

1. Be enabled
2. Be focused
3. Make sure
4. Use common sense.

These are discussed in more detail below.

Be enabled

Being enabled means putting in a reasonable effort before the project starts to ensure its successful completion. This includes:

- Getting clear management backing, including authorization to spend an appropriate amount of effort in the project and commitment to implement results. Nothing kills a project more effectively than lack of management support.
- Getting the right people involved. The most important people here are those who are directly involved in the process, who understand its operation and who will have to implement or will be affected by subsequent changes.
- Making sure the team understands the improvement process. Training is best done as close to the actual usage as possible, and may even be interleaved within appropriate stages.
- Getting a facilitator to help with the implementation of the improvement

process. This person is concerned only that the team is successful; they have no stake in any particular solution. Facilitating can be a key and highly skilled job.

• Making sure you have the authority to change the process. There is no point spending time in finding improvements that you will not be able to implement. This usually means either changing your own process or collaborating with other process owners in the improvement project.

Be focused

Being focused means paying close attention to the problem and the process during the whole project. This includes:

• Having an enthusiastic leader who cares deeply about the problem, the improvement process and the people in the team. Improvement teams should be led in a participative, not directive manner.

• Being focused on the needs of direct and indirect customers. The objective of any process is to satisfy the needs of its customers.

• Using clear objectives and plans to help the group pull together in the same direction towards the desired goal.

• Carefully selecting and using appropriate tools. The right tool in the right hands can be very incisive, cutting quickly through to the needed solution.

• Identifying the most effective things on which to focus from the many possible activities (selecting the 'significant few' from the 'trivial many').

• Keeping things simple. Although a degree of complexity may be required to understand sufficient detail to make improvements, excessive complexity causes undue effort and may significantly reduce the ease with which results can be communicated.

• Selecting items for action that the team is able to change. One of the traps in improvement projects is to find problems with suppliers and other people, rather than your own processes.

• Being tenacious in the face of seemingly insurmountable problems. When things do not work it is easy to give up, quoting bad tools, waste of time, etc. Sticking to objectives can transform failure into success.

• Being open to possibilities. When looking for potential problems, causes or solutions, it is easy to discount wild ideas which may be valid or which, when explored further, may lead to valid ideas.

• Identifying adverse effects of proposed changes on other people or processes. Good solutions for you can cause undesirable problems for others.

• Participating within an overall improvement programme and allowing others to learn from your experience.

Make sure

Making sure is at the heart of many quality activities, and it is particularly important when implementing change, as this helps to give confidence that improvements will work as expected. Activities include:

- As far as possible, basing decisions on verified facts and measured data, rather than opinions and hearsay. It is sometimes viewed as a management skill to be able to make snap decisions. This, however, can significantly reduce the chance of a successful project.
- Finding causes before solutions, to ensure that the root cause of a problem is being addressed, and not just symptoms or intermediate causes.
- Verifying assumptions and hypotheses. It is a trap to assume that because a tool has been used, the result must be correct.
- Checking that implemented changes work as expected. It is one of the laws of the universe that, even after careful verification of causes and trials of solutions, some solutions will not work when put into general practice.
- Learning from experience, including standardizing successes and finding and correcting the cause when things do not happen as expected.
- Documenting progress of the project. Writing things down enables unambiguous communication and allows previous decisions to be reviewed.

Use common sense

It has been said that common sense is uncommon, but it is a key tool in improvement projects. Common-sense activities include:

- Recognizing that what you get out of using a tool depends largely on what you put into it. Thus using verified data will give far more reliable results than opinions taken from a single meeting.
- Balancing effort with potential return. It is clearly worth putting a lot of work into a project that will double sales, but it is probably not worth this amount of effort to save five minutes a day in sorting mail.
- Only taking on tasks that you have a reasonable chance of completing in any given timescale. This does not mean shying away from challenges, but success should be given the best possible opportunity too.
- Not judging tools by their name. There are impressive sounding names which hide relatively simple tools. Some of these come from literal translations of the Japanese name!
- Not judging tools by their output. The value of some tools is as much in the doing and the thinking that they cause as in the final results. Other

tools have complex-looking results which are produced with quite simple methods and can be understood with a simple explanation.

- Using teams and tools for serious problems. Putting excessive effort into problems where the solution is obvious is trivializing the tools and techniques used, and can lead to them falling into disrepute.
- Making the work easier with available equipment. Computers can be used to organize information in databases, do calculations with spreadsheets and perform other tasks with specialized software. It may even be possible to connect the computer directly to measurement sensors.
- Knowing that quality improvement tools and techniques are not magic. It is not uncommon for people to assume that just using them will automatically guarantee success. On the other hand, it is also common for skepticism to prevent people from even starting to use them. Most tools at best only increase the chance of success (although this can be a significant increase).
- Balancing realistic expectation with enthusiasm and optimism. Expecting too little or too much can result in disappointment.
- Expecting there to be a learning curve for using tools and having patience when learning. It usually takes several attempts to get up to speed in using new tools and techniques. The key is to use the 'review' stage to try to determine honestly the key reasons why tools did or did not work as expected.

Part 2 : Concepts

In quality improvement, there are a number of basic concepts that cannot be described as tools in themselves, but a knowledge of them is particularly useful when using a number of the tools described in this book.

Processes and variation within them are a very common focus for activities, and the discussion in Chapter 1 is continued in Chapters 4 and 5. Chapter 6 focuses in on an area which can cause problems, examining some key points about taking measurements.

Many of the tools described are often used in groups, and Chapter 7 discusses some of the aspects of working together that may be considered when starting and working in groups.

4 Processes

Objective of chapter

To describe basic concepts of processes, particularly within the context of process improvement.

Processes are a fundamental concept within the arena of quality improvement, as all improvements can be made through gaining a better understanding of the processes involved. This chapter discusses processes and aspects of them with which tools commonly deal.

What is a process?

Processes are one of the 'Three Ps' of quality in business: People, Products and Processes, where products are *what* is done, and processes are about *how* it is done. Thus people use processes to produce products. The word 'products' here includes the end goal of all actions, which is often an intangible *service* rather than a more tangible product. Thus statements about quality often talk about 'products or services' rather than plain 'products'.

A way of contrasting quality in product and process activities is by viewing production of quality products as *doing the right thing* and quality processes are about *doing the thing right*, as in Fig. 4.1.

A succinct formal definition of a process is given in [Juran 88]:

> *'A process is a systematic series of actions*
> *directed towards the achievement of a goal'*

This phrase is expanded upon below.

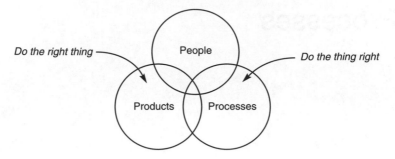

Fig. 4.1 Three Ps of quality in business

Actions within a process

Within a process, the 'series of actions' can be broken down into two types:
(a) A simple *action*, where something is *done*, and the subsequent action is always the same.
(b) A *decision*, where nothing is done other than to decide on what the subsequent action should be.

What makes the process systematic is that these actions are not performed randomly, but in a predefined sequence. The most common tool to show this sequence is a *Flowchart* (Fig. 4.2), which uses different symbols to distinguish the different types of action.

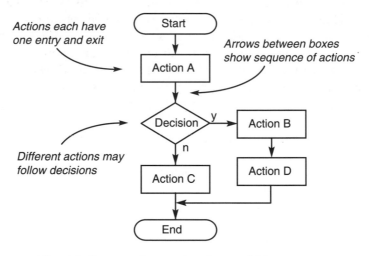

Fig. 4.2 Sequencing and actions within a process

Inputs and outputs

The goal of a process is usually the transformation of a set of *inputs* into a set of *outputs*, as shown in Fig. 4.3 (in practice, there are additional 'inputs' which are not transformed, such as machines, specifications, etc.).

Fig. 4.3 Process transforms inputs into outputs

This presents a problem when drawing diagrams of processes, as arrows may show either the sequence of actions, as in Fig. 4.2, or the inputs and outputs, as in Fig. 4.4. The approach that tools usually take is to do one or the other, but not both.

Suppliers and customers

The inputs to a process are the outputs from a previous or *supplier* process. The outputs of a process form the inputs to a later *customer* process. Processes thus link together to form chains of supplier and customer processes, as in Fig. 4.4.

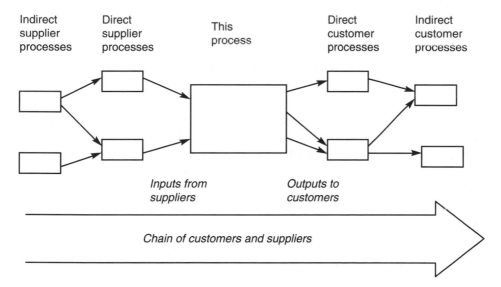

Fig. 4.4 Supplier and customer chains

In practice, there can be many customers of a process, as producing a faulty output may not only cause problems for the following process, but also (if the output is passed on in any way) for the other indirect customers further down the chain. Thus the customers of a design engineer include not only the production engineer, but production line workers, sales people and so on through to the end customer, as a bad design will affect all these people.

Nesting

Each process may itself contain other processes, which in turn may contain further processes. This *nesting* can make processes easier to understand at different levels, as shown in Fig. 4.5.

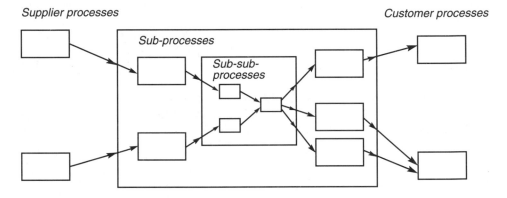

Fig. 4.5 Nesting processes

Thus the operation of an entire company may be considered as a single product, with inputs from suppliers, banks, etc., and outputs to customers, shareholders, etc. This may then be broken down into the major sub-processes, such as purchasing and manufacturing, each of which can be iteratively decomposed to an appropriate level (typically to individual roles). This can then be used in the analysis of company, department or personal processes, investigating how well processes interact and contribute to real customer needs.

Quality in the process

A quality process has the right inputs and performs the right actions to produce outputs that meet the needs of customer processes. There are four places where the quality can be specified and checked:

- *Entry criteria* define what inputs are required and what quality these must be to achieve the exit criteria. Entry criteria should be communicated to supplier processes, to become their exit criteria. If supplier processes are sufficiently well controlled, then there is no need to check inputs.
- *Task definitions* specify the actions within the process.
- *Validation definitions* identify test points within the process and define the tests and criteria for checking at these points. This enables problems to be caught close to their cause, reducing rework and scrap costs, and enabling problem causes to be addressed.
- *Exit criteria* define what outputs are required and what quality these must be to meet the needs of customer processes. Exit criteria may be derived from the entry criteria of customer processes.

Together, these make up what is known as the *ETVX model* (as in Fig. 4.6), which can be used to define the process and the quality required within it completely.

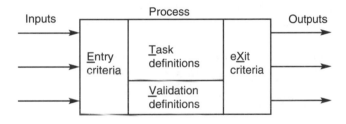

Fig. 4.6 The ETVX process quality model

In process improvement, it can be useful to apply this model to processes that are suspected of being troublesome, in order to identify measures to identify specific problems.

Process management

Process management involves the management of all aspects of a process, as described above. Basic actions may include:

- Finding the needs of customer processes and setting exit criteria accordingly.
- Deriving the requisite inputs, setting entry criteria and ensuring that supplier processes will meet them.

- Defining the actions, decisions and sub-processes within the process to:
  □ Check that inputs meet entry criteria.
  □ Transform the inputs into the required outputs.
  □ Check that the actions within the process produce correct results (validation criteria).
  □ Check that the outputs meet exit criteria.

- Recording, analyzing and acting upon the checks made.
- Determining the resources required to enact the process.
- Motivating and controlling the people within the process.
- Monitoring customer satisfaction and checking for changing needs.
- Improving the process further.

Process improvement

Taking the above descriptions into account, broad actions to improve processes may include:
- Changing exit criteria to define outputs that meet customer needs better.
- Changing the actions within the process either to achieve the above or to perform the same process more efficiently or more reliably.
- Changing entry criteria to achieve either of the above. This may mean working with a supplier to improve their process so that they can meet the new criteria.
- Changing validation criteria to detect problems within the process better.

In addition to validation activities, processes can be made more reliable by designing them for *mistake-proofing* and *robustness*.

Mistake-proofing (also called *Poka-Yoke*) involves designing the process so that it cannot be done wrongly. For example, a location peg may have a lug put on it, to prevent it being inserted the wrong way around, as in see Fig. 4.7.

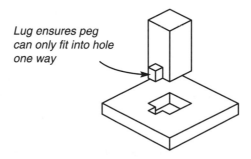

Lug ensures peg
can only fit into hole
one way

Fig. 4.7 Mistake-proofing

Other mistake-proofing examples include:

- Asymmetrically placed screw holes, so that parts cannot be assembled incorrectly.
- A computerized telephone dialer that, given a person's name, automatically selects and dials the correct number.
- A checklist of key activities that must be ticked off and signed before a customer order is dispatched.

Making a process robust involves using risk-management techniques to identify key causes of variation that cannot be eliminated, and taking measures to prevent them from upsetting the overall running of the process. This typically involves building redundancy into the process, and requires a balancing of costs against potential damage. Robustness examples include:

- Training several people in first aid, to cope with multiple accidents or absences.
- Allowing time in a project schedule for identified possible risks.
- Packing a parcel with polystyrene chips to prevent damage during transit.

Benchmarking

Another approach to improving processes is through *Benchmarking*, where the process is compared with a similar process, either in another part of the company or in another company, which is recognized as being superior.

Benchmarking against external companies processes may be done as a collaborative exercise, for example where several companies work together, sharing information on common key processes. Competitive benchmarking involves analysis of available information about a competing company (for example, financial performance or reliability levels). This data is then used as a goal for your own improvement efforts.

The ideal process against which to benchmark process is one recognized as being 'best in industry'. In practice, the best may not be known, or information on it may be unavailable. In practice, the best processes against which to benchmark are those where sufficient information is available to allow your own processes to be significantly improved.

Process Re-engineering

When processes are significantly out of date, making incremental improvements may not be enough and a more radical approach is required. *Business Process Re-engineering* (or *BPR*) implies going back to first principles and building processes from the ground up, starting with company goals and customer requirements and using whatever technology and methods are available to create an optimally effective and efficient business system.

BPR can run into problems where the significant change causes an equally significant reaction from the people involved, and results in the current cultural 'immune system' trying to reject the changes. To make BPR successful, as much if not more attention must be paid to the people as is paid to the processes, reassuring their fears and retraining them to work in the new organization.

See also

Chapters: Processes may be described with the Activity Network, Flowchart, Flow Process Chart, Gantt Chart, IDEF0, Relations Diagram and String Diagram. A process improvement framework is discussed in Chapter 1.

References: [Juran 88] clearly describes processes, process management and process improvement. [Deming 82] also has a clear view on process improvement and its benefits. [Radice 85] describes the ETVX model. [Shingo 86] and [Suzaki 87] detail mistake-proofing. Many other books in the bibliography discuss aspects of process management and improvement.

5 Variation

Objective of chapter
To describe concepts of variation within processes, particularly within the context of process improvement.

Variation is a major cause of quality problems and consequently many process improvement activities focus on identifying and reducing it. It is thus important to understand as much about variation as possible, even though its statistical nature can be disconcerting.

This chapter discusses the basic principles of variation, keeping the mathematical content to a minimum. In keeping with the style of the book, calculations are also minimized, consisting only of inserting numbers into simple formulae and using illustrated panels for calculations involving lists of numbers.

Understanding variation

The continuously variable nature of the universe is at the heart of the science of statistics, and at first glance can look very complex, particularly if approached from a mathematical viewpoint. This can lead to it being ignored, which is a pity, as even a simple appreciation of it can result in a reduction in haphazard attempts to control it, with a consequent saving in wasted time and degraded performance.

What is variation?

When a process is executed repeatedly, its outputs are seldom identical. For example, when a gun is successively fired at a target, as in Fig. 5.1, the bullets will not all pass through the same hole.

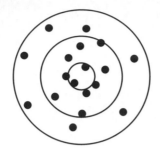

Fig. 5.1 Variation in output

This lack of repeatability is caused by the *variation* or *variability* in the process. If these causes are understood, then this can lead to the development of solutions to reduce the variation in the process and result in more consistent products which require less inspection and testing, have less rejection and failure, cost less to build, have more satisfied customers and are more profitable.

Causes of variation

Variation in process output is caused by variations within the process. These may be one or more of:
1. Differing actions within the process.
2. Differing effects within the process.
3. Differing inputs to the process.

As an example for each of these conditions, the variation in the placement of the bullet holes in the target may be affected by:
1. The gun being held or used differently.
2. Wear in the hammer mechanism causing the shell to be struck differently.
3. The bullets being of slightly differing shape or weight.

Thus, even if the first point is eliminated by putting the gun in a clamp and firing it remotely, the bullets will still not all hit the target in the identical position.

The reasons why variation occurs can be divided into two important classes, known as common and special causes of variation. These are discussed further below.

Common causes of variation

Within any process there are many variable factors, as indicated above, each of which may vary a small amount and in a predictable way, but when taken together result in a degree of randomness in the output, as indicated in Fig. 5.1. These seemingly uncontrollable factors are called *common causes of variation.*

Common causes of variation can seldom be eliminated by tinkering with the process. For example, consider the effect of simple adjustments to the clamped gun, as in Fig. 5.2:

1. The first hole is to the left of centre, so the clamp is rotated a little to the right.
2. If the clamp had been left alone, the second bullet would have gone a little to the right of centre, but as it has been moved right, the bullet now goes further to the right. As a reaction to this, the clamp is rotated somewhat more to the left.
3. The third bullet tends towards the left anyway, so the result is a hole even further to the left.

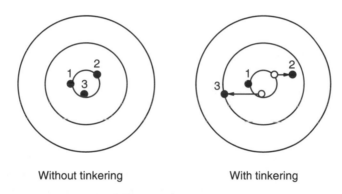

Without tinkering   With tinkering

Fig. 5.2 Effects of tinkering with common causes

It can be seen from this that it would have been better not to tinker with the clamp, and that the score would be more likely to improve if the whole system were understood first and then fundamental improvements made, such as building a better gun or making better bullets.

Special causes of variation

Special causes of variation are unusual occurrences which come from outside the normal common causes, for example where a shot goes outside the main grouping, due to someone tripping over the gunner as the gun is fired (Fig. 5.3).

Special causes can thus be addressed as individual cases, finding the cause for each occurrence outside the normal grouping and preventing it from recurring. This may be contrasted with the way that common causes must be addressed through the overall process.

The way that causes are addressed in a process improvement project is usually first to recognize and eliminate special causes, and then to find ways of improving the overall process in order to reduce common causes of variation.

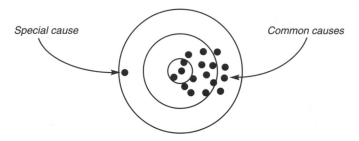

Fig. 5.3 Special and common causes of variation

Measuring variation

Variation is not simple to measure, as by its nature is random and individual events cannot be predicted. Despite this, a degree of measurement can be achieved by looking at how a number of measurements group together. Usually these items are selected with sampling methods.

The spread of measurements within a group enables special causes of variation to be distinguished from common causes of variation. Beyond this, the characteristics of how these random events are spread out can allow improvements in seemingly random chaos to be simply measured.

Distribution of results

It is common in processes for most measurements to cluster around a central value, with less and less measurements occurring further away from this centre. For example, the distribution of holes across the target will gradually spread out from a central, most common placement, as in Fig. 5.4.

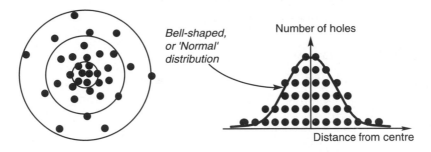

Fig. 5.4 Distribution of shots across target

The Normal distribution

The bell-shaped curve in Fig. 5.4 occurs surprisingly often and is consequently called a *Normal distribution* (or *Gaussian* distribution, after its discoverer) and has some very useful properties which can be used to help variation be understood and controlled.

The Central Limit Theorem

The reason for the common occurrence of this Normal distribution is either a natural distribution or the very useful and remarkable effect described by the *Central Limit Theorem*. This states that, even where the underlying population distribution is not Normal, the distribution of the averages of a set of samples *will* be approximately Normal.

This is clearly illustrated in Fig. 5.5, which shows the distribution of average values achieved by throwing all possible combinations of one, two, three and four dice.

With a single die, the distribution is rectangular, as there is one, equally likely way of achieving each number. With two dice, the distribution becomes triangular, as although there is only one way of averaging one (two ones), there are six ways of averaging the central value of 3.5 (1-6, 2-5, 3-4, 4-3, 5-2 and 6-1).

With three dice, the distribution becomes curved, and with four dice it is markedly bell-shaped, as there is still only one way of averaging one, but there are four ways of averaging 1.25 (three 1s and a 2) and so on up to 147 ways of averaging 3.5! A key use of this effect is that a predictable Normal distribution can be produced by measuring samples in groups of as few as four items at a time.

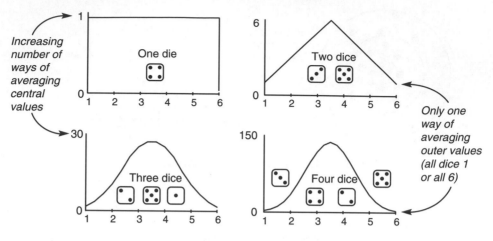

Fig. 5.5 Averages

Other distributions

A Normal distribution of measurement values does not always occur, and other distributions may be caused by various factors, conditions and combinations. Several of these are discussed in Chapter 23. It is a trap to use tools that expect a Normal distribution, such as Process Capability, when the distribution is not Normal.

Measuring distribution

The measurements of a process can vary in two different ways, in terms of their *centring* and their *spread*, as illustrated in Fig. 5.6.

The centring (also called *accuracy* or *central tendency*) of a process, is the degree to which measurements gather around a target value. The spread (also called *dispersion* or *precision*) of the process is the degree of scatter of its output values.

Ways of measuring centring

To measure the centring of a process requires that the centre point of the set of results be identified. The accuracy of the process can then be determined by comparing it with target values. There are three ways of measuring this centre point: the mean (or average), the median and the mode (see Fig. 5.7).

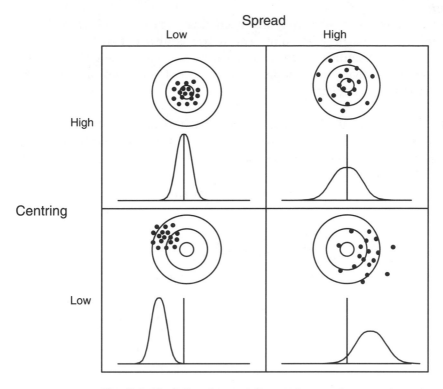

Fig. 5.6 Variation in centring and spread

Mean

The most common way of measuring the centre point of a set of measurements is with the average, or *mean* (i.e. the sum of all measurements divided by the total number of measurements).

The mean is useful for further mathematical treatment, as it considers all values (although a few extreme values can cause the mean to become unrepresentative of the rest of the values).

Median

If the measurements are listed in numeric order, then the *median* is the number half-way down the list. If there is an even number of measurements, it is half-way between the middle two numbers. The median is not distorted by extreme values, but it can be very unrepresentative of the other values, particularly in a distribution which is not symmetrical.

Mode

The *mode* is the most commonly occurring measurement. In a distribution graph, this is the highest point. The mode is also not distorted by extreme values, and is useful for measuring such as average earnings. However, there can be more than one mode, and it is not as good as the mean for mathematical treatment.

In a symmetrical distribution such as a Normal distribution, these three measures are the same. In an *asymmetrical* (or *skewed*) distribution, as below, there is a simple rule-of-thumb formula which can be used to estimate one, given the other two:

$$\text{Mean - Mode} = 3 \times (\text{Mean - Median})$$

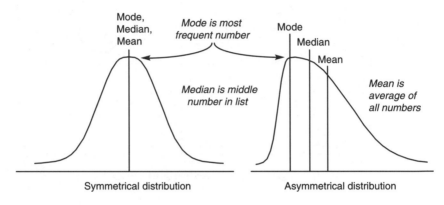

Fig. 5.7 Mean, median and mode

Ways of measuring spread

There are two main ways of measuring the degree of spread of a set of measurements: the range and the standard deviation.

Range

The range of a set of measures is simply the difference between the largest and the smallest measurement value. This is easy to calculate, but there are several problems with using it:

- Special causes of variation can cause an unrealistically wide range.
- As more measurements are made, it will tend to increase.
- It gives no indication of the data between its values.

Standard deviation

The standard deviation is a number which is calculated using a simple mathematical trick (calculating the square root of the average of squares) to find an 'average' number for the distance of the majority of measures from the mean, as in Fig. 5.8.

The standard deviation is of particular value when used with the Normal distribution, where known proportions of the measurements fall within one, two and three standard deviations of the mean, as in Fig. 5.9.

Thus, given a set of measures, the mean and the standard deviation can be calculated, and from this can be derived the probability of future measures falling into the three bands, provided that the distribution is Normal (a simple visual test for this is to draw a Histogram and look for the bell shape).

For example, if the gunner has an average score of 56 per target card, with a standard deviation of 6, then, provided the distribution is normal:

68.3% of scores will be 56 ± 6 (= between 50 and 62)
95.4% of scores will be 56 ± 12 (= between 44 and 68)
99.7% of scores will be 56 ± 18 (= between 38 and 74)

or, breaking out the six bands:

2.1% of scores will be between 38 and 44
13.6% of scores will be between 44 and 50
34.1% of scores will be between 50 and 56
34.1% of scores will be between 56 and 62
13.6% of scores will be between 62 and 68
2.1% of scores will be between 68 and 74

The remaining 0.3% of scores will be below 38 or above 74.

Calculating Standard Deviation

Calculation of the standard deviation of a list of numbers can be made easier by using a table:

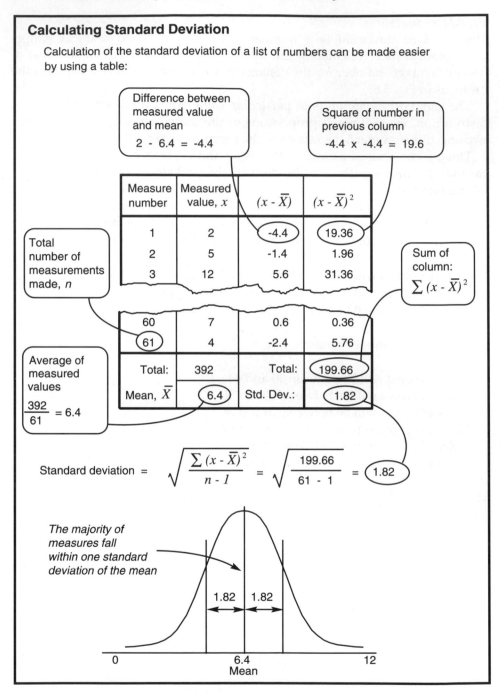

Standard deviation $= \sqrt{\dfrac{\sum (x - \bar{X})^2}{n - 1}} = \sqrt{\dfrac{199.66}{61 - 1}} = 1.82$

The majority of measures fall within one standard deviation of the mean

Fig. 5.8 Calculating the standard deviation

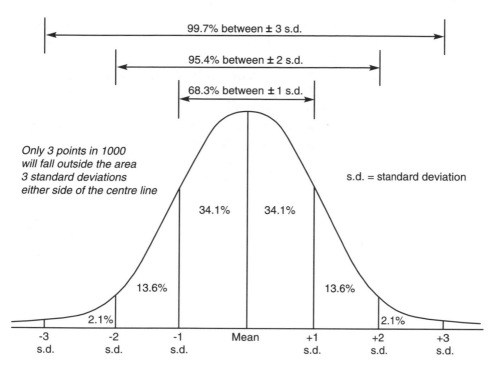

Fig. 5.9 Percentage bands across Normal distribution

Static and dynamic variation

The distribution of measurements as described above takes no account of time or sequence, as it is not important which measurement came first or last. This is *static* variation.

If the order in which measurements are made is known, then significant trends may be detected, which may be useful for catching a problem before it becomes serious. This is *dynamic* variation.

For example, if the gunner is initially accurate, but becomes less so as his arm tires, then this may not be detected from the final positioning of holes on the target - it could only be seen by plotting the positioning of the holes across time.

Dynamic variation is commonly measured using the Control Chart.

See also

Chapters: Tools for measuring Variation include the Control Chart, Histogram, Process Capability, Scatter Diagram and Design of Experiments.

References: Variation is covered in depth in books that delve more deeply into statistics. [Feigenbaum 86] discusses it in a manufacturing context. [Wadsworth 86] covers it well in a review of basic statistics. [Oakland 90] has a chapter on it. [Roy 90] and [Logothetis 92] discuss Taguchi's approach.

Other books discuss it and its importance more briefly, including [Juran 88] and [Deming 82].

6 Measurement

Objective of chapter
To identify key points about identifying and taking measurements.

When solving problems in a quality improvement or any other situation, tools and a structured framework are often used to help reach good decisions, but they alone are not enough. Whilst structure and tools may be considered as the engine of problem solving, they need the fuel of data to be effective. The confidence that can be put in any decision and the quality of the result are proportional to the accuracy of the information upon which the decision was based.

This chapter looks at ways to help find the right information that will enable effective decisions to be made.

Objectives

In any problem-solving or tool-usage situation, a desirable outcome may be described in the form of a statement of objectives. Sometimes this is implicit, but it is usually worth writing down in a short sentence, as this will help to achieve consensus within the project group, acting as a 'guiding star' for decisions and actions. One of those actions will be the collection of data in order to demonstrate whether objectives have been met. It makes sense if the statement is worded in a way that helps that data to be clearly identified.

For example, when setting the objective of an improvement project, the specifics of what is to be improved may be included in the objectives statement, such as, 'Increase the accuracy and timeliness of the order processing system'. In this case it is clear that accuracy and timeliness must be measured.

Questioning

When planning a project, even when using objectives, it may not always be clear what should be measured. A simple and effective approach to this is called the *goal-question-metric paradigm*, which uses a question as a bridge between objectives and measures. The approach is to ask questions about objectives that may help measures to be identified, particularly 'How will I know how well the objective is being approached?' and 'How will I know when the objective has been met?'. Other useful measures may be found by asking questions such as: 'How many?', How much?', 'When?', 'How useful?', 'How expensive?', 'How often?', 'Who?'.

For example, if the objective is 'make a better cake', then the questioning step may ask, 'How will I know a better cake?' and 'Who can tell me?', which then leads to measures such as comparison against a benchmark or focus group consensus.

Purpose of measurement

In measuring any process, there are two common reasons why measurements are made, being either an ongoing monitoring measurement or a more specific investigative one.

Monitoring measurement

Monitoring measurements act as indicators of the general health of the process, much as temperature gives an overall indication of the health of the human body. The measurement is made over a long period, so that trends and variation can be understood and points where specification limits or target values are exceeded may be identified.

Several considerations should be taken into account when identifying monitoring measurements:

- The measurement should identify the presence of problems, but not necessarily the cause. Breadth is thus more important than depth.
- The measurement should not be intrusive or upset the process in any way, as objective decisions can only be made through independent observation.
- Each measurement should be repeatable and made under similar conditions, so they may be compared on an equal footing.
- It should be possible for measurements to be made on a regular basis. This is easy where the process repeats frequently, such as on a production line, but can prevent identification of trends, etc., in processes with longer cycles, such as new product introductions.

- As it is made frequently, the measurement should be relatively inexpensive and easy to perform.

Investigative measurement

Investigative measurements are made specifically to find out more about known problems or causes. This may be likened to specific medical tests such as measuring blood pressure. The limited nature of an investigative measurement means that it may differ from monitoring measurement in several ways:

- The measurement may be intrusive.
- The cost of measurement is not particularly important.
- Many different measurements may be made, where each measurement covers a specific area in more detail.

Elements of measurements

Measurements may be more successfully selected and applied if their different parts and classifications are first understood. This section looks at aspects of measurements that may be taken into account when using them.

Type of measurement

Information gathered may be of two broad types: quantitative or qualitative. Each has its value, but they may be gathered and treated quite separately.

Quantitative information
The easiest type of information to measure and use is a numeric quantity. Numbers are precise and help clear decisions to be made. Tools which use quantitative data often work by using a combination of mathematical calculation and comparison of numbers against one another or against a fixed and critical value.

Most of the discussion in this chapter is about quantitative information.

Qualitative information
Quantitative data is not always available and not always enough. Qualitative information is non-numeric, typically appearing as written text. This often comes in 'chunks', where a phrase or sentence describes a single, independent piece of information. Tools which use qualitative data typically organize and structure these chunks relative to one another, thus revealing further

information.

Often, a situation is best described by a combination of numeric and non-numeric information, where the qualitative text helps to put the quantitative numbers into context, for example describing who was using a machine, where, under what conditions, etc.

Types of numeric data

When identifying what to measure, two main types of data should be taken into consideration, as each has applications where it is more useful.

Attributes

One of the simplest measurements that can be made in many situations is to count the number of items in a particular classification, such as the number of customers purchasing full insurance cover or the number of defects in each sheet of glass. This *attribute* measurement answers the question, 'How many?' and its simplicity often makes it a good starting point, with variable measurement being used when the problem area has been more narrowly identified.

Attributes are a good way of turning qualitative data into quantitative data, for example by counting employees who think they are significantly underpaid.

Variables

Beyond attribute measurement is *variable* measurement, where the question, 'How much?' is asked. Variable measurements have units, such as centimetres and kilograms. They also usually require more effort to collect than attributes, and the actual measurement usually requires the use of some form of measuring instrument.

Components of measurement

In any measurement, there are several components that must be taken into account when deciding what to measure.

Units

The measurement will be made in some kind of units. These should reflect the range of possible values, for example it is probably better to measure the length a piece of wood in millimetres rather than centimetres. Clearly stating the units to be used prevents situations where different people use different units and cause confusion in calculations and displays.

Scale

Many measurements are made in the form of numbers, as this is an absolute and flexible format, and the scale is simply the possible range of measured values. In some situations, however, numbers are not so useful, for example when identifying the possible actions of a customer upon finding a defective product.

In this case, the measurement scale is typically made up of a defined and discrete set of values. This can be useful when numbers are unclear, and it is easier to describe your satisfaction as 'high' or 'low' rather than '1' or '5'.

Target

There is often a target or goal value for the measurement. This may be a central value about which the measurement varies, or a distant target that is to be achieved, as in Fig. 6.1. The measurement can thus be usefully expressed as a difference from this ideal, rather than as an absolute value.

Limits

As well as a target value, there are often some kind of action limits, beyond which the measurement should not go. If the measured value falls outside such *specification limits*, then some kind of action may be defined, such as rejection of the measured item or an investigation into the cause of failure. On the other hand, it is desirable to beat target values.

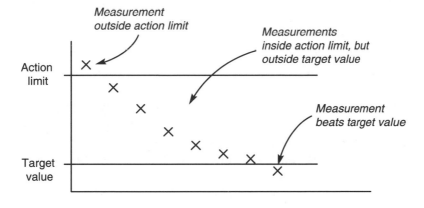

Fig. 6.1 Action and target values

Tool

The measurement may be made using some kind of measuring device. It is essential that this tool is accurate and reliable, as an uncertain measuring tool will result in worthless measurement values. Measurement tools include all methods of gathering data, from voltmeters to surveys. Each has constraints in use and the data given must be of a known accuracy to enable confident decisions to be made.

Process

If the measurement process is clear and well defined, then each measurement can be made in a consistent way, enabling successive values to be compared. Detailing the process also puts into perspective the actual work that has to be done to collect the data, and enables the requisite time and resource to be scheduled.

Details of the measurement process may include:
- Who is doing the measuring and how you will be sure they know what to do.
- When the measurement is done, including times, events and frequencies.
- What is to be measured, including items and sampling rules.
- The tools to be used, including calibration details.
- How the measurements are recorded, including design of Check Sheets.
- What is to be done with the completed data, including storage and actions.

How to measure

When taking measures, there are several approaches which can help to ensure that the right data is selected and collected in a way that helps with the subsequent analysis.

Stratification

When investigating a problem, a single general measurement is often insufficient and can cloak useful information. By measuring the situation in a number of different ways (*stratifying* or *segmenting* it), one or more 'cuts' may reveal new information that will allow specific corrective action to be identified, as in Fig. 6.2.

Common measurements used in stratifying data include:
- Raw materials and completed products
- Machines and tools
- People
- Processes and actions within them
- Time
- External factors, such as temperature and season.

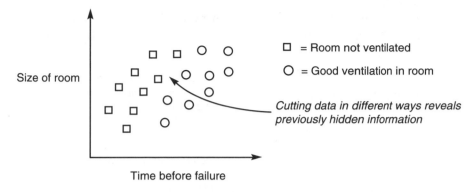

Fig. 6.2 Stratification

For example, a customer support organization counts the number of calls about each product, and find that a heater product is receiving a very high call rate. They have identified a problem, but cannot find out why without making more measurements. They therefore stratify the calls by taking intrusive measures, asking customers questions about suspected causes, such as the type of problem (failure, cutout, etc.), customer (age, occupation, etc.), how they are using the product (indoors/outdoors, hours of usage per day, etc.) and so on.

Sampling

In order to know *exactly* how a set of measured items behaves, they must all be measured, such as when determining the distribution of the values of a batch of electrical resistors. However, this is seldom possible, for several possible reasons:
  • There is a significant cost in measurement, for example when there are a large number of items or when it takes a long time to measure each.
  • Not all items may be available for measurement.
  • There may always be more items (an infinite population).
  • Measuring the item effectively destroys it.

In such cases, a limited *sample* may be measured, from which the characteristics of all other items (the *population*) are deduced. In order to be able to do this reliably, there are two factors that must be taken into account:
  • The sample must be large enough to contain a representative set of items from the population, to enable an accurate extrapolation for all other items

(see Fig. 6.3).

- The sample must be selected entirely at random, to ensure that no biases (intended or not) result in an incorrect picture of the rest of the population.

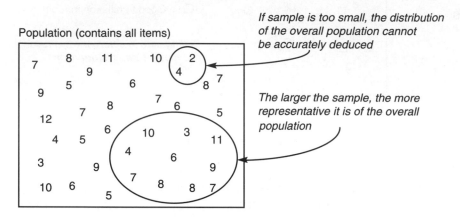

Fig. 6.3 Sampling from population

Most tool descriptions identify the size of samples that need to be taken to ensure a representative sample, so knowledge of statistics is not essential, although a deeper understanding in this area (or access to someone with this knowledge) can be very useful.

Recording data

When actually measuring data, it is important that the accuracy of the data is maintained through careful measurement and accurate instruments. This is best achieved through the use of a clearly defined data-collection process.

It is usually useful to collect not only the data to be used, but also information about the situation in which it was collected. This may include:

- The name of the person collecting the data.
- The date and time of collection.
- The method or process used for collecting data.
- Identification of any instruments used during data collection.

Where the data is to be collected by hand, then a Check Sheet may be designed to ease both the recording and interpretation of data.

A variable often overlooked when recording data is the person doing the job. The best way of reducing any potential variation from this source is through training. This need not be complex or long, but it should be enough for the person to understand how to use any instruments, operate any machines and reliably record all requisite data. It can help if they know how the information is likely to be used afterwards, as a fear that the information may be used to their disadvantage can tempt them to tamper with it.

See also

Many books on quality and tools contain general discussions on measurements and the use of data, including [Ishikawa 76], [Sinha 85], [Juran 88], [Oakland 90] and [Francis 90]. Sampling is discussed at length in [Grant 80], as well as the books above. [Basili 88] describes the goal-question-metric paradigm.

7 Teamwork

Objective of chapter
To describe key considerations about working in groups.

A group of people working together may have varying degrees of success in achieving their aims, and any lack of success in a project may be due to a number of factors that are not always clear. For example, a prestige project, staffed by well-trained experts with plentiful resources to hand, may be eclipsed by another smaller group of workers who achieve outstanding improvements through seemingly nothing more than lunchtime meetings and a few key process changes. Often, the difference lies not so much with the resources and skills available, but in the way the team works *together*, rather than as a group of individuals.

This chapter looks at some of the key points of how groups of people interact, and the factors that need to be taken into account to make teams successful.

Group formation

If a group of people are simply thrown together, they are not likely to immediately start working as a coherent team. To reach the state where they all comfortably know one another, know the task and know their role, they often pass through several stages, as in Fig. 7.1.

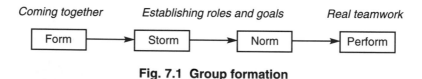

Fig. 7.1 Group formation

Form

In the formation stage, the group comes together for the first time. The people may be excited or anxious about the task ahead and their part in it and thus tend to spend their time in investigation of both the problem and the other people in the team. Because the problem is not yet known and the other people unproven in their new roles, judgments are usually suspended at this stage.

Storm

As the group starts to work together, the reality of assumptions and plans are tested, and disagreement and disillusionment can result when things do not turn out to be going as smoothly as expected. This results in revision of people's views, both of one another and also of the task and process used. Occasionally, groups never get past the storming stage as disagreements are so violent that people leave the team. It is a test of the leader's abilities in getting the team through this stage.

Norm

In the normalization stage, roles and relationships become established and the group starts to move forwards on its task. People accept one another's personalities and start to focus more on the problem in hand. Feelings at this stage tend to be ones of relief at having survived storming and being able to get down to work on the real problem. Normalization sometimes does not work well, as issues are not fully ironed out and the team may dip back into storming several times.

Perform

When personalities agree and activities are clarified, the team may then begin to really perform, focusing on the problem as a single unit. The real 'team' is born at this stage as a sense of friendliness and cooperation towards realistic goals develops. People know what they are doing and help one another selflessly as they work together towards team, rather than individual, objectives. It is at this stage that *synergy* becomes an effective tool, where the results of the group are noticeably better than might have been gained from working individually.

In practice, the degree to which teams perform will vary, and is often reflected in their results, which may range from the barely acceptable to a roaring success. Teams which perform well often survive in spirit well after the problem is solved and may re-form to work on other problems.

Beyond the Perform stage, the group dynamics still need to be maintained as, if the job gets too easy or too difficult, there may be a further *deform* stage where the group starts to break up through boredom or stress. If this is not recognized and corrected, then the group may self-destruct through argument, apathy or attrition.

Roles within the team

When teams are formed, it is normal for people to take different roles, according to their position, ability or character type. Formal roles are the external, defined positions that are associated with given responsibilities and are usually allocated according to the position or ability of each person.

Individuals in a team will also tend to adopt informal roles that depend more on their character than on any specific knowledge or position. Recognizing these behaviours can be very useful when helping the team to work together.

Formal Roles

In order for a team to work in an organized way towards their objectives, several formal roles are often allocated or decided on within the group. Although the leader is the most common role, other positions of specific responsibility can help give focus to specific activities and ensure formal tasks are completed.

Leader

The style of the group leader sets the style of how the group will operate. This style should be more participative than directive, as improvement groups often operate on a voluntary basis or where the work is outside their normal work scope. There also may be no official reporting line to the leader, who may be a peer or from another area.

A key objective of the leader is to motivate the rest of the team into having a strong focus on succeeding in their objectives. An active and effective way to achieve this is by working within the team rather than directing it from above. An important factor is that the leader should be respected by the team members, who will be willing to work together with him or her. The leader should also be clearly enthusiastic about solving the problem by using appropriate tools, rather than the less structured 'brainstorm and implement' sessions that often occur.

The leader should also have a good understanding of the improvement process being used and should be able to work closely with the facilitator.

Recorder

The information gathered, minutes of meetings, output from tool use and communications inside and outside the team forms the 'group memory' of the team. If this is not recorded and organized, it can result in the team itself becoming disorganized.

The role of the recorder (or *scribe* or *librarian*) is thus to record and gather all the data and present it in a format which the team can easily understand and reference. The key skills for the recorder are a clear and concise writing style and an ability to organize information for easy access.

Analyst

Measurements made during the project are seldom directly interpretable, and must be translated into an understandable format from which decision points may be identified. The analyst's key focus is on the measurement and interpretation of data to enable these decisions to be made.

The exact skills of the analyst will vary with the type of project, for example where detailed numerical measures are being made, a mathematical ability may be needed. Other projects may need an understanding of psychology, for example where the measurement is of people's opinions.

Expert

Experts in the team have specialized knowledge, for example about technical areas or key processes, and act as advisors and authorities in their field of expertise. It is important in an improvement team to either have appropriate expertise within the team or to have it readily available.

A chicken and egg situation can occur, where an expert is required to identify a problem, but the appropriate expert cannot be identified until the problem is known. This can result in the problem being circled, but not approached. The effect of this on the team is that experts may come and go, or may stay and become inappropriate people to have on the team.

Facilitator

The facilitator is not an actual team member, but is closely connected with the team, and especially with the team leader. This person is an expert in team dynamics and in the improvement process, and thus acts as an advisor and teacher. The facilitator never owns the problem, but does have a strong interest in the success of the group.

An effective way of allowing the facilitator to lead the team in specific activities, yet without undermining the leader's role, is for the leader to describe the objective and then to introduce the facilitator as someone who will help them achieve this. The facilitator then takes over, with the clear mandate of helping the group, whilst the leader sits *with* the group.

Informal roles

There are a number of models of interpersonal behaviour in groups that identify specific roles that people adopt, often unconsciously. It is important that these characters get on together, as subliminal conflict, where people react emotionally to situations they do not consciously recognize, can be particularly difficult to resolve.

In practice, behavioural style may vary along a spectrum between extremes. People may also act at different positions along the spectra, depending on the situation. Nevertheless, individuals do tend towards particular groups of behaviours and if these are recognized, a cohesive and effective mix may be found in the group to enable its members to work well together. A typical set of behavioural styles are as follows.

Social style: Self versus group

It is natural to consider one's own opinions and feelings as important, and many people are largely self-based in their thinking. However, people get on together by also thinking about others, and a person who is more group-based will consciously aim to bring the group together as a harmonious whole.

People with strong self-image may tend towards a leadership role, but unless they also consider the people in the team and the group as a whole, there is a danger of them becoming dictatorial, turning the focus away from the problem and onto personalities.

In effective groups, team members feel able to contribute their own ideas, but also take seriously the thoughts of others and work towards an agreeable solution. It is an important role of the leader to bring about this state of constructive cohesion.

Work style: Doer versus thinker

Some people have a practical work style, working to plan and taking pleasure in completing actions. Others are more interested in the reasons behind the actions, and may challenge conventional approaches.

In teams, a balance of both styles is needed, to ensure thoughtful beginnings and solid completions to team actions.

Thinking style: Divergent versus convergent

Divergent thinkers are good at brainstorming and coming up with unusual ideas. Convergent thinkers, however are good at judging and selecting items from a large set of possibilities.

Improvement teams often have an equal need for both styles of thinking, for example where divergent thinking is used to find possible causes, then convergent thinking is used to select likely key causes to be carried forward for further investigation.

Decision style: Intuition versus facts

In making decisions, a certain amount of personal judgment is required to be combined with the hard data available to help reach a conclusion. An intuitive decision maker tends to rely more on feelings and unidentified experience, whilst a factual decision maker will seek to increase confidence in a decision by seeking out and analyzing clear facts.

Quality improvement activities tend more towards the factual end of this spectrum, although there are some situations (often to do with people) where there is little hard data available, and an intuitive approach can yield good results.

Team meetings

A number of quality improvement and problem-solving tools are most effective when used with a group of people, each of whom may make a specific contribution. When the team meets, both the conduct of the meeting and the layout of the room should help them to work on the problem together, as one team.

Planning

Meetings are very expensive in terms of people's time and if there is no objective or agenda, then little is likely to be achieved. A short, focused meeting with a simple and clear objective is likely to be far more productive than a lengthy meeting with unspecified aims. The meeting is also more likely to be successful if the process and tools to use in the meeting are identified beforehand and a facilitator brought in as appropriate.

It is thus worth spending time before the meeting identifying the objective of the meeting, how this may be achieved and how any blocks to progress may be overcome.

Room layout

When sitting together, all members of the team should feel equally able to contribute. A long, rectangular table can isolate people at the ends; the best shape is a simple circle.

When working with a whiteboard or flipchart, people should sit in a wide semicircle or arc, facing the work area. This will help them to focus on the problem, rather than one another. Attention to the problem can be further helped by clearly displaying the objective of the meeting, for example on a single sheet of flipchart paper which is taped to the wall.

In the meeting

When the objective and process is agreed by all, the meeting simply becomes a matter of following this plan.

It often occurs that one or two people will dominate any meeting and will tend to do all the talking. This prevents or inhibits other people from making useful input to the team. Other people may also be naturally reticent or unwilling to become involved.

It is one of the tasks of the team leader to enable and encourage contributions from *all* members of the team, which may require specific attention to be paid to both dominant and reluctant individuals.

At the end of the meeting, all decisions, actions, responsibilities and timescales should be agreed and clear to everyone. These key points may be reinforced in a written meeting summary (not detailed minutes).

Successful teams

In summary, teams can be helped to be more successful by considering a few key points:

- Smaller groups are usually more focused and successful. Larger groups are slower and more conservative. Around three or four people is a good size for a problem-solving team, although up to ten can work.
- If formal and informal team roles are complementary, the team will find it easier to work together on the problem without conflict and are more likely to have requisite skills available for specific tasks.
- A successful team has a sense of cohesion and focus, having worked through to the 'perform' stage. The problem is well understood and 'owned'. They believe they can succeed and are committed to success.
- When the team is focused is on solving the problem, advantage is taken of any available ways of achieving this, including tools, training and facilitation.
- People are more likely to accept changes when they have been involved in the decision-making and implementation processes.

Finally, it is worth noting that research has clearly shown than teams learn faster, come up with more ideas and make better decisions and than individuals working alone. The only disadvantage is that this usually requires a greater total effort. If the potential benefit of team problem-solving is considered worthwhile, then the investment has a good chance in paying off with effective results.

See also

[Scholtes 88] and [Robson 93] discuss many aspects of problem solving in groups. Belbin 81] and [Adair 86] describe the effect of different personality types in groups. [Shaw 81] and [Argyle 83] focus on general interpersonal behaviour. Books on the subtler forms of communication, such as [Morris 77], [Pease 81] and [Pease 85] can also help interpersonal understanding. [Frank 90] and [Doyle 76] describe ways of making meetings effective.

Part 3 : Tools

The remainder of this book is dedicated to the description of a large number of tools. Each chapter is typically around ten pages long and has a common format, as described in the preface.

The overall objective of each chapter is to enable practical use of the tools, and as complete a description as possible is given. The only places where this has been reduced is in tools where the full mathematical content would be beyond the scope of this book.

To help with finding tools, these chapters are organized in alphabetic order. Thus once the name of a tool is known, its description can be easily found.

8 Activity Network

What it's for

To schedule dependent activities within a plan.

When to use it

- Use it when planning any project or activity which is composed of a set of interdependent actions.
- Use it to calculate the earliest date the project can be completed, and to find ways of changing this.
- Use it to identify and address risk to completing a project on time.
- It can also be used for describing and understanding the activities within a standard work process.
- The resulting diagram is useful for communicating the plan and risks to other people.

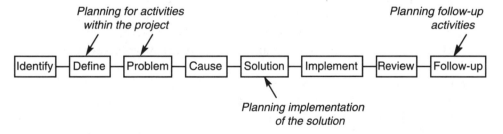

Fig. 8.1 Possible uses in improvement project framework

How to understand it

A project is composed of a set of actions or tasks which usually have some kind of interdependency. For example, before an axle can be turned, it must first be designed, the metal must be purchased, etc. This type of complex system is much easier to understand through the use of diagrams than through textual description, as actual interconnections between tasks can be shown.

The Activity Network diagram displays interdependencies between tasks through the use of boxes and arrows, as in Fig. 8.2. Arrows pointing into a task box come from its predecessor tasks, which must be completed before the task can start. Arrows pointing out of a task box go to its successor tasks, which cannot start until at least this task is complete.

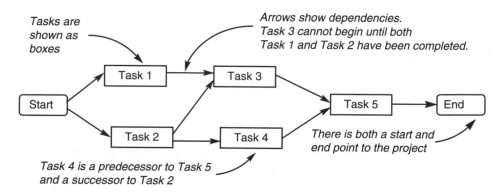

Fig. 8.2 Activity Network

In a network such as this, the points where arrows meet are called *nodes*. Thus, as there are tasks (or activities) at these points, it is also known as an *Activity-on-Node* Diagram. It is usually easier to work with than the alternative *Activity-on-Arrow* Diagram, where the arrows represent tasks.

There are a number of attributes that can be associated with a task, such as the person doing it and the resources they need to do the job. One of the most important of these is the time required to complete each task as, once this is known, the actual calendar dates for tasks can be calculated. This is done using the *Critical Path Method* (or *CPM*). Once the start date for the overall project is known, this will give the earliest and latest start dates for each task.

The amount of time that a task can be delayed without affecting the completion time of the overall project is known as the *slack time* or *float*. Slack can either be regarded as a 'safety margin' or as wasted time. The total of all slack times for all tasks in the project gives the total time wasted, and may be reduced if the tasks can be rearranged.

When people and resources are allocated to tasks, it may also be necessary to rearrange tasks so that people do not have to work overtime to work on more than one task at once. This is called *levelling* or *resource smoothing*.

The *critical path* through the diagram is the sequence of tasks which have zero slack time. Thus, if any task on the critical path finishes late, then the whole project will also finish late. There is always at least one critical path. In Fig. 8.3, tasks 1 to 3 form the critical path, whilst tasks 4 and 5 may be delayed without affecting the completion date of the project.

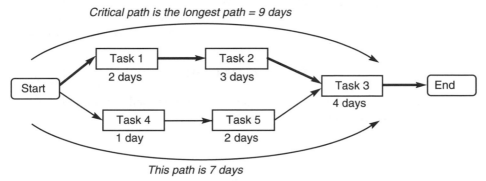

Critical path is the longest path = 9 days

This path is 7 days

Task 4 or Task 5 could, between them, start or finish up to 2 days late without delaying the end of the project. This path thus has 2 days slack in it.

Fig. 8.3 Critical path

It is possible to have what appears to be a task which takes no time to complete. This is called a *checkpoint* or *milestone*, and is usually included in the diagram to highlight an important point in the project.

The Activity Network can be used to identify risk in the plan. Typical areas where there is a danger of the schedule being slipped are illustrated in Fig. 8.4 and include:

- Anywhere on the critical path.
- Where there is a long sequence of tasks, each with a single predecessor and successor. If any task is delayed, it will delay all of its successor tasks. Also, a small risk of delay for each task adds up to a large delay for the overall task sequence.
- Where a task has many predecessors. If any one predecessor task is delayed, then the task will also be delayed.
- When a resource or person that may become unavailable is used in any of the above situations, the risk is compounded.
- Where there are many tasks running at one time, particularly if there are

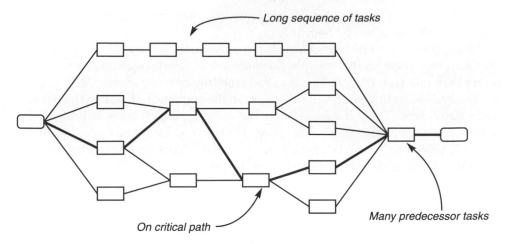

Fig. 8.4 **Areas of risk**

several risky ones. A risk here is that management will not be able to cope with simultaneous failure.

Example

A project team in a chain store, working on a problem with the customer response process, came up with a solution that required careful implementation. They decided to use an Activity Network to plan and manage this stage, with the key objective of implementing the solution with no degradation of service to customers at any time.

They used cards with a Tree Diagram to identify the tasks that would need to be done, then transferred the bottom-level tasks, one at a time, to the Activity Network and completed this with effort estimations and dependency links between tasks, as in Fig. 8.5. They then entered it into a computer system to calculate timings, perform resource smoothing and help reduce slack time.

The plan showed that the time and effort in implementation would fall outside their budgeted figure. They consequently took the plan to the steering committee to get authority to spend additional time on the project. The implementation went very smoothly.

Other examples
- A funeral director maps out the tasks involved in a funeral, paying attention to how multiple funerals might overlap. By rearranging tasks, he enables one more funeral to be fitted into a day, thus increasing customer responsiveness along with business volume.

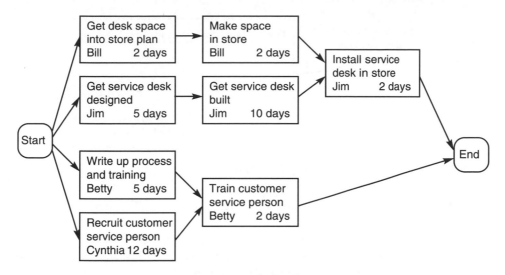

Fig. 8.5 Example

- A production group in an electrical goods manufacturer measures and maps out the tasks required to build a toaster. They redesign and reallocate tasks to reduce the critical path time.
- A quality department team use an Activity Network to plan and agree with all departments the tasks for implementing a new quality management system.

How to do it

1. Define the key objective of the plan, for example, 'to lay all paving stones in a street to a given pattern'. This forms the basic boundary of the project and lets you identify when the job is done.

2. Identify other constraints which may affect the actual planned actions. These typically will be around work, time and cost. For example, where the job must be done within a week, within a set budget, using available manpower, to government standards, and with minimum noise and disruption to local residents.

3. Identify the actual tasks that need to be done. This may be done through the use of a Tree Diagram (in this case, only the bottom-level tasks will be used in the Activity Network).

   Write a short description of each task onto 3" x 5" cards. Also make

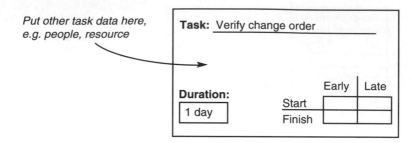

Fig. 8.6 Task card

space for earliest and latest start and finish dates, as in Fig. 8.6.

4. Write on each card the time that the task will take. Other information may also be included, such as the person (or persons) who will perform the task, the extra tools or resources required, etc. At this time, the person's name may not be known, but the required skill level should be known as this might affect the time estimate.

 When writing in the time, try to use the same units for each task. For example, put them all in hours or all in days. This will make calculations easier.

 The task durations will normally be within an order of magnitude of one another. Thus if most tasks are several hours long, but there is one task with a duration of three weeks, then this may well be an indication that this task should be broken down further.

5. Start from the beginning, and ask which tasks must be done first. Place these cards to the left of the working area. If there is more than one, place them spaced out one above the other.

6. For each task just placed, find the task cards which must *immediately* follow and place these to the right, as in Fig. 8.7.

 If a task should start part-way through another task, then break the second task down into two or more tasks to enable clear start and finish links to be made.

 If the cards becomes squashed up or it is not clear from the positioning which card follows which, take a little time to rearrange them so the correct sequence is clear and there is space for subsequent cards to be added.

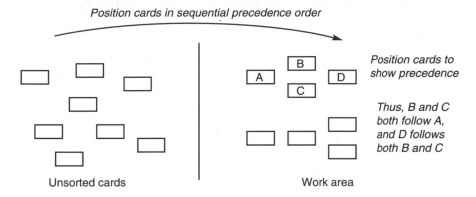

Position cards in sequential precedence order

Position cards to
show precedence

Thus, B and C
both follow A,
and D follows
both B and C

Unsorted cards   Work area

Fig. 8.7 Positioning cards

7. Repeat step 6 until there are no more task cards to place.

   If the sequence of tasks is not clear, it can be easier to start with a central, well-understood task, and identify tasks which must go before and after it. Another strategy is to start at the end and work back to the start by asking of each task, 'What task must be done before I can do this?'.

   Sometimes tasks may be found that should be placed in a part of the diagram that has already been laid out. If this happens, simply rearrange the diagram to fit in the new card.

   If new tasks are identified during this process, just write up a new card.

8. Complete the links between tasks by drawing lines in the work area between cards. To do this, the cards need to be quite firmly attached to a work area that can be drawn on, such as a whiteboard or large sheet of paper.

   When drawing the links, use arrows to indicate which task follow which. The order of tasks is made clearer if the tasks generally flow from left to right.

   The early and late times for each task can now be calculated and the critical path identified.

9. Starting with the tasks at the beginning of the diagram, complete the early start and early finish for each task in turn, following the arrows to the next task, as in Fig. 8.8. A task cannot be completed until all of its predecessors have been completed.

   The early start of a task is the same as the early finish of the preceding task. If there is more than one predecessor task, then there are several

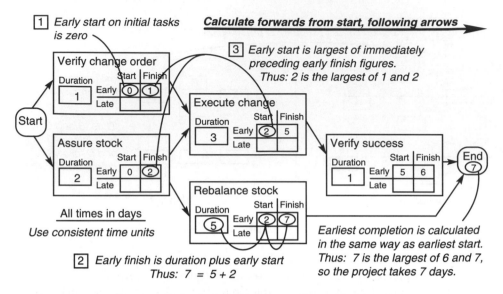

Fig. 8.8 Calculating early start and early finish

possible early start figures. Select the *largest* of these.

The early finish for each task is simply the early start plus the duration of the task. The final calculation is for the earliest completion time for the project. This is calculated in the same way as the early start date.

10. Starting with the tasks at the end of the diagram, complete the late start and late finish for each task in turn, following the arrows in the reverse direction to the previous task, as in Fig. 8.9. A task cannot be completed until all of its successors have been completed.

    The late finish is the same as the late start of the succeeding task (for the final tasks in the project, this is equal to the earliest completion date, calculated in step 9). If there is more than one successor task, then there are several possible late figures. Select the *smallest* of these.

    The late start for each task is simply the late finish minus the duration of the task. The final calculation is for the earliest completion time for the project. This is calculated in the same way as the early start date.

11. Calculate the slack time for each task as the difference between the early and late times, as in Fig. 8.10.

    Also identify the route through the diagram where the slack time on each task through the route is zero. This is called the *critical path*, as any slippage in these tasks will affect the overall project completion date.

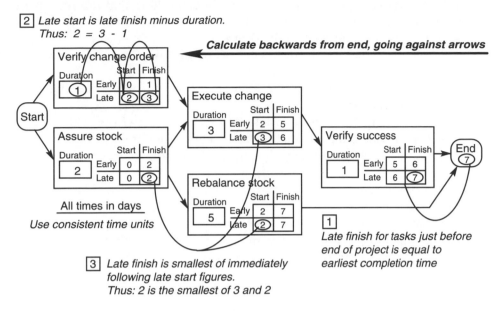

Fig. 8.9 Calculating late start and late finish

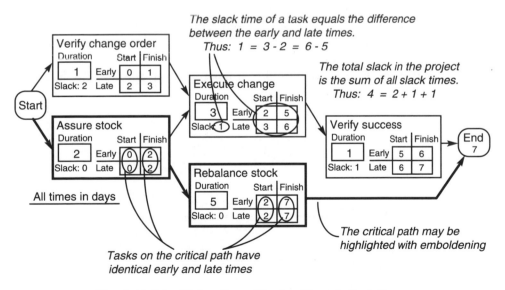

Fig. 8.10 Identifying the critical path and slack times

12. Evaluate and act upon the results, including checking that the final plan meets any constraints identified in step 2. Actions may include:
    • Reducing the total slack in the project by rearranging tasks.
    • Preventing people from having to work overtime by allocation, reallocation and task rearrangement.
    • Identifying risky parts of the plan and reducing risks by reallocation or rearrangement.
    • Recalculating the early and late times to find the effect of the above actions on the critical path, the project completion time and the slack.
    • Rebudgeting to account for the effects of rearrangement or allocation.

13. Start the tasks, using the diagram to help manage the project. Management actions may include:
    • Substituting actual durations of tasks into the diagram.
    • Re-estimating future task durations, using known task durations.
    • Adding, modifying or removing tasks.
    • Rearranging the resources used.
    • Recalculating the early and late times to find the effect of the above actions.

Practical variations

• The *Activity-on-Arrow Diagram* reverses the style of Activity-on-Node Diagram shown above, with tasks being represented by arrows, as in Fig. 8.11. The actual style used is often a simple matter of taste, although the Activity-on-Node Diagram lends itself better to the use of cards, and does not need dummy activities (which appear as dotted lines and have no name or duration).

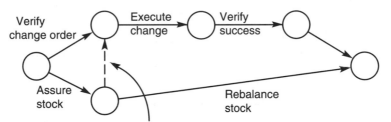

Dotted line is 'dummy activity' to ensure that 'Execute change' starts only after both 'Verify change order' and 'Assure stock' are completed

Fig. 8.11 Activity-on-arrow diagram

- Where tasks are related, as in Tree Diagram families, it can be useful to number them (as in Fig. 8.12) or otherwise indicate their relationships (for example, by naming their parents). Now when the cards are laid out within a network, the original tree structure can still be seen.

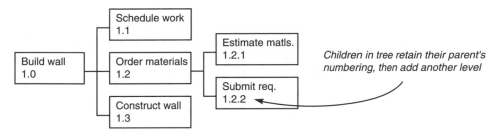

Fig. 8.12 Numbering tasks in tree

- In large projects, where there can be hundreds of tasks, it can be useful to break up the plan into independent pieces. To keep this easy to manage, inter-plan dependencies should be minimized or eliminated.

  The sub-plans can either be a set of sequential plans, where one is completed before the next is started, or nested plans, where a single task in a 'high-level' plan is exploded into a complete sub-plan. Nested plans are particularly easy to do when building plans off Tree Diagrams, with the high-level branches forming the top-level plan and the sub-plans containing the lower level tasks.

- The *Delphi Method* is a method of gaining consensus within a group, which may be used to agree on task duration estimates. This is performed by first asking for task estimates, then sending a summary of responses back out to the team members, inviting them to modify their views in light of this feedback. This is repeated until sufficient consensus is reached.

  A simple method of finding a 'middle point' from the final set of estimates is to use the following formula:

  'Middle' = (Lowest response + (4 × Average response) + Highest response) / 6

Notes

The Activity Network is sometimes called an *Arrow Diagram* or *PERT Chart*, where PERT stands for Programmed Evaluation Review Technique.

There are special computer programs for working with Activity Networks, which are often referred to as Project Management software. These perform the critical path calculation, along with other tasks such as levelling and cost calculations.

See also

Chapters: The Activity Network can be viewed as a special form of Relations Diagram. Display final timings in a Gantt Chart. Use a Tree Diagram to break down tasks.

References: [Mizuno 88] and [Brassard 89] each have a chapter on it. [Gitlow 90] and [Oakland 93] cover it more briefly. [Page-Jones 85] discusses its use for project management.

9 Affinity Diagram

What it's for

To structure a large number of discrete pieces of information.

When to use it

- Use it to bring order to fragmented and uncertain information and where there is no clear structure.
- Use it when information is subjective and emotive, to gain consensus whilst avoiding verbal argument.
- Use it when current opinions, typically about an existing system, obscure potential new solutions.
- Use it, rather than a Relations Diagram, when the situation calls more for creative organization than for logical organization.

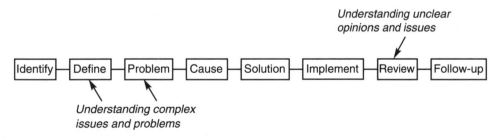

Fig. 9.1 Possible uses in improvement project framework

How to understand it

It is not unusual when working on a project to find a chaotic situation where there are many individual pieces of information held by different people, but no clear picture of the overall problem. The result is often that there are a number of theories and significant disagreement about which is right.

Affinity Diagrams bring order into such uncertain situations by organizing the pieces of information into related groups and then describing the primary characteristic of each group with a 'header' or 'affinity' title. This process can be repeated so that a hierarchy of groups is built up, as in Fig. 9.2.

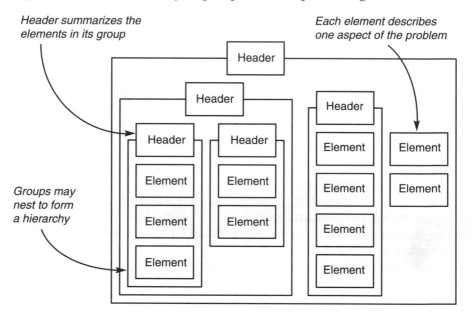

Fig. 9.2 Affinity Diagram components

A key difference between the Affinity Diagram and other tools is that it builds the hierarchy 'bottom-up', starting from the basic elements and working up, as opposed to starting from the top header and working down.

Affinity Diagrams are most commonly built using the 'KJ' method (named after Kawakita Jiro, its originator), which aims to stimulate creative, 'right-brained' thought, rather than logical 'left-brained' thought, by banning discussion during the building of the diagram. The concept of left- and right-brained thinking comes from Nobel-prize winning work that identified how the left hemisphere of the brain is used more for logical, verbal activity, whilst the right hemisphere is used more for creative, non-verbal activity. By deliberately not using left-brained speech, the KJ method encourages the creative right brain to become more active. This silent activity also has the benefit of avoiding discussions that could become heated or otherwise drift away from the real problem at hand.

The result of building an Affinity Diagram should be a problem that is better understood, particularly in the way the individual elements of it fit together into related groups.

Affinity Diagrams are often most useful when they break the problem into fairly small groups which have creative headers. Large groups of elements (typically five to ten or more), particularly with predictable headers such as 'Finance' can indicate that the elements were classified using a logical existing system, rather than by creative affinity grouping.

A good affinity group may have elements that at first sight do not seem to fit well together and have an unusual header, but which when considered with an open mind is understood and throws new light on the problem.

Example

The personnel department of a food supermarket chain store identified a high resignation rate of good checkout staff. There was information available from exit interviews about their reasons for leaving, but this was disorganized and there was no clear area that they felt they could address. They decided to use the KJ method and an Affinity Diagram to try to better understand why these people were leaving (see Fig. 9.3).

As a result, the checkout process was investigated further and eventually completely redesigned. This included a redesigned booth and hourly breaks for operators. Consequently, there were significantly fewer leavers (and as a bonus, customer satisfaction increased).

Other examples
- The design department of a manufacturer of porcelain figurines brainstorm new product ideas. This results in a lot of interesting snippets, but no clear direction. They use an Affinity Diagram to organize and understand the results and find a whole new product line in natural animal figures that reflect current environmental concerns.
- A marketing group have done a customer survey and want to organize the unstructured comments given in the section of 'how could we better serve your needs'. They copy each comment, word for word onto cards and use an Affinity Diagram. The result is a clear segmentation of needs.
- A production cell team use an Affinity Diagram to help organize their thoughts about possible improvement projects before presenting them to their supervisor. The result is clear agreement on key points.

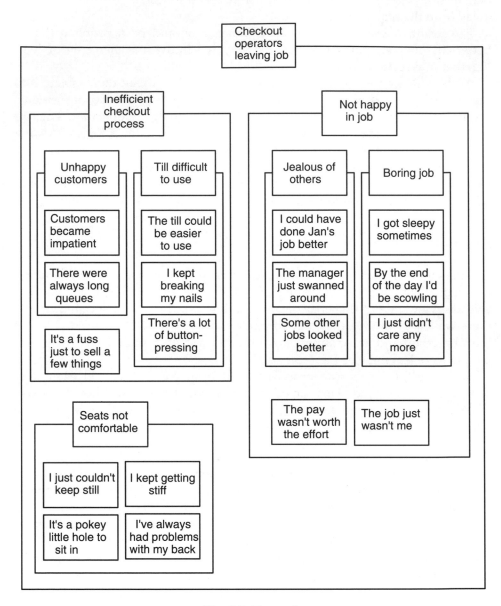

Fig. 9.3 Example

How to do it

1. Form a team of between four and seven people to work on the problem. The ideal group has a good understanding of the problem, works well together and has complementary, rather than supplementary, knowledge. They also have a tendency to think creatively about problems.

2. Define the task in such a way such that the problem is clear, but there is scope for creative thought around it. For example, use 'Design attractive rainwear for 13 to 15 year old girls' rather than 'children's mackintoshes'. In the meeting, display this prominently.

3. Collect data about the problem, for example using Brainstorming, Nominal Group Technique or Surveys. Where data is *verbal*, such as from interviews and observations, record the actual words spoken.

4. Transfer the data onto 3" x 5" cards (one item per card), making sure that what is written is understandable as an individual item. This can be helped by using a complete sentence, and by avoiding abstract terminology. For example, 'Bright colours get you noticed' rather than 'luminous'. If a mixture of subjective and objective data is used, differentiate them for later reference, for example with an asterisk.

5. Shuffle the cards (to remove any patterns that may influence their placement in step 6) and spread them out in a 'parking area' so that they can all be seen. There should be enough space in front of the parking and organization area for the team to freely move.

6. *Silently*, the group reads the cards and moves them one by one from the parking area into the organization area, placing together those that seem to be most closely related, as in Fig. 9.4.

   Use feeling and impression to group cards rather than conventional classifications, such as common keywords and clichés (this is particularly important if you are trying to shed new light on an old problem). Aim for small groups of cards; four or less is good, up to about ten is acceptable.

   Cards may be moved between groups, which can result in people moving cards back and forth in silent debate until one person capitulates. If they persist, the leader or facilitator may have to assist.

   This stage ends when the movement of cards ceases. There may be a few cards left in the parking area which do not fit into any groups.

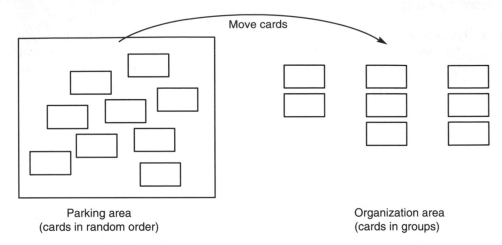

Parking area
(cards in random order)

Organization area
(cards in groups)

Fig. 9.4 Moving the cards

7. Discuss each group, aiming to identify the common characteristics of the group. This may result in cards being moved to or from other groups. Create a header card to summarize the spirit of the group, either by selecting an appropriate card from within the group or by writing a new one.

   Put the header cards at the top of each group, either at the top of a column (as in Fig. 9.5) or physically on top of the group with the other cards attached below it. Mark the header cards, for example with a bold border, to distinguish them from other cards. If the header card is to be moved away from its group, a numbering system can be used to enable it to be put back later.

8. Repeat the process, building up a multi-level tree made up of groups which contain other groups and individual cards. To do this, treat any existing group as a single card, titled as the header card.

   If there are a number of small groups, then clip the group cards under the header card and return them to the parking area before repeating from step 6 until there is only one composite group left.

   If there are a few, larger groups, it may be easier to leave them in place and identify any grouping of these by discussion.

9. The cards and groups may then be documented in a single diagram for communication, discussion, etc.

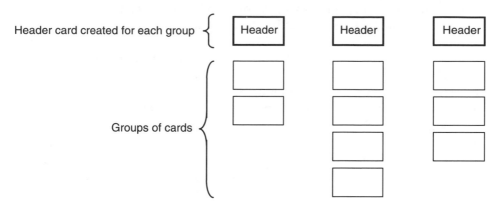

Header card created for each group

Groups of cards

Fig. 9.5 Adding header cards

Practical variations

- Use adhesive memo notes, instead of cards. These stay where they are put, and can be used to sort the notes vertically, on a whiteboard or flipchart. A disadvantage with these is that they are not as durable as card.
- Use different style conventions for showing groups. For example, with group headers not in boxes and groups in rounded boxes (Fig. 9.6).

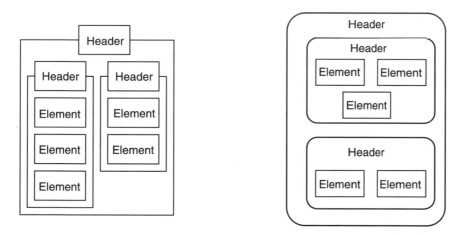

Fig. 9.6 Different display styles

- If cards are used, stop them from moving by attaching them to the organization area, either with reusable adhesive pads or by using a pinboard.
- Do it quickly, to ensure that only feelings and intuition are used to sort cards.
- Do it slowly and carefully, thinking of the real meaning of each card.
- Create one group at a time, selecting only cards from the parking area that fit together in the current group.
- Where there is disagreement (typified by silent moving of cards back and forth), allow people to create a duplicate card, so two or more groups can simultaneously contain the same card. Mark the duplicate cards to indicate their status. This effectively causes an overlap between groups (which may be shown as such on the final diagram).
- Allow group members to write new cards during the KJ session, possibly starting with no cards at all.
- If the resultant diagram has many lines close to one another, then groups may be highlighted by the use of colour or line weight.
- Use flipchart paper for the organization area, and draw vertical lines to create four columns per sheet. Use one column for each group. This makes it easier to sort cards within a limited space. It also prompts for groups to be split if they get too big to fit in one column.
- Keep it simple with only one level of sort (so there is no hierarchy of headers), as in Fig. 9.7.

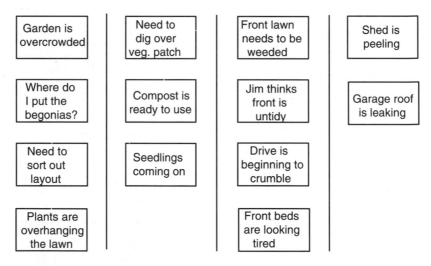

Fig. 9.7 Simple, single-level sort

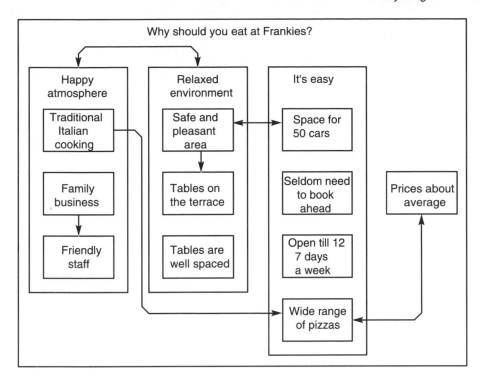

Fig. 9.8 Showing relationships with arrows

- When the diagram is complete, add arrows between items and groups to show significant relationships, as in Fig. 9.8. This is useful where the structure of the problem is mostly hierarchical, but has some interrelationships, and usually illustrates it better than a Relations Diagram.

Notes

Affinity Diagrams are one of the second seven tools.

See also

Chapters: Use it to organise ideas generated from Brainstorming. The principles can also be used to help build, 'bottom up', any tree-shaped tool, including Cause-Effect Diagram, Decision Tree, Fault Tree Analysis, Process Decision Program Chart or Tree Diagram. The result of any complex use may be shown with a

Relations Diagram.

References: [Mizuno 88] has a chapter on it and include many examples. [Asaka 90], [Brassard 89] and [Gitlow 90] give detailed instructions for its use. [Oakland 93] has a section on it and discusses it relative to the other second seven tools.

10 Bar Chart

What it's for

To show the differences between related groups of measurements.

When to use it

- Use it when a set of measurements can be split into discrete and comparable groups, to show the relative change between these groups.
- Use it when there are multiple sets of measurement groups, to show the relationship and change within and between groups.
- Use it, rather than a Line Graph, to display discrete quantities rather than continuing change.
- Use it, rather than a Pareto Chart, when a consistent ordering of bars is wanted. This can ease recognition and comparison of current and previous charts.

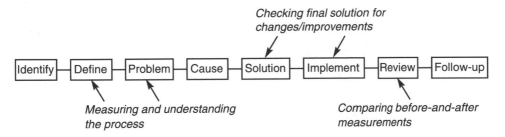

Fig. 10.1 Possible uses in improvement project framework

How to understand it

Numeric measurements may be organized in tables to make them easier to understand, but this format still lacks visual impact, with trends and relative sizes difficult to discern.

The Bar Chart shows measurements in discrete physical bars, as in Fig. 10.2. The area of the bar is proportional to the size of the measurement, and gives a better *visual* impression of its size than a point or vertical line. Where there is more than one bar, then the *relative* sizes can be seen, even between physically separated bars. Even complex trends across multiple bars may be apparent (although Line Graphs and Control Charts can be better for measuring trends).

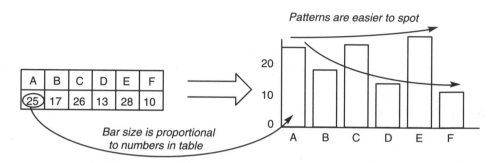

Fig 10.2 Table of numbers versus Bar Chart

The Bar Chart is a flexible format which can be used in a wide number of situations (this may be contrasted with the specific purpose of the Histogram or Pareto Chart). The independent nature of each bar enables even quite disconnected items to be compared.

Example

A corporate finance department regularly reported expenses of group companies in a Bar Chart, which was then used to help identify improvement opportunities (see Fig. 10.3). It was noticed that the company with the highest expenses also had the highest overhead costs. A subsequent project to improve this situation broke down these costs further, using a Pareto Chart. Solutions to the problems were found through the experiences of another group company that had already succeeded in reducing its overheads to the lowest in the group.

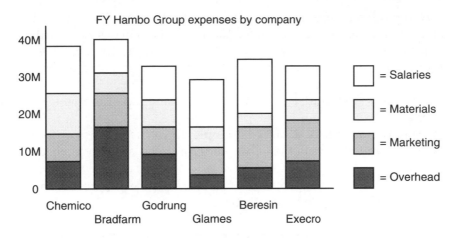

Fig 10.3 Example

Other examples

- A school advertises its improved capability by using a Bar Chart to show the increasing number of exam passes at each grade, across several years.
- A lathe operator, when making a presentation to management about potential improvements, puts the contents of his check sheet into an attractive coloured Bar Chart.
- A software project manager tracks weekly defect arrival, using a Bar Chart in which the defects are broken down further by severity. Thus in one chart, she can see an increase in the arrival of critical defects, even when the overall arrival rate is decreasing.

How to do it

1. Identify the purpose of the Bar Chart, including the questions it may answer and decisions that may be made from it. Common uses include:
   - Analyzing the change in measurements across time.
   - Analyzing the change in measurements for each of a set of related subjects.
   - Showing the above with additional breakdown within each measurement point.
   - Comparing several separate sets of measures.

2. Decide on the data that must be displayed in the chart in order to meet the purpose of step 1.

A typical measurement is of all events of a specific type within a defined time period. For example, 'Value of all cosmetics sales within one financial year'. There may be several data ranges, for example, 'Sales figures for this year and last year' (which are to be compared in the chart).

3. Identify how individual bars are to be made up. Common methods include:
   - Subdivision of total data. For example, all cosmetics sales by month.
   - Subdivision by item. For example, 12 months' sales by each cosmetic type.
   - Combination of the above. For example, each bar is one month's sales, subdivided again by cosmetic type.

4. Select the number of bars in the chart. If multiple groups of bars are to be shown, avoid over-complication by limiting the number of these groups. As a guideline, it should be possible to clearly see the colour or shading of each bar on the final chart. Typically, this will result in a limit of around 10 to 15 bars.

   For example, a year's sales figures are better shown as 12 monthly bars, rather than 52 weekly bars. However, if this year's sales are being compared with those of the past 2 years (using groups of 3 bars), then it may be better that each bar represents 3 months, which will again result in 12 bars on the chart.

5. Draw a sample chart, and check if it can meet its purpose, both in readability and in the decisions that may be made from it. If necessary, revise the above decisions.

6. Collect the data, for example with a Check Sheet. The results may be displayed in a table, such as Table 10.1.

   Ensure that the data collection process gives reliable data, for example by using trained people.

Table 10.1 Data for plotting in Bar Chart

Sales (Millions)	Year 1	Year 2	Year 3
Product A	12	14	18
Product B	22	12	6
Product C	15	17	16

7. Plot the chart, using appropriate scales. Label it to identify it uniquely and help with any subsequent decision making.

8. Review the chart and act on any identified decision points, such as:
   - Bars above or below target value.
   - Bars of unexpected height, particularly relative to other bars.
   - Trends across sets of bars.

Practical variations

A number of practical variations are shown in Table 10.2, below and on following pages.

Table 10.2 Variations on Bar Charts

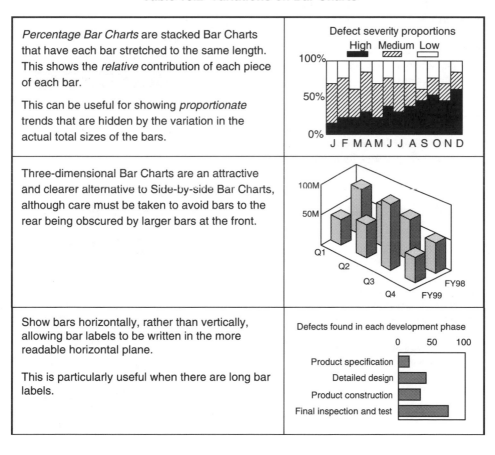

Percentage Bar Charts are stacked Bar Charts that have each bar stretched to the same length. This shows the *relative* contribution of each piece of each bar. This can be useful for showing *proportionate* trends that are hidden by the variation in the actual total sizes of the bars.	Defect severity proportions
Three-dimensional Bar Charts are an attractive and clearer alternative to Side-by-side Bar Charts, although care must be taken to avoid bars to the rear being obscured by larger bars at the front.	
Show bars horizontally, rather than vertically, allowing bar labels to be written in the more readable horizontal plane. This is particularly useful when there are long bar labels.	Defects found in each development phase

Table 10.2 Variations on Bar Charts (cont.)

Side-by-side Bar Charts have multiple bars at each measurement position, and are typically used to compare two or three related sets of measurements. As this reduces the width of bars and increases the complexity of the chart, it imposes a practical limit on the number of groups that can usefully be shown.	**Projected financing** Income Expense Loans
Stacked Bar Charts have single bars which are split into several pieces. They are typically used to sub-classify the values at each measurement position. Note how no space between bars reduces the independence of each bar and emphasizes continuous change.	**Defect severity** High Medium Low
Pictorial Charts use pictures or symbols instead of continuous bars. This gives a more dramatic format and emphasizes the number represented by the bar.	**Casualty treatments, May '99** 10 20 30 40 50 Men Women Children
Use negative and positive bars to show negative and positive aspects of a measurement set (such as revenue and expenditure). It can also be useful to superimpose a line graph, showing such as an overall trend.	**Defect fix progress** Reported Fixed To do

- The *Pie Chart* is closely related to the Percentage Bar Chart, in that it highlights the proportionate (rather than absolute) size of a set of data, using angle rather than length to show relative proportions. Where more than one Pie Chart are shown together, the diameter can be used to indicate the total size, as in Fig. 10.4. Other variations on Pie Charts include 'cutting out' key segments and using 3-D effects.

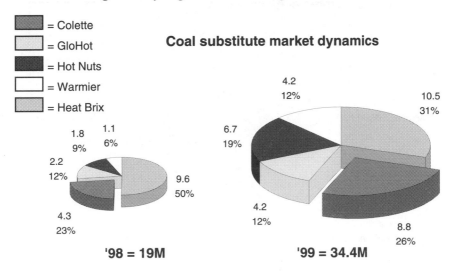

Fig. 10.4 Pie Chart

- The *Band Chart* is a cross between the Percentage Bar Chart and the Pie Chart, as it shows a single set of figures as a percentage. It is similarly useful for comparing proportionate differences between two or more sets of figures, as in Fig. 10.5.

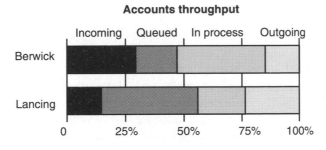

Fig. 10.5 Band Chart

- A *Radar Chart* (or *Glyph*) is a Bar Chart with individual bars arranged in a circle and lines drawn between the top of each 'bar'. This is useful for showing performance relative to limits or other measurement sets, with crossing lines highlighting changes, as in Fig. 10.6. Radar charts are useful for showing improvements of the same system or for comparing different items, such as in competitive analysis.

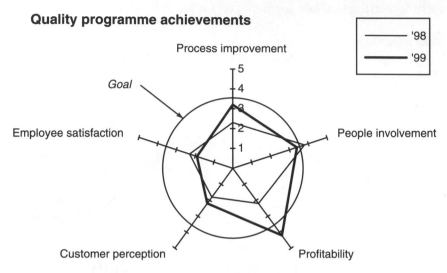

Fig. 10.6 Radar Chart

- Use a graphic picture to show the presence/absence or size of measured items. The picture may be something relevant to the data being displayed, such as a boat for naval information.

Notes

Bar Charts are one of the first seven tools.

See also

Chapters: Gantt Charts, Histograms and Pareto Charts are special cases of Bar Charts. Check Sheets can display data in bars.

References: Bar Charts are often discussed within the context of graphs in general, including in [Ishikawa 76], [Asaka 90] and [Oakland 90]. Some variations are shown in [Rose 57] and [Wadsworth 86].

11 Brainstorming

What it's for

To creatively generate new ideas.

When to use it

- Use it when new ideas are required, to generate a large list of possibilities.
- Use it when a solution to a problem cannot be logically deduced.
- Use it when information about a problem is confused and spread across several people, to gather the information in one place.
- The creative synergy of a Brainstorming session is also useful in helping a team bind together.

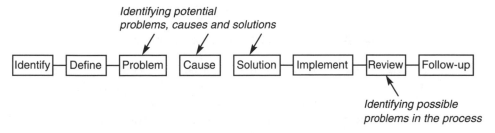

Fig. 11.1 Possible uses in improvement project framework

How to understand it

To live in society, we learn to conform in our thinking as well as our actions, to the degree that we acquire psychological blocks against being different. A consequence of this is that when we try to think of new ideas, our minds work against us, for example by convincing us that unconventional thinking will be ridiculed.   As a result, we often use habitual thought patterns to jump to solutions that are easy to find, but are not necessarily the best approach.

Brainstorming bypasses these blocks and enables the mind to reach its full creative potential by suspending judgment, removing the fear of failure and encouraging the use of *divergent thinking* to achieve a long list of ideas. True divergent thinking differs from conventional thinking, in that the list will contain illogical and unconventional ideas as well as logical and obvious ones. In practice, good solutions are often found within the conventional thinking zone. In the creative zone, however, the abandonment of conventional thought can unearth brilliant new solutions.

It is common to follow the divergent thinking of a Brainstorming session with a more logical *convergent thinking* session to organize and reduce these ideas to one or more which will be used, as in Fig. 11.2.

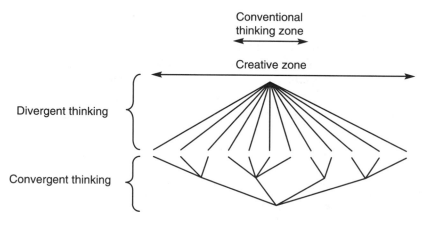

Fig. 11.2 Divergent and convergent thinking

Brainstorming works well in groups, because of the effects of *synergy*, where the effect of people working together is greater than it would be if they had worked individually. For example, one person's (possibly ridiculous) idea can trigger further and possibly more valuable ideas in other people.

The size of the group is important, as if it is too small, some synergy may be lost, but if it is too big, it can become too chaotic or people may hold back for fear of appearing silly.

The creative activity of brainstorming uses 'right brained' thinking in the same way as the Affinity Diagram. It is common for people not to consider themselves as being particularly creative, but actual results and consequent confidence can be significantly improved with practice.

It is useful for a person who is not involved in the creative session to act as facilitator. The purpose of this role is to maintain a non-threatening context, while keeping the participants' minds open and focused solely on the problem. This person owns the process, whilst the Brainstorming group owns the problem. A good facilitator can make a lot of difference, especially if they are skilled at 'opening people up' and encouraging them to be more experimental than they would normally dare to be.

A separate recorder may also be employed to write down the ideas, allowing the facilitator to maintain this focus on the group.

Strictly speaking, Brainstorming is only for creating a list of new ideas. In practice, it tends to be also used for the collection of less creative opinions, and often also includes a voting session to select items for further action.

Example

The picnic committee surveyed a sample of the workforce about what they wanted in it. The most popular request was for a themed event (not just the same old sitting around eating sandwiches). The committee knew the constraints: limited cost and distance. The chairman asked the works manager to facilitate a Brainstorming session so he could join the group.

The meeting started with the facilitator introducing himself and the recorder (his secretary) and laying down the ground rules. The problem, 'Theme for a company picnic' was pinned to a wall and two flipcharts were set up to record ideas where everyone could see them. The meeting started:

Facilitator:	Mike, you start.
Mike:	How about Country and Western?
Facilitator:	Fine. Jane, you're next in line ...
Jane:	Cowboys and Indians.
John:	No, we did that a couple of years ago ...
Facilitator:	Sorry, John, can we stick to the rules? No criticism of any kind, no matter what.
John:	Sorry, Jane. Ok ... horse racing.
Celia:	Dog racing!
...	
<later>	
Jane:	Green.

Sandra: (laughing) Sky-blue pink with purple dots!

John: Yes! Aeroplanes! We could hold it at the local airfield, and have plane rides ...

Facilitator: Sounds good, John, but let's discuss details later. Ken, you look like you're thinking about something.

...

<later>

Facilitator: Ok, we seem to have a good set of ideas. Now it's time to find the best ones. Can you all come up and put three crosses against your favourite idea, two against the next one, and then one each against three 'runners up'.

<a little later>

Facilitator: Right. The top three, aeroplanes, clowns and hats are clearly more popular than any of the others. Let's take a little time to discuss them. Jane, could you tell us why aeroplanes would be a *good* theme? [Jane did not vote for aeroplanes].

<later>

Celia: We could have a funny planes theme, or an aeroplane hat competition.

Mike: Mmm. Fun in the air could include things like kite flying.

<later>

Facilitator: The suggested theme is 'Clowning about in the air'. Are we all agreed, then, that this is the joint recommendation of this group?

The result of the meeting was the whole group enthusing about a theme that was a synthesis of a straight suggestion with an idea which was sparked off by a ridiculous bit of fun. The picnic was a great success.

Other examples
- A management team uses a Brainstorming format to collect opinions on the validity of a draft training strategy.
- A workgroup of people who use compressed air tools Brainstorm for ideas to reduce the noise made by their tools.
- A group of accountants use a Brainstorming session to find ways of reducing tax payments without transgressing the law.

How to do it

1. Start with a clear, open and unambiguous statement of the problem that you want to address. Thus 'Theme for company picnic' is better than 'Possible formal celebration this summer'.

2. Appoint a facilitator to organize and run the Brainstorming meeting. Look for a person who is skilled in facilitating, who has no strong opinions about the problem and who the potential Brainstorming group will respect in that role. If possible, also appoint a recorder (if this is not possible, the facilitator may take this role).

3. Form a group of between five and eight people who may contribute to the problem. Look for complementary, rather than supplementary knowledge, to allow for the broadest range of inputs. Try to avoid including people who may antagonize or inhibit one another.

4. Lay out the meeting room with participants facing one wall, on which is a whiteboard or flipchart. Thus they face the problem, not one another. Prominently display the description of the problem to solve, which may be of the form, 'How can we ... ?'

5. In the meeting, the facilitator focuses the group by describing the four rules of Brainstorming (which he will help to drive during the meeting):
   (a) *No criticism or debate*. Absolutely no negative talk allowed. Focus on the problem, not each other. Suspend judgment until later.
   (b) *The sky is the limit*. The wilder the ideas the better. Crazy ideas often lead to useful ideas.
   (c) *Quantity rather than quality*. The more ideas you have, the more chance of a useful one appearing.
   (d) *Mutate and combine*. Key off each other's suggestions, changing and mixing existing ideas in order to create new ones. Even slight variations or 'misinterpretations' are valid.

   The facilitator will also maintain a psychologically 'safe' environment during the meeting, upholding the 'no criticism' rule and also preventing other factors which might inhibit contributions, such as the presence of tape recorders or observers. Interruptions should also be prevented, as these may disturb the flow of ideas.

6. Start generating ideas, making sure that everyone can contribute. For example, start by taking turns in 'round robin' fashion to add ideas, then drop into a free-for-all when the first burst of ideas has run out.

7. As the ideas are suggested, the recorder writes each one down on the whiteboard or flipchart, so that they are all in full view of the participants.

8. Ways to regenerate flagging ideas include:
    - Build a private list of ideas beforehand, and dip into it when ideas run out or get stuck in a rut.
    - Stop for a while, and just *look* at the ideas generated so far. Look again for mutations and combinations.
    - Take a break. Rest the mind. Do something to take thoughts away from the problem for a while. Even consider leaving the conclusion of the meeting for several days, allowing people to come back and add new ideas at odd moments.
    - Have a 'wild idea' session, where the main objective is to come up with outlandish ideas.
    - Improve on promising ideas by talking about, 'What I like about this idea ... '.
    - Use one or more of the variations below.

9. When there are no more ideas to add, discuss the listed ideas, looking to identify the better ideas rather than eliminating those which are not so good. The ideas can be reviewed in the light of known constraints, such as time and cost, again looking positively for how they can be used within these constraints.

10. If there is no clear agreement on the best idea, or if there is any chance of participants being reticent, identify a voting system to decide (see Chapter 40).

    The facilitator confirms that this is a group decision, and that all support the final choice.

Practical variations

- Include someone in the team who is known for being creative, but who is completely naive about the problem. They can help to open up new possibilities.
- If your morals permit, drink a little alcohol to help reduce inhibitions (but not so much as to fog the brain!).
- Remove the thinking constraints of the normal work environment by moving the Brainstorming session to a less conventional situation. Factors that can be changed include time, location, dress. For example, have an informal session one evening in a local bar.
- Help people to relax by telling some jokes. Laughter is always good, provided you laugh together, and not at one another. A mark of a good Brainstorming sessions is that the people involved *enjoyed* themselves.

- Before starting to write down ideas, have a silent period during which participants think about the problem. They may, if they wish, write down ideas to call out later.
- Leave the final list pinned to a wall or sent as a copy to team members so they can look at it in odd moments. This can allow late ideas to be added and allows an incubation period, where some thought can be given before starting any subsequent selection process. This can help to prevent any immediate discounting of 'ridiculous' ideas.

   A possible danger with this is where strong individuals informally canvass other team members to back their favourite idea. On the other hand, diving straight into a selection process immediately after Brainstorming can result in the excitement of creation carrying over and impractical ideas being selected.
- Start with a session to come up with ways of restating the problem, looking at it from different angles. Start each restatement with 'How to ...'. The result will be a list of additional stimuli for the main Brainstorming session.
- Have a warm-up session to 'stimulate the creative juices', using a subject about which it is easy to be creative.
- Write the ideas on cards or adhesive memo notes, to enable the ideas to be subsequently organized using other techniques, such as the Affinity Diagram or Relations Diagram.
- Use a standard checklist to prompt for more questions, For example:
   - Replace with something else?
   - Add or extend in some way?
   - Rearrange the parts?
   - Reduce or simplify?
   - Combine diverse elements?
   - Change the sequence?
   - Vary the variables?

- Identify blocks that may have to be overcome by reversing the problem statement. For example, ask, 'How could we prevent people coming to a company picnic?'. This is particularly useful where the subject has emotional connotations and the team is uncomfortable with it.
- After an idea has been selected, brainstorm again to identify possible snags and problems by asking, 'How can this idea fail?'.
- Write ideas in an unclear fashion, then ask people who did *not* create the idea to interpret it. The originator may then say what they were thinking. A simple way of doing this is to use only single words, such as 'opening' or 'red'.

There are many other methods of creating new ideas, which can be used either as modifications to or as replacements of straight Brainstorming. These include:

- *Brainwriting* is based on the 'mutate and combine' rule. In this system, each participant starts with a large sheet of paper, and writes about an idea for around three minutes. The papers are then shuffled and redistributed and each person continues developing the same idea that is already on the sheet. After five rounds, pin the papers to the wall, discuss and vote.
- *Braindrawing* uses the same rules as brainwriting, only instead of writing about the idea, each person does a drawing about the idea and passes it on to the next person who continues the drawing. This helps the creative, non-verbal right brain to be optimally used, and can be effective where the team has a creative block.
- *Rightbraining* encourages the development of partial thoughts by making partial drawings, as in Fig. 11.3. Combine the partial drawings into creative combination drawings.

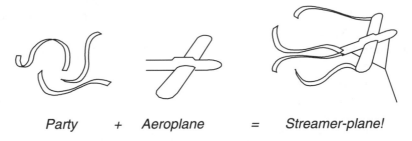

Party   +   Aeroplane   =   Streamer-plane!

Fig. 11.3 Rightbraining

- *Attribute Listing* involves generating a separate list of attributes of the problem, then looking for new ideas through modification of these. For example, attributes of a picnic might include fun, music, games, family, etc. An idea from this could be a for a rock music theme, including a family group kareoke competition.
- In *Morphological Analysis,* the most important dimensions of are problem are identified, then all relationships between these are examined. For a picnic, these could be cost to the company, attendance on the day or the enjoyment engendered. An idea from this could be to survey employees on possible events, showing them the overall cost and possible charges to cover popular but too expensive attractions.

- In *Synectics*, conventional thought and jumping to solutions are avoided as the leader only gradually reveals the full problem, adding more information as the group solves the more general problems first. Thus the picnic discussion may start with a discussion about motivation, then discussing the company as a family, involvement of employees' families and what family groups enjoy doing. This should result in a deeper understanding of the overall problem, which should in turn lead to a better solution. Thus the idea for a picnic could be turned into a weekend camp, where people can get to know each other better.
- *Lateral Thinking* forces new ideas by taking new paths that deliberately avoid conventional thinking. Thus any 'logical' ideas are banned. This requires an open attitude that suspends judgment, looking for ways in which unconventional ideas can be realized.

Notes

Brainstorming is widely used, but there is limited agreement on the detail of how it is to be done. The name is often used for a general collection of thoughts within a group, whether it is creative or simple collation of known facts. Selection, often through Voting, is also often considered to be a part of Brainstorming.

See also

Chapters: Many tools can use the result of Brainstorming, including Affinity Diagram, Cause-Effect Diagram, Decision Tree, Failure Mode and Effects Analysis, Fault Tree Analysis, Force-Field Diagram, Gantt Chart, Process Decision Program Chart, Prioritization Matrix, Relations Diagram, Surveys, Tables, Tree Diagram, Value Analysis and Voting. The Nominal Group Technique is similar to Brainstorming, but less creative.

References: The original description of Brainstorming is in [Osborn 57]. Since then, a great deal has been written on creative thought. [Rawlinson 81] is a more recent book on the subject, including a detailed description plus tips and variations. There are many other descriptions of how to brainstorm, including [Fisher 81], [Scholtes 88] and [Asaka 90] although there is often some variation between each description. [Kotler 88] discusses several variations on idea generation within the context of creating new products. [DeBono 67] is the original book on lateral thinking.

Many of his other books, such as [DeBono 71], discuss and extend this. [Gordon 61] describes Synectics in detail. A number of other books give ways of increasing creativity, including [Parnes 62], [Adams 74], [Ray 89], [Juniper 89] and [Foster 91].

12 Cause-Effect Diagram

What it's for

To identify and structure the causes of a given effect.

When to use it

- Use it when investigating a problem, to identify and select key problem causes to investigate or address.
- Use it when the primary symptom (or effect) of a problem is known, but possible causes are not all clear.
- Use it when working in a group, to gain a common understanding of problem causes and their relationship.
- Use it to find other causal relationships, such as potential risks or causes of desired effects.
- Use it in preference to a Relations Diagram where there is one problem and causes are mostly hierarchical (this will be most cases).

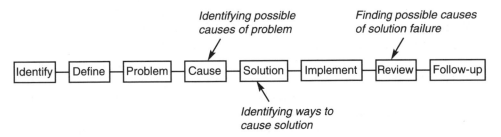

Fig. 12.1 Possible uses in improvement project framework

How to understand it

Solutions to problems are often not easy to find, and those that at first appear to be obvious may address only symptoms rather than the true cause of the problem. Identifying causes as an intermediate step makes solutions both easier to find and also more likely to address the problem fully.

Causes tend to appear in chains, where one cause is caused by another, and so on. Thus an accident may be caused by a puncture, which is caused by a weak tyre wall, which is caused by imperfections in the rubber, etc. One cause may also be caused by a combination of other causes. Thus the puncture may be caused by a rough road surface and by sudden braking, as well as a weak tyre, as in Fig. 12.2.

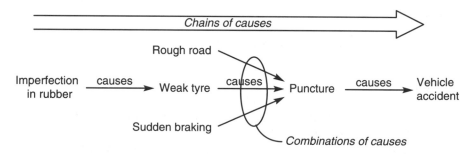

Fig. 12.2 Chains and combinations of causes

The Cause-Effect Diagram uses a specific layout to display the hierarchy of causes, as in Fig. 12.3. The angled lines enable more detail to be added than lines at right angles to one another, especially in an informal situation where causes are being added 'on the fly'. Each line indicates either a named cause or a *cause area* which contributes to the cause line to which it is attached. A cause area is not a cause, but may contain causes. For example, a tyre may be a cause area but may not be a cause of an accident. A smooth or punctured tyre can be a cause. Cause areas tend to be nouns, whilst causes tend to use verbs.

When determining causes of a problem, the important causes that need to be addressed are seldom all known, let alone the effects of individual causes on the problem and on one another. The Cause-Effect Diagram is often used to address this by acting as an organizing structure within a Brainstorming session, in which case the causes on the final diagram may be a combination of known, suspected and other possible causes.

The Cause-Effect Diagram is often the result of divergent thinking about causes, and must be followed by convergence into the *key causes* which are to be addressed by further action. To prevent ineffective solutions, these need to be verified as being actual causes before finding solutions for them.

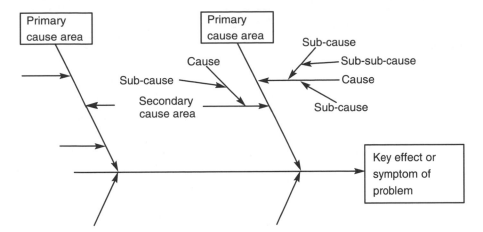

Fig. 12.3 Elements of Cause-Effect Diagram

Root causes are those at the ends of chains of causes, and which do not have any sub-causes. Root causes of key causes are often worth addressing.

A lopsided diagram can indicate an over-focus in one area, a lack of knowledge in other areas, or it can simply indicate that the causes are focused in the denser area. A sparse diagram may indicate a lack of general understanding of the problem or just a problem with few possible causes.

Example

The managing director of a weighing machine company received a number of irate letters, complaining of slow service and a constantly engaged telephone. Rather surprised, he asked his support and marketing managers to look into it. With two other people, they first defined the key symptom as 'lack of responsiveness to customers' and then met to brainstorm possible causes, using a Cause-Effect Diagram, as in Fig. 12.4.

They used the 'Four Ms' (Manpower, Methods, Machines and Materials) as primary cause areas, and then added secondary cause areas before adding actual causes, thus helping to ensure that all possible causes were considered. Causes common to several areas were flagged with capital letters, and key causes to verify and address were circled.

On further investigation, they found that service visits were not well organized; engineers just picked up a pile of calls and did them in order. They consequently set up regions by engineer and sorted calls; this reduced traveling time and increased service turnaround time. They also improved the telephone system and reviewed their suppliers' quality procedures.

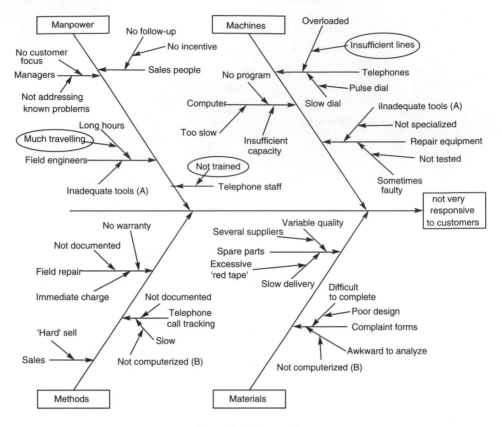

Fig. 12.4 Example

Other examples

- A sales team, working to increase the number of customers putting the company on their shortlist for major purchases, identifies through a survey that the key problem is that the customers perceive the company as a producer of poor-quality goods. They use a Cause-Effect Diagram to brainstorm possible causes of this.
- A pig farmer gets swine fever in her stock. To help ensure it never recurs, she uses a Cause-Effect Diagram to identify possible causes of the infection, and then checks if they can happen and implements preventive action to ensure none can happen in future.
- A wood turner notices that his chisels sometimes become blunt earlier than usual. He uses a Cause-Effect Diagram to identify potential causes. Checking up on these, he finds that this happens after working with oak. Consequently, he resharpens the chisels after turning each oak piece.

How to do it

1. Form a small team of people to work on the problem. Ideally, their knowledge and skills will be complementary, to give a broad but expert group. If it has not been already defined, meet first to define the key symptom or effect of the problem under scrutiny. Aim for a brief, clear phrase which describes what is happening to what, such as, 'Low sales of MkII Costor'.

   Make sure that only a single effect is described, as this may result in several sets of causes. For example, an effect of 'damp and dirty conditions' could have different causes of dampness and of dirt.

2. Write down the key effect or symptom at the center-right of the page (or whiteboard or flipchart, if you are doing it in a group), and draw a spine horizontally from it to the left.

3. Draw the main cause area 'ribs' (typically around four to six), one for each of what appears to be the primary cause areas. If these are uncertain, then the 'Four Ms' (Manpower, Methods, Machines and Materials) provide a good starting point, as in Fig. 12.5.

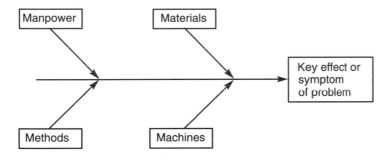

Fig. 12.5 'Four Ms' cause areas

4. Use Brainstorming to build the diagram, adding causes or cause areas to the appropriate ribs or sub-ribs as they appear.

   If a cause appears in several places, show the linkage by using the same capital letter next to each linked cause, as in Fig. 12.4.

   Beware of adding 'causes' which are actually solutions. These often are expressed as a negative; further consideration may find a truer cause. For example, a better cause than 'no heating' may be 'low ambient temperature', as it opens up the possibility of additional practical solutions, such as 'installing insulation'.

Beware also of things which are knock-on effects, rather than causes, e.g. given an effect of 'Inadequate telephone system', a sub-cause may be 'Insufficient lines', but 'Dissatisfied staff' is a knock-on effect.

Ways of finding more causes include:
- Keep asking 'Why?'. A popular phrase is, 'Ask Why five times'.
- Look at the diagram without talking. Look for patterns.
- Take a break. Do something to take your mind off your current line of thought.
- Involve other people, especially those who have expertise in the problem areas.
- Leave the chart on the wall for a few days to let ideas incubate and encourage passers-by to contribute.

If the diagram becomes lopsided or cramped, you may want to reorganize the diagram with different major ribs.

5. Discuss why the found causes are there. Look for and circle key causes which require further attention. Avoid having too many key causes, as this may result in defocused activities. If there is no clear agreement, use a Voting system.

6. Consider the key causes again. Are any more important than others? If so, put a second circle around them, or put numbers next to them to show their relative priority.

7. If necessary, gather data to confirm key causes are real, and not just assumed. Repeat the process as necessary.

8. Plan and implement actions to address key causes.

Practical variations

- Add 'mini' Cause-Effect Diagrams at each point along a Flowchart or any other relevant diagram, to identify potential problems, as in Fig. 12.6. This can also be done in a Force-Field Diagram.
- Do it in two stages. First ask '*What* could be a cause?', identifying all cause areas (e.g. under 'machines' this could be car, phone, computer, etc.), then ask '*How* could it cause problems?' to find possible causes in each of these areas (e.g. under 'phone' could be 'no visual communication', 'interrupts other activities', etc.). This is a rigorous approach that will result in a very

dense diagram, but which may help to find unexpected causes.

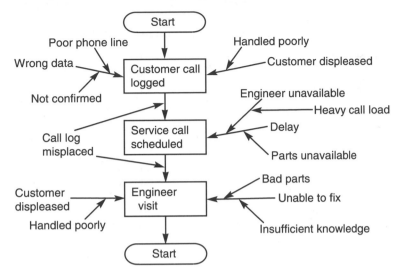

Fig. 12.6 Cause-Effect on Flowchart

- Write down all causes in a simple list before building the chart. An Affinity Diagram can then be used to organize the causes, to help find the main cause areas.
- Differentiate cause areas from actual causes, for example by circling or underlining them.
- Start with a fairly quick pass at identifying causes, select key causes from these, and then to home in on these key causes, tracking back to root causes. This can speed up the process, but can also result in other causes being missed.
- The 'four Ms' are sometimes called the 'four Ps' which are People, Process, Product and Plant. Common additional major cause areas include Programmes, Policy, Plans, Environment, Maintenance, Management, Money, Measurement.
- Indicate differing confidence in causes, for example, where there is a mixture of measured, unmeasured and speculative causes, show the difference by putting a box around measured causes and underlining unmeasured causes.
- Start with a *desired* effect, and determine what must be done to cause it.
- Start with an effect on the *left* of the page and determine the possible knock-on effects, as in Fig. 12.7.
- Start with an effect in the *middle* of the page and expand its causes to the left, and its knock-on effects to the right.

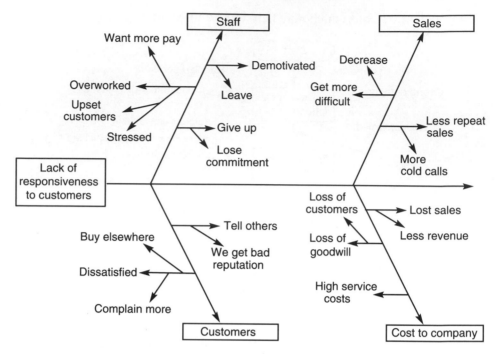

12.7 Showing possible knock-on effects

Notes

The Cause-Effect Diagram is one of the first seven tools. It is also called a *Fishbone Diagram*, because of its shape, or an *Ishikawa Chart*, after its originator, Kaoru Ishikawa, who first used it in 1943.

See also

Chapters: Use it to identify causes of a key problem as identified in a Pareto Chart, Voting or Prioritization Matrix. Use Brainstorming to identify possible causes. It can be used to extend a Flowchart or Force-Field Diagram to show causal chains. The Relations Diagram is an alternative tool where causes have complex interrelationships. The Cause-Effect Diagram is a specialized form of Tree Diagram.

References: [Ishikawa 76] contains a chapter on Cause-Effect Diagrams, and is the most common reference. [Asaka 90] and [Oakland 90] covers them in fair detail, whilst other books contain briefer descriptions, including [Wadsworth 86] and [Sinha 85].

13 Check Sheet

What it's for

To manually collect data in a reliable, organized way.

When to use it

- Use it when data is to be recorded manually, to ensure the data is accurately recorded and is easy to use later, either for direct interpretation or for transcription, for example into a computer.
- Use it when the recording involves counting, classifying, checking or locating.
- Use it when it is useful to check each measurement as it is recorded, for example that it is within normal bounds.
- Use it when it is useful to see the distribution of measures as they are built up.

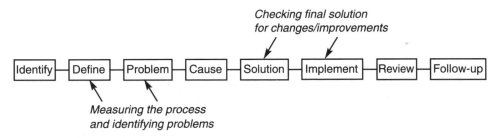

Fig. 13.1 Possible uses in improvement project framework

How to understand it

If data is collected in a disorganized way, it is likely to end up as a jumble of numbers on a convenient scrap of paper, where the numbers are easily misunderstood and the paper may be lost. By collecting it in an organized way, fewer mistakes are likely in the collection, transcription, understanding and storage of the data.

A Check Sheet is simply a sheet of paper organized to simplify and standardize manual data collection and to ease interpretation of results. The simplification is characterized by the use of checks or marks to record events, rather than recording these as numbers or text, as in Fig. 13.2. This enables one Check Sheet to contain a large number of recorded data points.

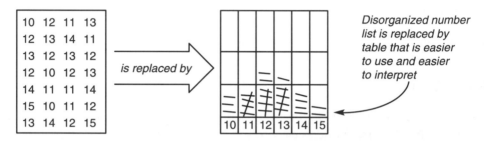

Fig. 13.2 Simplifying and standardizing manual data recording

There are three main uses of Check Sheets. Firstly, they can be used to count items, either as a simple count of different items, such as defects, or to show the distribution of a set of measurements. Simple counts may be displayed as a Pareto Chart, whilst distribution may be displayed as a Histogram. When counting items, the Check Sheet also is useful as the overall picture is built up in front of your eyes as you add individual items. Secondly, they may be used to show the physical location of something, such as defects on a manufactured item. This is useful for finding significant bunching of measurements which may then help to find problems. Lastly, they may be used to help prompt for an action and consequently be ticked to certify that a particular action has been carried out.

In interpreting and analyzing Check Sheets, identified problems may be broken down further by using the other information on the sheets about the circumstances where the measurements were made. A danger in interpretation is in not having or using this information and making assumptions that localized problems are more widespread than they are. For example, a defect log from a single product line may be wrongly generalized to cover all product lines.

Example

The paint bay team in a car manufacturer had the objective of discovering and removing the main causes of paint blemishes in doors. To achieve this, they concluded that they needed to determine the number and location of each type of blemish. They also defined the process to capture data on one form for each paint lot. They used a combination of a Defective Item Check Sheet and a Location Plot, as in Fig. 13.3.

Paint bubbles were the most common problem, and were investigated first. The grouping led the team to investigate the paint programming, where it was discovered that the paint robot was hesitating at corners. Reprogramming the robot significantly reduced the number of errors. Further analysis found that varying paint viscosity was causing runs.

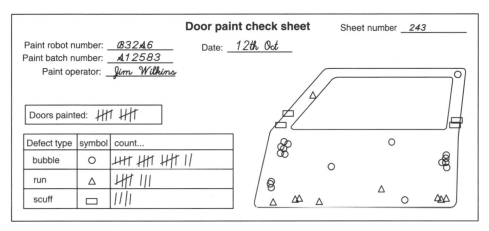

Fig. 13.3 Example

Other examples

- A customer response group use a Check Sheet to track the time band during the day when each customer calls. They then ensure that there are enough people available to cope with the heavy load periods. This reduces fatigue and increases customer satisfaction.
- A drinks retailer has a Check Sheet to log the types of purchase made, and changes her stock and displays to expand the range in the more popular types of wine. The result is a measurable increase in turnover.
- A garage uses a Checklist to ensure all service points are completed. The engineer then signs it and gives a copy to the customer as an assurance. This significantly reduces service omission errors.

How to do it

1. Identify the end objectives of the measurement, such as what questions are to be answered and what decisions are to be made. Consequently, identify what data needs to be collected, and in what format. Common uses for Check Sheets include:
    *   Measuring the distribution of a set of measurements.
    *   Counting and classifying defects into various types.
    *   Identifying the physical location of defects.
    *   Verifying that actions have been completed.

2. Identify the data that needs to be collected about the process. This should include all variables which could be problem causes or could contribute to variation in results, such as date, time, operator, batch number, machine reference, etc.

3. Identify the period and circumstances of data collection and consequently estimate the maximum number of measurements per Check Sheet.

    If samples are being taken (as opposed to measuring everything), make sure that these are planned carefully, for example by taking sufficient measurements at appropriate points in the process.

4. Design the Check Sheet, aiming to ease the collection, transcription and interpretation processes. A typical form includes:
    *   An area for the data about the process.
    *   An area to collect the main data, organized so that it may be visually interpreted. This should be large enough to contain the maximum expected number of data elements (step 3).
    *   Columns or rows to total the data, ready for transcription (typically into a computer, for later reference or further analysis).
    *   Other information about the situation where the data was collected that may help decision making, such as operator, date, machine, weather, etc.

    Common designs for Check Sheets are discussed under *Practical variations*, below.

5. Ensure the Check Sheet works as intended by testing it, preferably in a live situation.

6. Ensure users are able to use the Check Sheets properly. This may include

training, adjusting work instructions, etc. In any case, the data recording should not be too intrusive.

7. Collect the data, ensuring all required data is entered onto the form and can be clearly read. Ensure that representative samples are being taken for the conclusions that will be drawn from the results (for example, assumptions about everyone cannot be made if only one person is using it).

8. Interpret and use the results as planned.

Practical variations

- A *Process Distribution Check Sheet* measures the frequency of a single item across a range of measures, visually showing the distribution, as in Fig. 13.4. These are interpreted as histograms.

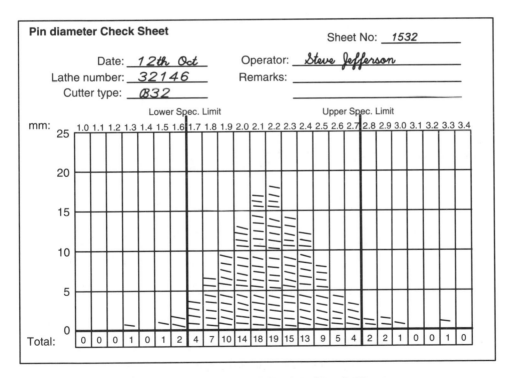

Fig. 13.4 Process Distribution Check Sheet

- A *Defective Item Check Sheet* counts and classifies defects by type, as in Fig. 13.5. If the expected ordering is known (e.g. the Pareto sequence), then the Check Sheet can be designed with this ordering set up, so any deviation may be detected. These may be interpreted as Pareto Charts (and can be redrawn as such).

Typing test analysis		Date: *12th Oct*
Typist: *Kelly Hall*		Test: *R324*
Examiner: *Jay Brown*		
Type of error	**Count**	**Score**
Reversed letters	ⱶⱶⱵ	5
Missing letters	ⱶⱶⱵ |||	8
Extra letters	ⱶⱶⱵ	5
Wrong letters	ⱶⱶⱵ ⱶⱶⱵ	10
	Total errors:	28

Fig. 13.5 Defective Item Check Sheet

- A *Location Plot* (or *Defect Location Check Sheet* or *Concentration Diagram*) uses a picture of the item to mark defect positions, as in Fig. 11.6. Problem areas are usually indicated by clustering of marks.

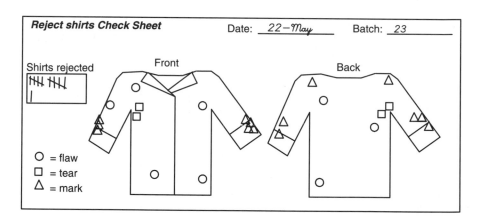

Fig. 11.6 Location Plot

- A *Defective Cause Check Sheet* aims to correlate cause and effect, by including possible causal factors, such as time of day, operator, machine and location. It can also be used as a part of a controlled experiment. In order to correlate many factors, it can get quite complex (and be quite a design challenge!).
- A *Checklist* (or *Check-up Confirmation Check Sheet*) contains a list of actions or results of actions which are ticked as they are done (such as during the service of a motor vehicle). The complete checklist then becomes a certificate of completion. Simple checklists are often a good solution for problems where important activities can be forgotten.

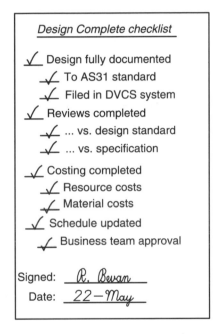

Fig. 13.6 Checklist

- A *Work Sampling Check Sheet* is used to analyze how time is spent, by classifying the type of activity being done at randomly selected moments throughout the day.
- A *Travelling Check Sheet* moves with a product through production and forms a complete running record of all tests and inspections. This can form a useful certificate of completion.

Notes

Check Sheets are also known as *Data Collection Sheets*. Where they are used for counting, a commonly used name is *Tally Chart*. They are one of the first seven tools.

See also

Chapters: Check Sheet marks may be built up as a Histogram. Results of classifications may be shown in a Pareto Chart.

References: [Ishikawa 76] and [Asaka 90] discuss Check Sheets in detail. [Wadsworth 86] contains a number of examples and variations. They are also discussed more briefly in [Feigenbaum 86] and [Oakland 90].

14 Control Chart

What it's for

To identify dynamic and special causes of variation in a repeating process.

When to use it

- Use when investigating a process, to determine whether it is in a state of statistical control and thus whether actions are required to bring the process under control.
- Use it to differentiate between special and common causes of variation, identifying the special causes which need to be addressed first.
- Use it to detect statistically significant trends in measurements; for example, to identify when and by how much a change to the process has improved it.
- Use it as an ongoing 'health' measure of a process, to help spot problems before they become significant.
- It is only practical to use it when regular measurements of a process can be made. Typically this is in processes that repeat within a reasonably short space of time.

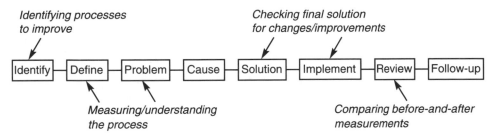

Fig. 14.1 Possible uses in improvement project framework

How to understand it

Chapter 5 (on variation) shows that when a process is run repeatedly, even under apparently stable conditions, measurements made of it will seldom be identical. A Histogram can be used to show the static distribution of a set of these measurements, but this does not show dynamic trends, for example where successive measurements may indicate a significant change within the process (see Fig. 14.2).

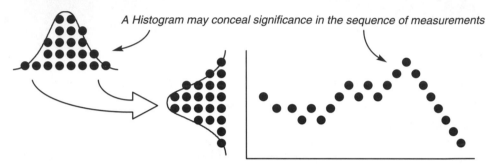

A Histogram may conceal significance in the sequence of measurements

Fig. 14.2 Dynamic variation

A Control Chart usually has three horizontal lines in addition to the main plot line, as shown in Fig. 14.3. The central line is the average (or *mean*). The outer two lines are at three standard deviations either side of the mean. Thus 99.7% of all measurements will fall between these two lines (this is described in more detail in Chapter 5).

The top line is called the *upper control limit* and the bottom line is called the *lower control limit*, as points falling outside these bounds are considered

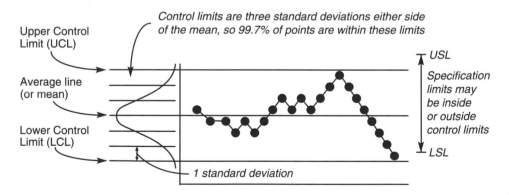

Fig. 14.3 Control limits

as being out of control. These limits are often abbreviated to UCL and LCL. Although control limits are straight lines for most types of Control Charts, there are some types of chart where they are different for each plotted point, as in Fig. 14.6.

Note that specification limits are not related to control limits. Specification limits say what the process results *should* be, whilst control limits show what the process is *actually* doing.

The actual calculations of control limits varies with the type of measurement being portrayed (this is for mathematical reasons). Measurements which answer the question, 'How *much*?' are called *variables* (e.g. weight, time, voltage). A further identification is that they are measured in quantitative units, such as grams and seconds. Non-variable measurements are called *attributes*. These ask, 'How *many*?', measuring countable items, such as the number of defective items or the number of actual defects in a batch (note the difference: one defective item may contain several defects).

Each point on a variables Control Chart is usually made up of the average of a set of measurements. This is for two reasons.

Firstly, it results in a predictable Normal (bell-shaped) distribution for the overall chart, due to the Central Limit Theorem, as described in Chapter 5.

Secondly, this will result in tighter control limits. This is because the averaging effect in each group smooths out individual high and low measurements, resulting in a Control Chart that can detect smaller changes in the process than one which plots one point for each measurement. This is illustrated in Fig. 14.4, which shows how the same shift in average results in a greater likelihood that a narrow distribution will detect this change. In a Control Chart where each point represents the average of a set of measurements, this would result in points outside the control limits that would not be outside the limits of a Control Chart where each point represents a single measurement.

Two Control Charts must be drawn when tracking variables, because just measuring the average of subgroups could result in significant variation *within* the subgroups being missed, as illustrated in Fig. 14.5. It may also be noticed here that the control limits for the range chart are not symmetrical about the central average line. This is because although the average chart has a Normal distribution, the distribution of the range chart is skewed. It is also common for the lower control limit of a range chart to be on the zero line, as a negative value would be nonsense.

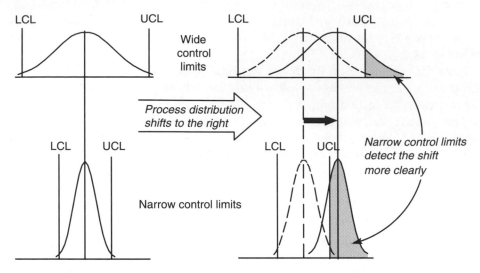

Fig. 14.4 Effect of spread on sensitivity to change

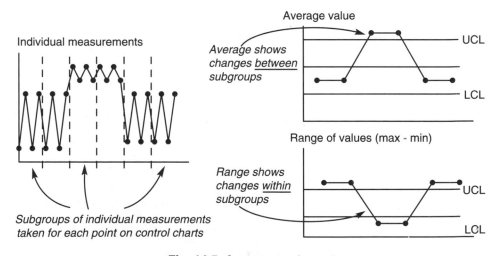

Fig. 14.5 Average and range

Interpretation of the Control Chart requires identification of significant factors such as points which fall outside the control limits or patterns which repeat seven or more times. A significant point or pattern will indicate that the process is 'out of control'. This does not necessarily mean that it is wildly wrong, but it does indicate that it is not statistically stable. Conversely, a statistically stable process may have unsatisfactorily wide variation.

When significant patterns or points are found, then assistance with identifying possible typical causes may be found by using a Cause-Effect Diagram. These include changes in people, the actions they carry out, the tools and machines used, the raw materials and the general environment. Basic patterns to look for and possible interpretations are shown in Table 14.1.

Table 14.1 Interpreting patterns in Control Charts

Control Chart	Name	Description	Possible interpretation
	Special cause of variation	Point outside control limits.	Something unusual has happened. e.g. Person was interrupted.
	Shift	Seven or more consecutive points, all on one side of the central average line.	The overall average has changed. e.g. Showing result of process improvement.
	Trend	Seven or more consecutive points, all increasing or decreasing in value.	Gradual change in the process. e.g. A tool is wearing out.
	Cycle	Seven or more repeating patterns (possibly over several points).	Time-related effect. e.g. People changing with shifts.

Example

An accounts department started an improvement project to try to reduce the number of internal purchase forms that its users completed incorrectly. As an overall measure of their success, they used a p-type Control Chart to measure the proportion of purchase forms that were not completed correctly. This was chosen, rather than measuring the actual number of defects, because any number of defects on a form required about the same effort to revise.

Each point on the chart represented all purchase forms for one day. This was chosen as it allowed a 25-point chart to be drawn reasonably quickly. This subgroup size was permissible as, even though the number of forms in each group was less than 50, the number of defective forms in each subgroup was more than 4.

A Pareto Chart indicated that the development department made most mistakes, and a survey indicated that they did not understand the form. On the 15th of the month, a half-hour training class was held for the development people. Table 14.2 and Fig. 14.6 shows the calculation and Control Chart for the month. It can be seen that after the training, there were nine points in a row below the centre line indicating a statistically significant improvement.

In the next month, the proportion defective was further reduced by extending the training to other departments. Before long, there were so few wrongly completed purchase forms that the subgroup period had to be extended to one week.

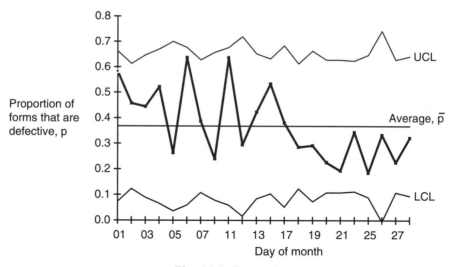

Fig. 14.6 Example

Table 14.2 Example

Day of month	Number of purchase forms, n	Number of defective forms	Proportion defective, p	LCL	UCL
01	24	14	0.583	0.073	0.663
02	35	16	0.457	0.123	0.613
03	27	12	0.444	0.090	0.646
04	23	12	0.522	0.066	0.670
05	19	5	0.263	0.036	0.700
06	22	14	0.636	0.060	0.677
07	31	12	0.387	0.108	0.628
10	25	6	0.240	0.079	0.657
11	22	14	0.636	0.060	0.677
12	17	5	0.294	0.017	0.719
13	26	11	0.423	0.084	0.652
14	30	16	0.533	0.104	0.632
17	21	8	0.381	0.052	0.684
18	35	10	0.286	0.123	0.613
19	24	7	0.292	0.073	0.663
20	31	7	0.226	0.108	0.628
21	31	6	0.194	0.108	0.628
24	32	11	0.344	0.112	0.624
25	27	5	0.185	0.090	0.646
26	15	5	0.333	0.000	0.742
27	31	7	0.226	0.108	0.628
28	28	9	0.321	0.095	0.641

Average proportion defective = 0.368 (this gives the centre line).

Other examples

- A production team in a glass manufacturer uses a c-chart to measure flaws in sheets of float glass. They address problems that the chart highlights until it becomes stable, then use it as an ongoing monitoring measurement. As other improvements are made, the control limits gradually reduce.
- A customer manager uses a p-chart to measure the weekly proportion of customer feedback forms that contain one or more critical complaints about the company's major product. A detected upward trend results in an early correction of a new service routine.
- A lathe operator uses X-bar and R control charts to show the variation of

cut shafts. When a shift towards a control limit is detected, he finds that the cutting tool is wearing, and so replaces it, bringing the process back into control.

How to do it

1. Identify the objective of using the Control Chart. Typically this will be either to detect defects or to monitor a suspect or critical process. For example, 'to monitor the accuracy of a breakfast cereal packet filling process'.

   The process selected should repeat sufficiently often to provide enough measures to be able to plot a Control Chart.

2. Identify the actual measurement to be made, including what to measure, and where in the process to measure it. Select the measurements based on their ability to identify problems or defects.

   Focus the measurement to minimize the likely variation. For example, a separate Control Chart for each of several identical canning lines will be more likely to identify problems on one line than using one chart for all the output of all lines, where significant variation on one line may be swamped by measures from the other lines.

   Reduce waste by identifying the measurement at the earliest point in the process where problems may be detected.

   The actual measurement should be reasonably easy to carry out.

3. Identify the type of Control Charts to use. This will depend on the type of measurement being made. Fig. 14.7 uses a simple chart to ease selection.

   A number of points may be taken into consideration when identifying the type of Control Chart to use:
   - Variables charts are useful for machine-based processes, for example in measuring tool wear.
   - Variables charts are more sensitive to change than Attributes charts, but can be more difficult both in the identification of what to measure and also in the actual measurement.
   - Only use an Individuals (X) chart when few measurements are available (e.g. when they are infrequent or are particularly costly. These charts are less sensitive to change than the Averages (X-bar) chart. They can also have an unusual (non-normal) distribution, in which case the Control Chart is not a suitable tool (use a Line Graph instead).

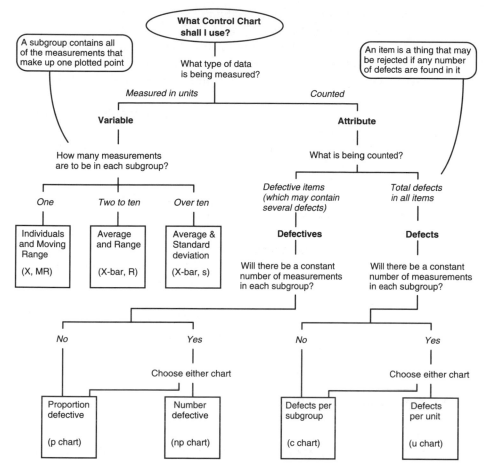

Fig. 14.7 Selecting the type of Control Chart

- The Standard Deviation (s) chart is easier to calculate if a statistical calculator or computer spreadsheet is used. If one of these is available, then the s-chart may be consistently used instead of the Range chart.
- Attribute charts are useful for both machine- and people-based processes. Data for them is often readily available and they are easily understood. It can thus be easier to start with these, then move on to Variables charts for more detailed analysis.
- u- and c-charts give a measure of *how* defective units are (unlike p- and np-charts).
- In a u-chart, the defects within the unit must be independent of one another, for example, 'component failures on a printed circuit board'.

- Use a u-chart for continuous items, such as fabric. An example measure is 'defects per square foot of cloth'.
- A c-chart is a useful alternative to a u-chart when there are a lot of possible defects on a unit, but there is only a small chance of any one defect occurring. For example, 'flaws in a roll of material'.

4. Choose the *subgroup*. This is the group of measurements that will make up each plotted point on the Control Chart.

   Each subgroup typically contains the same number of measurements, although p- and c-charts are bounded by events, such as time (e.g. measurements per week), people or batches. In any case, there should be enough measurements in each subgroup to make the chart statistically correct and Table 14.3 gives guidelines for this.

   The subgroup should be selected with the aim of (a) making the measurement *within* each subgroup as consistent as possible, whilst (b) maximizing the chance of highlighting differences *between* subgroups. Considerations include:
   - Synchronizing measurement points with other process variables. For example, measure weekly rather than every four days.
   - Using experience to determine subgroups, for example, known tool wear rates.
   - Using larger subgroups, as they result in Control Charts which are more sensitive to change.
   - Using smaller subgroups when they are expensive or time-consuming.
   - Measuring more frequently when significant variation can occur over a short period.
   - Initially measuring more, then reducing measurements as the data is understood.
   - Using consecutive measurements, rather than a random sample, as this will result in less variation within the subgroup, with tighter, more sensitive control limits.
   - Selecting subgroup measurement which seldom results in zero value points. For example, counting customer complaints per hour when there are only one or two per day, will give many points plotted on the zero line.

5. Prepare for measurement. This should aim to make measurement as simple and error-free as possible. If possible, automate the measurement process. If measurements are to be collected by hand, design a data collection form that eases both the collection and the subsequent calculations.

Table 14.3 Subgroup size

Type of chart	Number of measurements taken for each subgroup
Individuals and Moving Range (X, MR charts)	1 or 2
Average and Range (X-bar, R charts)	2 to 10 (typically 4 or 5)
Standard deviation (s chart)	Typically 10 or more (may be less)
Proportion defective (p chart)	50 or more (individual subgroups may vary). May be less if there are 4 or more defects per unit
Number defective (np chart)	50 or more. May be less if there are 4 or more defects per unit
Defects per unit (u chart)	50 or more (individual subgroups may vary)
Defects per subgroup (c chart)	50 or more

Ensure that the people involved with the collection of data and construction and interpretation of the Control Chart are able to perform their tasks efficiently and accurately. Train them as appropriate, including the use of practical trials.

6. Make the measurements as planned in step 5.

7. Calculate mean and upper and lower control limits, using Figs. 14.8 to 14.14. Note that although most control limits are straight lines, the p- and u- charts may have control limits that are different for each plotted point.

   Sometimes a lower control limit is calculated as less than zero, but as it is impossible for the plot to go below zero, the lower control limit is set at the zero line.

Calculations for Average and Range Control Charts

1. Calculate basic averages from measured values

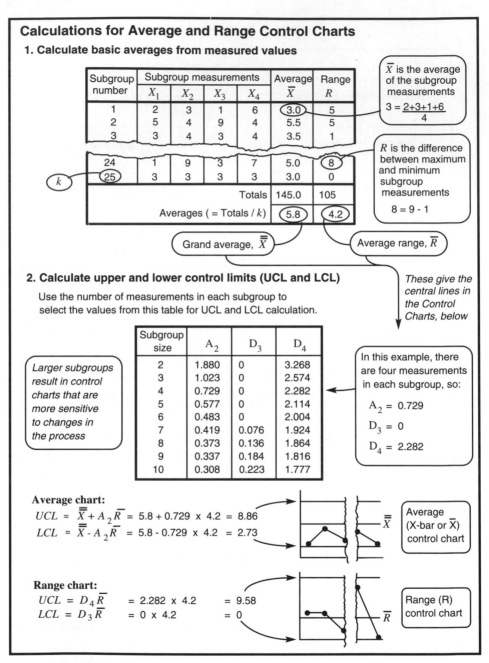

Subgroup number	Subgroup measurements				Average $\bar{X}$	Range R
	X_1	X_2	X_3	X_4		
1	2	3	1	6	(3.0)	5
2	5	4	9	4	5.5	5
3	3	4	3	4	3.5	1
24	1	9	3	7	5.0	(8)
(25)	3	3	3	3	3.0	0

$\bar{X}$ is the average of the subgroup measurements

$$3 = \frac{2+3+1+6}{4}$$

R is the difference between maximum and minimum subgroup measurements

$$8 = 9 - 1$$

Totals: 145.0   105

Averages (= Totals / k)   (5.8)   (4.2)

Grand average, $\bar{\bar{X}}$ Average range, $\bar{R}$

2. Calculate upper and lower control limits (UCL and LCL)

Use the number of measurements in each subgroup to select the values from this table for UCL and LCL calculation.

These give the central lines in the Control Charts, below

Subgroup size	A_2	D_3	D_4
2	1.880	0	3.268
3	1.023	0	2.574
4	0.729	0	2.282
5	0.577	0	2.114
6	0.483	0	2.004
7	0.419	0.076	1.924
8	0.373	0.136	1.864
9	0.337	0.184	1.816
10	0.308	0.223	1.777

Larger subgroups result in control charts that are more sensitive to changes in the process

In this example, there are four measurements in each subgroup, so:

$A_2 = 0.729$

$D_3 = 0$

$D_4 = 2.282$

Average chart:

$UCL = \bar{\bar{X}} + A_2\bar{R} = 5.8 + 0.729 \times 4.2 = 8.86$

$LCL = \bar{\bar{X}} - A_2\bar{R} = 5.8 - 0.729 \times 4.2 = 2.73$

Average (X-bar or $\bar{X}$) control chart

Range chart:

$UCL = D_4\bar{R} = 2.282 \times 4.2 = 9.58$

$LCL = D_3\bar{R} = 0 \times 4.2 = 0$

Range (R) control chart

Fig. 14.8 Calculating Average and Range (X-bar, R) Control Charts

Calculations for Individuals and Moving Range Control Charts

1. Calculate basic averages from measured values

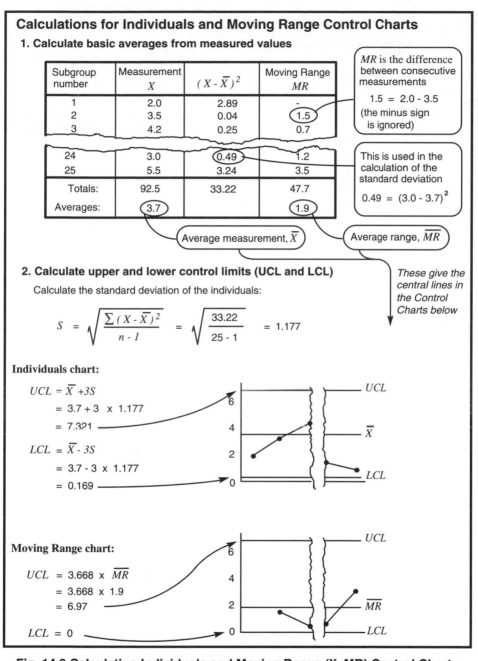

Subgroup number	Measurement X	$(X - \bar{X})^2$	Moving Range MR
1	2.0	2.89	-
2	3.5	0.04	1.5
3	4.2	0.25	0.7
24	3.0	0.49	1.2
25	5.5	3.24	3.5
Totals:	92.5	33.22	47.7
Averages:	3.7		1.9

MR is the difference between consecutive measurements

1.5 = 2.0 - 3.5
(the minus sign is ignored)

This is used in the calculation of the standard deviation

$0.49 = (3.0 - 3.7)^2$

Average measurement, $\bar{X}$

Average range, $\overline{MR}$

2. Calculate upper and lower control limits (UCL and LCL)

These give the central lines in the Control Charts below

Calculate the standard deviation of the individuals:

$$S = \sqrt{\frac{\sum (X - \bar{X})^2}{n - 1}} = \sqrt{\frac{33.22}{25 - 1}} = 1.177$$

Individuals chart:

$UCL = \bar{X} + 3S$

$= 3.7 + 3 \times 1.177$

$= 7.321$

$LCL = \bar{X} - 3S$

$= 3.7 - 3 \times 1.177$

$= 0.169$

UCL

$\bar{X}$

LCL

Moving Range chart:

$UCL = 3.668 \times \overline{MR}$

$= 3.668 \times 1.9$

$= 6.97$

$LCL = 0$

UCL

$\overline{MR}$

LCL

Fig. 14.9 Calculating Individuals and Moving Range (X, MR) Control Charts

Calculations for Standard Deviation Control Chart

1. Calculate average and standard deviation for each subgroup

Subgroup number	Measurements X_1	X_2	X_{19}	X_{20}	Average $\overline{X}$	Std.Dev. s
1	2	3	1	6	3.2	2.2
2	5	4	9	4	4.5	1.2
3	3	4	3	4	5.2	1.5
24	1	2	3	7	6.6	1.7
25	3	3	3	3	3.7	0.5
Totals					145.0	28.2
Averages					5.8	1.1

$\overline{X}$ is the average of the subgroup measurements
$$3.2 = \frac{2+3+...+1+6}{20}$$

s is the standard deviation of each subgroup
$$s = \sqrt{\frac{\Sigma(\overline{X}-X)^2}{(n-1)}}$$
$$= \sqrt{\frac{(6.6-1)^2+...+(6.6-7)^2}{(20-1)}}$$
$$= 1.7$$

Average std. dev., $\overline{s}$
1.1 = 28.2 / 25

2. Calculate upper and lower control limits (UCL and LCL)

Use the number of measurements in each subgroup to select the values from this table for UCL and LCL calculation.

This gives the central line in the Control Chart below

Subgroup size	A_2	B_3	B_4
10	0.308	0.284	1.716
11	0.285	0.321	1.679
12	0.266	0.354	1.646
13	0.249	0.382	1.618
14	0.235	0.406	1.594
15	0.223	0.428	1.572
16	0.212	0.448	1.552
17	0.203	0.466	1.534
18	0.194	0.482	1.518
19	0.187	0.497	1.503
20	0.180	0.510	1.490
21	0.173	0.523	1.477
22	0.167	0.534	1.466
23	0.162	0.545	1.455
24	0.157	0.555	1.445
25	0.153	0.565	1.435

In this example, there are 20 measurements in each subgroup, so:
$A_2 = 0.180$
$B_3 = 0.510$
$B_4 = 1.490$

The A_2 figures are for calculating limits for the Average chart, which is usually drawn alongside the Standard Deviation chart

$UCL = B_4\overline{s}$ = 1.490 x 1.2   = 1.788
$LCL = B_3\overline{s}$ = 0.510 x 1.2   = 0.612

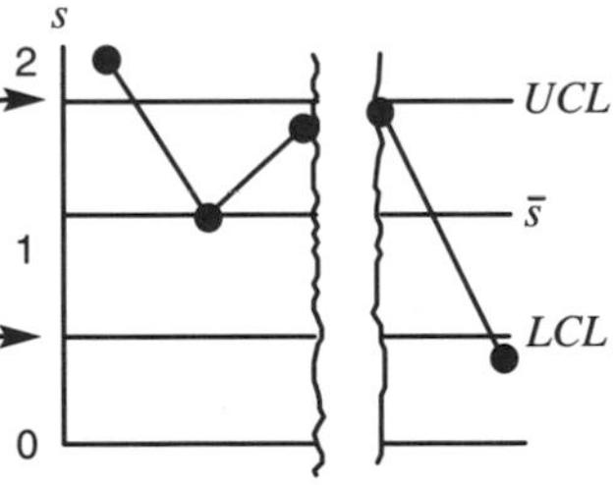

Fig. 14.10 Calculating Standard Deviation (s) Control Chart

Calculations for Proportion Defective (p) Control Chart

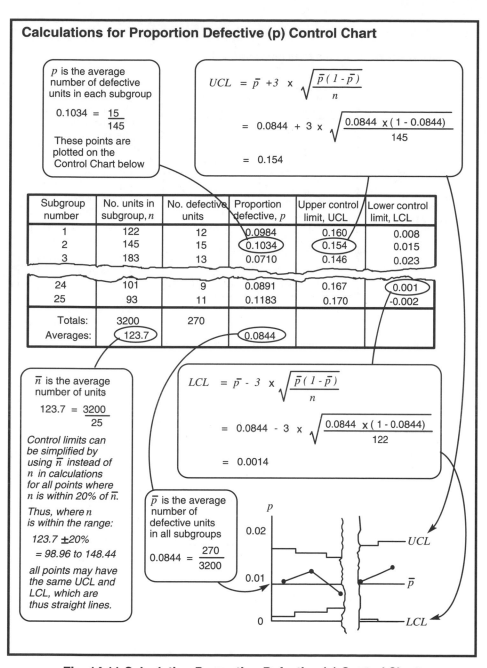

p is the average number of defective units in each subgroup

$0.1034 = \dfrac{15}{145}$

These points are plotted on the Control Chart below

$$UCL = \bar{p} + 3 \times \sqrt{\frac{\bar{p}(1-\bar{p})}{n}}$$

$$= 0.0844 + 3 \times \sqrt{\frac{0.0844 \times (1 - 0.0844)}{145}}$$

$$= 0.154$$

Subgroup number	No. units in subgroup, n	No. defective units	Proportion defective, p	Upper control limit, UCL	Lower control limit, LCL
1	122	12	0.0984	0.160	0.008
2	145	15	0.1034	0.154	0.015
3	183	13	0.0710	0.146	0.023
24	101	9	0.0891	0.167	0.001
25	93	11	0.1183	0.170	-0.002
Totals:	3200	270			
Averages:	123.7		0.0844		

$\bar{n}$ is the average number of units

$123.7 = \dfrac{3200}{25}$

Control limits can be simplified by using $\bar{n}$ instead of n in calculations for all points where n is within 20% of $\bar{n}$.

Thus, where n is within the range:

123.7 ±20%

= 98.96 to 148.44

all points may have the same UCL and LCL, which are thus straight lines.

$$LCL = \bar{p} - 3 \times \sqrt{\frac{\bar{p}(1-\bar{p})}{n}}$$

$$= 0.0844 - 3 \times \sqrt{\frac{0.0844 \times (1 - 0.0844)}{122}}$$

$$= 0.0014$$

$\bar{p}$ is the average number of defective units in all subgroups

$0.0844 = \dfrac{270}{3200}$

Fig. 14.11 Calculating Proportion Defective (p) Control Chart

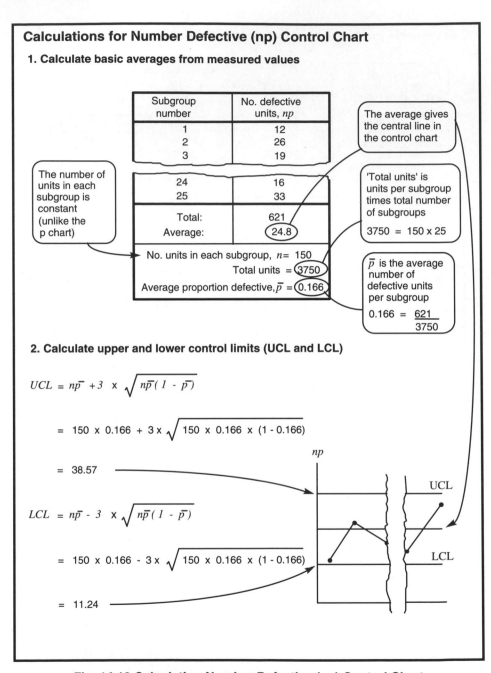

Calculations for Number Defective (np) Control Chart

1. Calculate basic averages from measured values

Subgroup number	No. defective units, np
1	12
2	26
3	19
24	16
25	33
Total:	621
Average:	(24.8)

The average gives the central line in the control chart

The number of units in each subgroup is constant (unlike the p chart)

'Total units' is units per subgroup times total number of subgroups

3750 = 150 x 25

No. units in each subgroup, n= 150
Total units = (3750)
Average proportion defective, $\bar{p}$ = (0.166)

$\bar{p}$ is the average number of defective units per subgroup

$$0.166 = \frac{621}{3750}$$

2. Calculate upper and lower control limits (UCL and LCL)

$$UCL = n\bar{p} + 3 \times \sqrt{n\bar{p}(1 - \bar{p})}$$

$$= 150 \times 0.166 + 3 \times \sqrt{150 \times 0.166 \times (1 - 0.166)}$$

$$= 38.57$$

$$LCL = n\bar{p} - 3 \times \sqrt{n\bar{p}(1 - \bar{p})}$$

$$= 150 \times 0.166 - 3 \times \sqrt{150 \times 0.166 \times (1 - 0.166)}$$

$$= 11.24$$

np

UCL

LCL

Fig. 14.12 Calculating Number Defective (np) Control Chart

Calculations for Number of Defects (c) Control Chart

1. Calculate basic averages from measured values

Sample number	No. defects in sample, c
1	24
2	8
3	12

The size of each sample is constant. (same number, weight, area, length, etc.)

24	15
25	23
Total:	405
Average, $\bar{c}$:	(16.2)

The average gives the central line in the control chart

$$16.2 = \frac{25}{405}$$

2. Calculate upper and lower control limits (UCL and LCL)

$$UCL = \bar{c} + 3 \times \sqrt{\bar{c}}$$

$$= 16.2 + 3 \times \sqrt{16.2}$$

$$= 28.27$$

$$LCL = \bar{c} - 3 \times \sqrt{\bar{c}}$$

$$= 16.2 - 3 \times \sqrt{16.2}$$

$$= 4.13$$

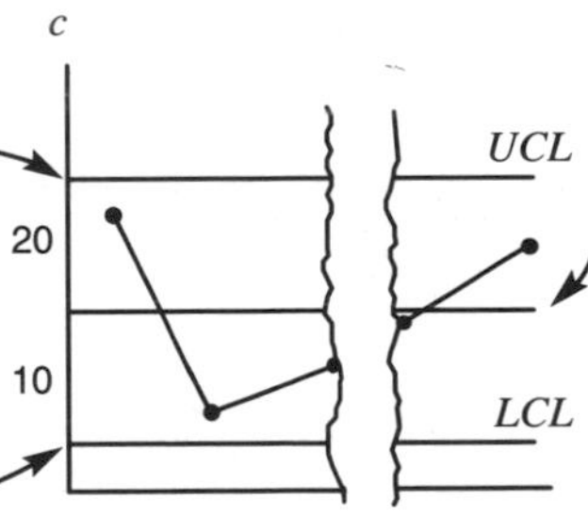

c

UCL

20

10

LCL

Fig. 14.13 Calculating Number of Defects (c) Control Chart

Calculations for Defects per Unit (u) Control Chart

1. Calculate basic averages from measured values

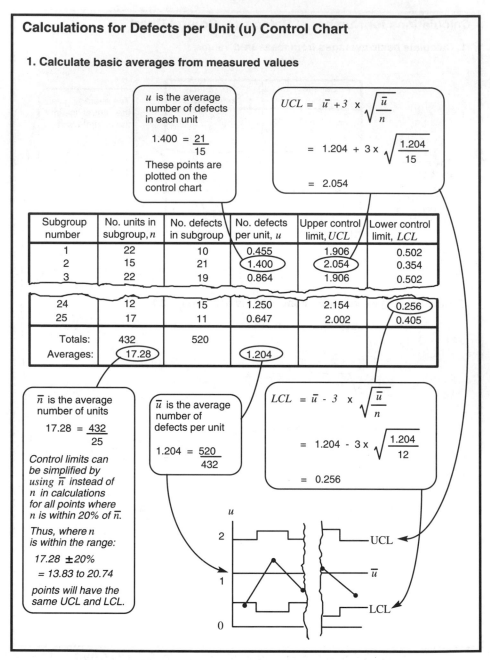

u is the average number of defects in each unit

$$1.400 = \frac{21}{15}$$

These points are plotted on the control chart

$$UCL = \bar{u} + 3 \times \sqrt{\frac{\bar{u}}{n}}$$

$$= 1.204 + 3 \times \sqrt{\frac{1.204}{15}}$$

$$= 2.054$$

Subgroup number	No. units in subgroup, n	No. defects in subgroup	No. defects per unit, u	Upper control limit, UCL	Lower control limit, LCL
1	22	10	0.455	1.906	0.502
2	15	21	1.400	2.054	0.354
3	22	19	0.864	1.906	0.502
24	12	15	1.250	2.154	0.256
25	17	11	0.647	2.002	0.405
Totals:	432	520			
Averages:	17.28		1.204		

$\bar{n}$ is the average number of units

$$17.28 = \frac{432}{25}$$

Control limits can be simplified by using $\bar{n}$ instead of n in calculations for all points where n is within 20% of $\bar{n}$.

Thus, where n is within the range:

17.28 ±20%

= 13.83 to 20.74

points will have the same UCL and LCL.

$\bar{u}$ is the average number of defects per unit

$$1.204 = \frac{520}{432}$$

$$LCL = \bar{u} - 3 \times \sqrt{\frac{\bar{u}}{n}}$$

$$= 1.204 - 3 \times \sqrt{\frac{1.204}{12}}$$

$$= 0.256$$

Fig. 14.14 Calculating Defects per Unit (u) Control Chart

8. Draw the chart. This should include:
   - One plotted point for each subgroup, with a line drawn between successive points.
   - Horizontal lines for each of the central line, upper control limit and lower control limit.
   - Labelling and other information to uniquely identify the chart and help with any subsequent investigation.

9. Interpret the chart, looking for significant patterns and points (use Table 14.1), and act on the results. Typically this will involve finding the cause of any identified significant set of points, followed by devising a method of correcting the problem. This can require a fair amount of effort, as the Control Chart shows when to look, but not where.

Practical variations

- Another significant set of points that can be identified on a Control Chart is a *bias*, where more points that might be expected are on one side of the centre line. They need not be sequential, as in a shift. Significant sets are:
  - Ten out of eleven consecutive points on one side of the centre line.
  - Twelve out of fourteen consecutive points on one side of the centre line.
  - Fourteen out of seventeen consecutive points on one side of the centre line.
  - Sixteen out of twenty consecutive points on one side of the centre line.

- Draw one additional horizontal line two standard deviations away from either side of the central average line (these occur at two-thirds of the way towards the control limits for most Control Charts - this excludes range charts, which do not have a symmetrical distribution). These lines are called the *Upper Warning Limit* (UWL) and the *Lower Warning Limit* (LWL), and catch additional sequences that may indicate out-of-control situations. Warning limits are illustrated in Fig. 14.15.

  Additional sequences (to those in Table 14.1) that may now indicate out-of-control situations include:
  - Two out of three consecutive points are between a warning limit and the corresponding control limit.
  - Three out of seven consecutive points are between a warning limit and the corresponding control limit.
  - Five or more points which are all increasing or decreasing (a trend) and which cross a warning limit.

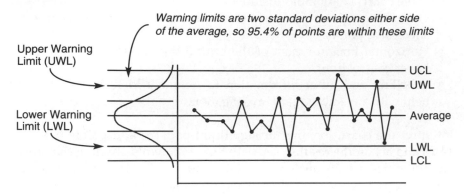

Fig. 14.15 Warning limits

- Draw a third and fourth line in addition to the warning limits, at one standard deviation either side of the central average line. Additional sequences to check for now include:
    - Fifteen consecutive points which lie entirely between these two lines.
    - Four or more consecutive points beyond one of these lines.

- If the cost of looking for problems in the process is high and the consequence of problems is not serious, then wider control limits may be used, for example at four standard deviations from the central average line. Conversely, control limits may be tightened, for example to two standard deviations, if the cost of looking for problems is low and the consequence of problems is serious.
- A *Multi-Vari Chart* is a simple way of showing the ranges of each of a set of samples, where the range is shown by a vertical line, as in Fig. 14.16. Each line typically represents between 3 and 5 measurements. Specification limits are used instead of control limits, so it can be seen whether any items are getting near or exceeding these constraints.
- A variation on the Multi-Vari Chart is the *Box Plot*, where the simple line is enhanced with a box to show the middle 50% of measurements, with a line to show the central measurement (the median). Each sample is thus visually divided into four *quartiles*. This requires a number of measurements per sample (typically at least 25).

    A variation on this is to change the box width in order to show any change in sample size.

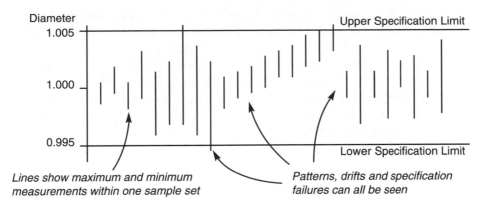

Fig. 14.16 Multi-Vari Chart

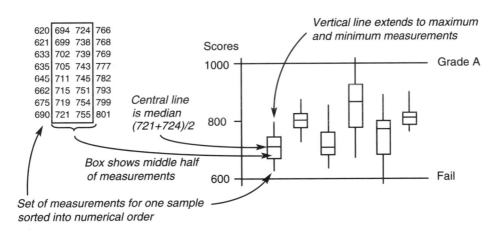

Fig. 14.17 Box Plot

Notes

Control Charts were defined by Walter Shewart. Control limits are sometimes also called *Action Limits*.

See also

Chapters: Other tools for measuring Variation include the Histogram, Process Capability, Scatter Diagram and Design of Experiments.

References: Control Charts are discussed in detail in a number of books. [Grant 80] has ten chapters on them. [Wadsworth 86] has five chapters. [Owen 93] has nine chapters. [Juran 79] and [Asaka 90] have explicit details for constructing them. [Oakland 90] dicusses them and their application in detail, without recourse to too much mathematics.

15 Decision Tree

What it's for

To select from a number of possible courses of action.

When to use it

- Use it when making important or complex decisions, to identify the course of action that will give the best value according to a selected set of rules
- Use it when decision-making, to identify the effects of risks.
- Use it when making plans, to identify the effects of actions and possible alternative courses of action.
- Use it when there are chains of decisions, to determine the best decision at each point.
- Use it only when data is available, or can reasonably be determined, on costs and probabilities of different outcomes.

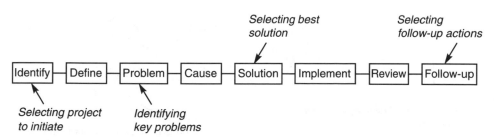

Fig. 15.1 Possible uses in improvement project framework

How to understand it

Making decisions can be difficult when future events are uncertain and can give widely varing results. For example, where there are several possible improvements to a product, each of which has a different cost and where each has several possible failure modes. The decision then becomes a 'numbers game', where the aim is to identify those actions which will give the best results whatever events may occur.

The Decision Tree is used to evaluate possible actions and subsequent events in order to gain a numerical value by which the best action can be selected, as illustrated in Fig. 15.2. Actions and possible subsequent events on the diagram are differentiated by the shape of the point from which they spread, with numeric values indicating the best decision at each point.

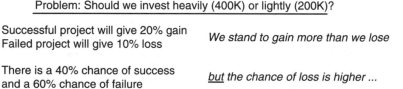

Problem: Should we invest heavily (400K) or lightly (200K)?

Successful project will give 20% gain
Failed project will give 10% loss

We stand to gain more than we lose

There is a 40% chance of success
and a 60% chance of failure

but the chance of loss is higher ...

... so, we use a Decision Tree to identify the gains we really value:

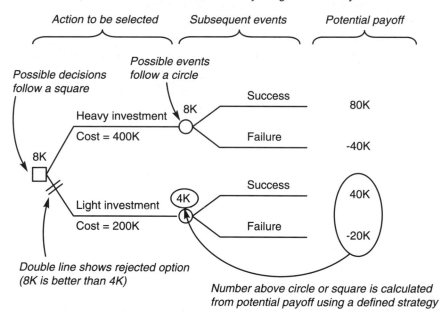

Fig. 15.2 Elements of Decision Tree

A key part of using the Decision Tree is in selecting the strategy for determining the real present value of the potential payoffs. For example, an approach based on minimizing loss may be selected in preference to one which focuses on the probability of events occurring. Various strategies and their affects on choice are illustrated in Fig. 15.7.

Decision Trees can deal with more than just one set of actions and subsequent events, as the occurrence of an event may trigger another decision point. For example, a project failure might require the appropriate contingency action to be selected. Thus Decision Trees can become quite deep as chains of possible events and decisions are considered. To increase the space on the page for multiple levels, it is common to use codes instead of phrases for actions and events, as in Fig. 15.3, although this can reduce the immediate readability of the diagram.

Decision Trees are constrained in the same way as other data-driven tools in that their value is very much affected by the accuracy of the data being used. Thus, for example, if probabilities are rough estimates rather than extrapolations of measured trends, then the results must be considered in this light.

Example

The management team of a manufacturer of space heaters were trying to decide whether to release a revolutionary new heater, or whether to continue testing it. Releasing it immediately would ensure good sales, as no other manufacturers had anything like it. However, this would be at an estimated 10% risk of serious problems which would result in halving the revenue. Another six months testing would reduce the chance of problems to 5%, but at an estimated 8% risk of a comparable heater being introduced by the competition. They decided to use a Decision Tree to calculate the Expected Monetary Value (EMV) of the options in order to help decide what to do.

Figure 15.3 shows the figures and the Decision Tree. The final figures indicated that in terms of EMV, the options had very similar value, as the threat of competition canceled out the gains in reliability. They followed this up by repeating the calculations with a small range of probability figures, to investigate the sensitivity of the model. This showed that a change in problem risk had the greatest effect, so they decided to continue testing.

Other examples
- A machine shop team use a Decision Tree to balance the possible future demand for increased productivity with methods of achieving this. They find that a 10% increase can be best met with training and improved work

processes, but a further 10% increase will require new machinery.
- The safety team in a power plant use a Decision Tree to understand the overload situation and to develop contingency measures for unacceptable hazards.
- A doctor investigating a disease uses a Decision Tree to understand the possible effects of using imperfect tests and possible developments.

Probabilities and codes

		Problems P	No problems NP	Competition C	No competition NC
R	Release now	10%	90%	—	—
T	Test more	5%	95%	8%	92%

Payoff (sales)

	Problems (sales - 50%)	No problems	EMV calculations (= value of actions)
Release now	50K	100K	50K x 0.1 + 100K x 0.9 = 95K
Test more			78K x 0.08 + 97.5K x 0.92 = 95.24K
Competition (sales -10%)	40K	80K	40K x 0.05 + 80K x 0.95 = 78K
No competition	50K	100K	50K x 0.05 + 100K x 0.95 = 97.5K

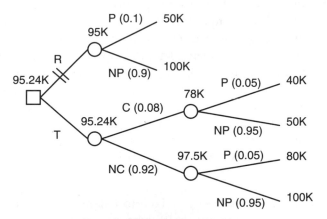

Fig. 15.3 Example

How to do it

1. Identify the objective of the decision-making process. Typically this involves maximizing something desirable, such as profit, sales or satisfaction, or reducing something undesirable, such as defects, time taken or scrap.

2. Identify constraints on the decision making. These will effectively act as additional sub-objectives, and can be used to prevent the objective being achieved at the expense of other goals. For example, an objective to increase short-term profit could be fulfilled at the expense of longer term investments, unless some reasonable constraints are defined.

3. List the set of possible actions to be considered as ways of achieving the objectives. For example, if the objective is to increase productivity, options may include new machinery and revised working practices.

   This should be a relatively short list, typically of between two and four actions, particularly if the Decision Tree is to be multi-level, in order to minimize the complexity of the final Tree. This may start as a longer list which is first whittled down to a few strong contenders amongst which the best choice is difficult to identify.

4. List the possible events that may follow on from each of the actions identified in step 3. Limit this to a few events which constitute all possibilities, for example, 'sales increase', 'no change' and 'sales decrease'.
   Events may be dependent or independent, as follows:
   * *Dependent events* are a direct consequence of performing an individual action, and are thus different for each action. For example, the action of increasing furnace temperature to reduce firing time may also result in more scrap through cracked pots.
   * *Independent events* do not depend on the actions, and are just as likely to happen whatever action is taken. For example, the dynamics of the national economy are not affected by an investment in a new product, yet may still affect future sales.

5. For each action (step 3) and event (step 4), determine a value that describes the gain that will be achieved if this combination occurs. This is commonly called the *payoff* or *outcome* and may be shown in a *payoff table*, as in Fig. 15.4.
   This measurement will require a common unit, related to the original objective (step 1). This is typically a financial measure, but can be others,

Return on advertising campaign

Events / Actions	E1 Rising market	E2 Falling market
A1 Prime-time spread	30	14
A2 Targeted sectors	20	18
A3 Low-level	15	21

Fig. 15.4 Payoff table

such as time, efficiency, etc. It can be useful to include the cost of performing the actions in this figure, rather than just using the return gained. Thus 'profit' or 'return on investment' may be better than simple 'revenue'.

6. The basic Decision Tree can now be drawn. Start with a small square on the left of the page with lines radiating for each possible action (step 3). At the end of each line, draw a small circle with one line coming out of it for each possible subsequent event (step 4). At the end of each of these lines write in the payoff (step 5). Actions and events may either be written in full or as codes from a table, such as in Fig. 15.4. The final diagram will look something like Fig. 15.5.

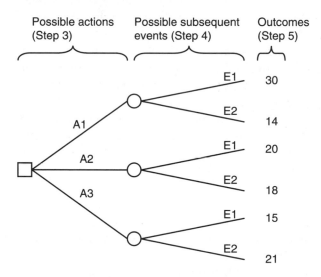

Fig. 15.5 Basic Decision Tree

7. Decide how to select the best actions by using a defined strategy to determine the 'real' value of the payoffs identified in step 5. Common strategies are outlined below and illustrated in Fig. 15.8, which shows how different strategies can result in different activities being selected.

   - *Maximin*, which looks for the best worst-case situation, and is the 'pessimist's choice'. Thus, in Fig. 15.8, A2 is selected.
   - *Maximax*, which seeks to maximize to profit by selecting the option with the highest potential return. It can thus be viewed as the 'optimist's choice'. Thus, in Fig. 15.8, A1 is selected.
   - *Minimax Regret* or *Opportunity Loss*, which takes the conservative approach of seeking to minimize the loss incurred should the best action not be taken. Thus, in Fig. 15.8, A1 is selected.
   - *Expected Monetary Value*, or *EMV*, includes the concept that an item which is less likely to occur is also worth less. This is a very common strategy, based on the sound statistical and financial principle that effective value is equal to actual value multiplied by probability of occurrence. Thus, in Fig. 15.8, A2 is selected.
   - *Expected Opportunity Loss*, which combines the Minimax Regret with the statistical principles of EMV to give a conservative statistical approach. Thus, in Fig. 15.8, A3 is selected.
   - *Utility* puts other personal values on events and actions. For example, actions may be rejected if there is any risk whatsoever of loss.

8. If the strategy calls for it (e.g. if it is EMV or EOL), determine the probability of each action/event combination. It can be very difficult and expensive to get accurate figures, and decisions may need to be made on the value of accuracy. For example, it may be worth spending thousands on a market survey when changing a product line, but a less accurate estimate may be adequate when deciding what lockers to put in a changing room.
   Ways of determining these figures include:
   - Asking people in surveys of customers, employees, etc.
   - Measuring aspects of processes, such as time taken, defects, etc.
   - Identification and extrapolation of previous trends.
   - Investigating variation.

Probability figures are usually shown as being between 0 (no chance) and 1 (certainty), although percentages may be more familiar and can be used instead as they are directly equivalent. Event probabilities, particularly for dependent events, can be shown in a table, as in Fig. 15.6.

Probability of finding defects after specific test type

Events / Actions	Serious defects found in use	Other defects found in use	No defects found in use	Total
Saturation test	0.02	0.08	0.90	1.00
Limited test	0.05	0.15	0.80	1.00

Event probabilities for each action total 1.0 (or 100%)

Fig. 15.6 Probabilities of dependent events

The final figures may be written on the Decision Tree diagram. Put them in parentheses underneath the appropriate event lines.

9. Calculate the value of each action, using the strategy selected in step 7, and write this above the circle at the end of the action's branch on the tree drawn in step 6. For example, if an Expected Opportunity Loss strategy is being used, as in Fig. 15.8, then the tree from Fig. 15.5 will appear as in Fig. 15.7.

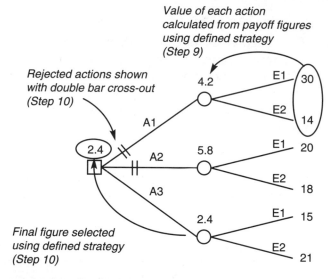

Fig. 15.7 Adding action values (for EOL strategy)

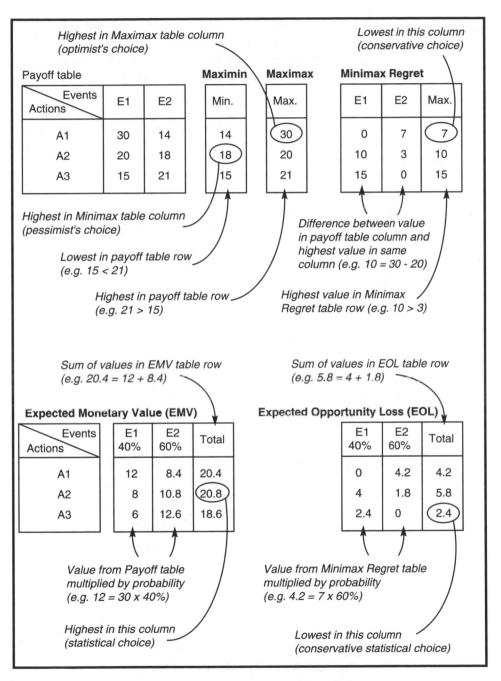

Fig. 15.8 Calculations for decision strategies

10. Select one of the values from step 9, again using the defined strategy of step 7 (typically it will be the largest or smallest value). Write this value above the square box where the action branches meet. This indicates the action selected, so cross out the rejected actions with double lines, as in Fig. 15.8.

11. If required, the tree may be extended with another set of decisions, using steps 3 to 10. This caters for consideration of what possible actions and events might occur, if any or all of the events in the first stage occur. This is typically used in complex situations where there is no payoff before several sets of actions and events. In this case, delay calculation until the tree is complete and then ripple back the values in the same way as step 9. The result will be a multi-level Decision Tree, as in Fig. 15.9.

12. Carry out the selected actions and check the events and payoff occur as expected. If they do not, identify causes for another round of process improvement.

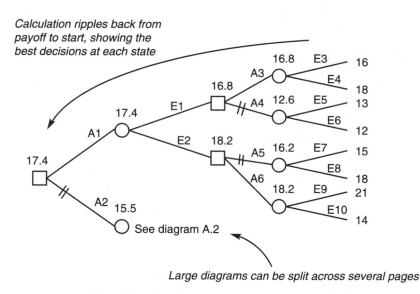

Fig. 15.9 Multi-level Decision Tree

Practical variations

- When the complete Decision Tree is large, break it into separate sub-trees. This makes it easier to calculate and understand.
- Use a Prioritization Matrix both to select the possible actions to consider and to identify the subsequent events.
- Sometimes multiple events occur between actions. These can be handled by rippling back the calculation, as in Fig. 15.3.
- Use the Decision Tree with the Activity Network, to plan for alternative project actions.
- A *Probability Tree Diagram* uses a Decision Tree just to break down sequences of possible events. If probabilities of individual events are known, then overall probabilities can be calculated by multiplying at each level, as in Fig. 15.10. Note that the final set of probabilities still sums to 1, as it represents all possible outcomes.

Problem: I need to test the solar panel with at least 2 out of 3 days sunny.
There's a 90% chance of sun each day. What's the chance of success?

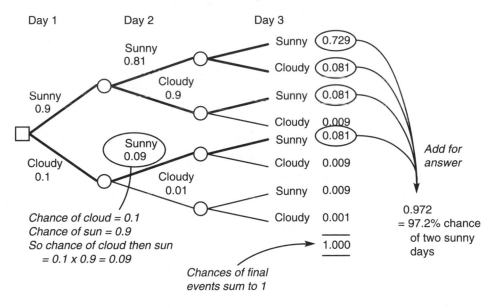

Fig. 15.10 Probability Tree Diagram

Notes

Decision Trees originated in financial and marketing decision making, although they can be used for many other situations.

See also

Chapters: The Decision Tree is a specific type of Tree Diagram. Use Brainstorming, Nominal Group Technique or Surveys to help identify risks and subsequent actions. Use a Prioritization Matrix to select actions and events. Failure Mode and Effects Analysis, Fault Tree Analysis and Process Decision Program Chart also investigate risk.

References: Decision Trees tend to be discussed in specific books on decision making. [Hamburg 70] covers the calculations in one section. [Moore 88] discusses their use in detail, with many examples.

16 Design of Experiments

What it's for

To understand the effects of different factors in a given situation.

When to use it

- Use it when investigating a situation where there are many variable factors, one or more of which may be causing problems.
- Use it when variable factors may be interacting to cause problems.
- Use it when testing a solution, to ensure that there are no unexpected side-effects.
- Use it when there is not the time or money to try every combination of variables.

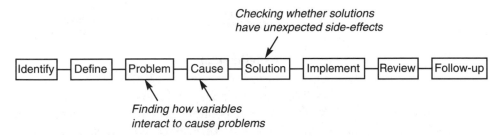

Fig. 16.1 Possible uses in improvement project framework

How to understand it

In many problem situations, it is a common mistake to assume immediately that the most obvious factor is the sole cause, and to devise a solution based on this assumption. It is also common to be surprised when the solution is not as effective as hoped. For example, a horticulturist may find that a fertilizer causes leaf burn in warm weather and immediately assumes that temperature is the only cause. However, the only way to *know* this is to recognize all possible contributory factors and to perform a series of experiments where these factors are varied in a controlled way. Thus the horticulturist might recognize humidity and illumination as additional factors that can affect the biochemical reactions within leaves.

When performing an experiment, there are two things that can be changed: *factors* and their *levels*. A factor is a measurable item such as humidity or temperature, which, when changed, might affect the result of the experiment. The levels of the factor are the set of values, such as 20 or 30°C, that the factors may have. In any experiment, there are a number of *trials* in which the levels of a fixed number of factors are varied, as in Fig. 16.2.

There are fixed number of variable factors

Trial number	Temperature (°C)	Humidity (%)	Illumination (lux)	Leaf burn (%)
1	20	20	10	18
2	22	30	20	23
3	24	40	30	45
4	28	50	40	48

There may be a large number of trials

Each factor may be varied within a fixed set of levels

The results of each trial depends on the factors and levels

Fig. 16.2 Experimental trials

The complete set of possible combinations of levels and factors in an experiment is called the *full factorial*, and is often too large to perform a trial using each combination. A significant part of 'Design Of Experiments' is in determining what subset of the full factorial (or *fractional factorial*) should be selected for trial. A common approach is to vary just one factor, keeping all other factors at constant levels, but this can result in an incomplete picture as

Trial no.	Window 1	Window 2	Door	Result (°C chg.)
1	Open	Open	Open	-8
2	Open	Open	Closed	-3
3	Open	Closed	Open	-5
4	Open	Closed	Closed	-2
5	Closed	Open	Open	-6
6	Closed	Open	Closed	-2
7	Closed	Closed	Open	-1
8	Closed	Closed	Closed	0

A full factorial experiment tries all combinations of factors and levels, but can be very costly

So a representative fraction may be selected

1	Open	Closed	Closed	-2
2	Closed	Open	Closed	-2
3	Closed	Closed	Open	-1

But the common approach of varying just one factor misses any interaction effects

Fig. 16.3 Factorials and fractions

the effect of interactions between factors is ignored, as illustrated in Fig. 16.3.

A set of trials that forms a consistent and complete experiment follows several rules. A *balanced* experiment ensures 'fairness' by requiring that the different levels of each factor occur equally often. In an *orthogonal* experiment, the effect of different factors can be separated out so separate causes can be identified (a test for this is shown in Fig. 16.4). The effects of all factors should also be measurable or *estimable* to a reasonable degree.

In practice, many experiments can be simplified by using only two levels of each factor. This may occur naturally or it may be used when a single change in level will show whether the factor is significant or not.

Once the experiment is completed, the problem is to determine the real effects of each individual factor. There are statistical approaches to this, but a simple and effective way is to plot the average values of each factor and level, both individually and in combination, as in Fig. 16.5. The most significant individual factor will thus have the steepest line, although this will also depend on the levels used. Significant combinations of factors will have lines with large angles between them (a good sign of significance is where the lines cross one another).

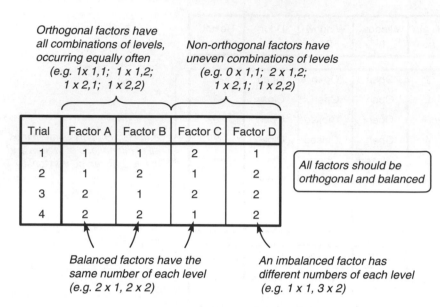

Fig. 16.4 Balance and orthogonality

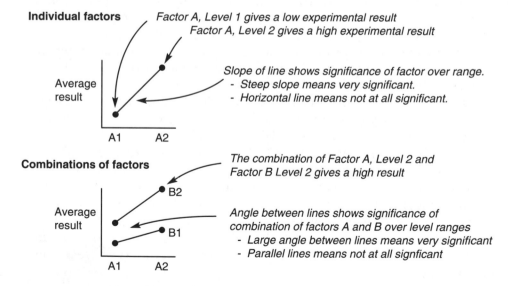

Fig. 16.5 Plots of experimental results

Example

The marketing group in an airline wanted to increase the number of business class seats sold on its off-peak flights. Key factors were identified as advertising level and pricing strategy. They trialled two advertising campaigns and three pricing strategies in geographically separate but demographically similar areas. As there was a small number of possible trials, they performed a full factorial experiment, as in Fig. 16.6. The results showed in the individual effects plots that the level of advertising campaign was significant and that pricing had a non-linear effect on seats sold. This was confirmed in the interaction effects plot, which showed that the first advertising level was ineffective whatever the pricing, and the second advertising level was most effective when coupled with the second pricing strategy.

Other examples

- A plastic moulding workshop wants to reduce injection moulding rejects and thus perform a set of experiments which change injection pressure, mix temperature and setting time. Analysis of the results shows a combination of temperature and setting time as the most significant factor. Further experiments find the optimum combination of these.
- A market research team designs an experiment to determine which factors will most influence customers to purchase a product. They run a survey which asks questions about several levels of price, packaging and delivery. Unexpected results include a high sensitivity to price-delivery combinations. Consequently, a premium-rate couriered delivery service is set up and proves to be very popular.
- A yacht design team aims to improve speed through changing the shape of the boat's sail. Rather than try random shapes, they identify the key sail parameters and then design and perform a set of experiments with each factor set at two levels. They follow this up with multi-level experiments for the two most significant factors found in the first experiment set. The result is a new sail that increases speed by 5%.

Trial	Advertising level, A	Pricing strategy, P	Seats from 4 random flights	Total
1	1	1	28, 26, 21, 32	107
2	1	2	25, 28, 21, 29	103
3	1	3	23, 26, 22, 28	99
4	2	1	29, 33, 32, 28	122
3	2	2	42, 44, 39, 45	170
4	2	3	36, 40, 39, 35	150

Averages of seat counts

Individual effects		Pairs of interaction effects	
A1	25.75	A1 x P1	26.75
A2	36.83	A1 x P2	25.75
P1	28.63	A1 x P3	24.75
P2	34.13	A2 x P1	30.50
P3	31.13	A2 x P2	42.50
		A2 x P3	37.50

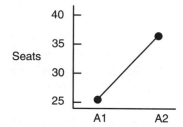

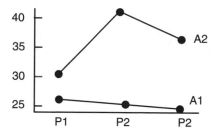

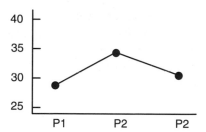

Fig. 16.6 Example

How to do it

1. Identify the objective of using experiments. Typically, this may be one of:
   - Finding true causes of problems.
   - Finding how causes interact.
   - Finding the best solution to a problem.
   - Testing a solution to ensure it has no undesirable side-effects.

2. Define what is to be measured to show the results of the experiment. It will make the experiment much easier if this is a single measurement that can be easily and accurately performed. Be clear about other factors, such as who, when and how the measurement will be made.

3. Identify the factors that are to be controlled during the experiment. Consider all things that may affect the measured result, then select those that are to be varied and those that are to be held steady or otherwise monitored. As with step 2, any measurements should be clearly defined. Examples of factors include price, dimensions, temperature, errors, brands of fertilizer, age ranges.

   When there are many factors, reduce the list of those that are to be varied by selecting those known to affect the result and those whose effects are uncertain. It might also be appropriate to perform a series of experiments, starting with a smaller subset of 'high-probability' factors.

4. For each factor selected in step 3, identify the set of levels that the experiment must consider. This will typically be a small set of possible values such as 20, 24 and 28°C; 'GroFast' and 'EasyGrow'; present and absent.

   There will be fewer trials to perform and the subsequent analysis will be easier if very few levels of each factor are selected. Two levels are sufficient for many cases, as this will show whether changing the factor level changes the experimental result. Three or more levels can be used to check for a non-linear response.

   Select the levels to be representative of the range of normal values. Thus they should be sufficiently separated to be able to identify changes over the normal operating range, but not so spread as to meet any boundary effects, such as where a liquid boils.

   Ensure the factors can be controlled and measured at these levels. If they cannot be controlled, then it may be sufficient to measure them and sort them into ranges.

5. Select the actual trials to take place. There are a number of possible ways of doing this, depending on the type of experiment being performed. Some simple methods are described in the section on practical variations, below. Other more complex methods are described in the references at the end of the chapter..

   The decision on how many trials to perform may include economic factors, such as time, effort and cost. For example, crash-testing of vehicles is expensive and time consuming and is impractical to do too often.

   When trials are selected, check that they are balanced, with the different levels of each factor occurring the same number of times. Also check for orthogonality, with each pair of factors having each combination of levels occurring the same number of times (as in Fig. 16.4).

6. Perform the trials as planned. This may be a simple set of experiments or may require significant organization and funding. In any case, be careful in controlling factors at the selected levels and in measuring and recording results.

   Consecutive trials should not have any chance of affecting one another; if this could happen, perform trials in random order.

   Results may be recorded in a simple table, such as in Fig. 16.7, which shows one trial per row, with levels and results on the same row. This will help analysis, as results may be visually correlated with the selected factor levels.

7. Analyze the results. A simple approach is to average and plot results for each factor, level and combination, as in Fig. 16.7. More complex methods are given in the references.

   Where there are more than two levels, this will result in lines through more than two points. If the lines are not straight, then this indicates a complex effect.

8. Act on the results. This will depend on the objectives from step 1, and thus may be one of:
   • Eliminating what is now a known cause.
   • Selecting the most effective solution to a problem.
   • Acting to remove undesirable side-effects.

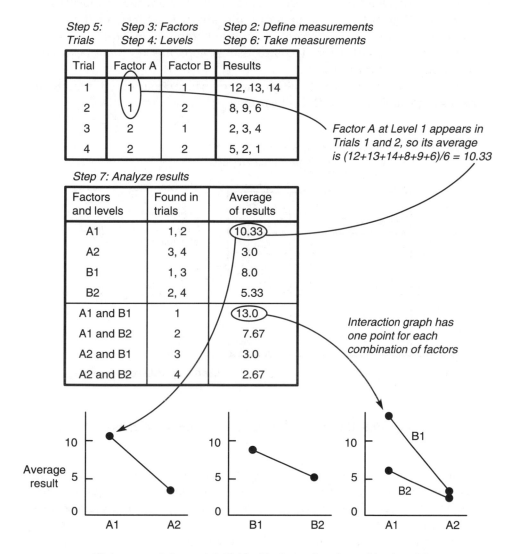

Step 5:   Step 3: Factors   Step 2: Define measurements
Trials   Step 4: Levels   Step 6: Take measurements

Trial	Factor A	Factor B	Results
1	1	1	12, 13, 14
2	1	2	8, 9, 6
3	2	1	2, 3, 4
4	2	2	5, 2, 1

Factor A at Level 1 appears in Trials 1 and 2, so its average is (12+13+14+8+9+6)/6 = 10.33

Step 7: Analyze results

Factors and levels	Found in trials	Average of results
A1	1, 2	10.33
A2	3, 4	3.0
B1	1, 3	8.0
B2	2, 4	5.33
A1 and B1	1	13.0
A1 and B2	2	7.67
A2 and B1	3	3.0
A2 and B2	4	2.67

Interaction graph has one point for each combination of factors

Plot one graph for each individual factor and each combination of factors

Fig. 16.7 Analyzing results

Practical variations

• Use a Matrix Diagram to select a subset of trials from the full factorial, as in Fig. 16.8. Rows and columns are allocated to factors and their levels such that each square represents a unique combination. Squares are then shaded to represent actual trials to use. A separate key may be used to describe the factors and levels.

   Results may be recorded on the same matrix, and summed in matching boxes opposite the factor/level headings.

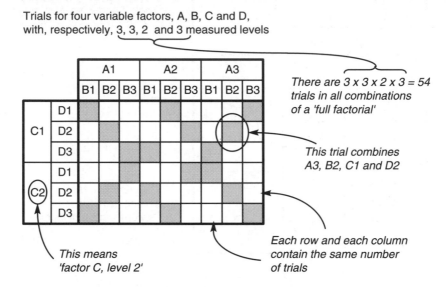

Fig. 16.8 Using a matrix to select a subset of trials

• A *Latin Square* is a simple method of selecting a small set of trials in a situation where there are several factors and levels. The square simply ensures that each level occurs once for each factor by rotating the levels around the factors for each successive trial, as in Fig. 16.9. If the resulting pattern may affect the result, the trials may be performed in random order.

   Latin squares have a fairly significant constraint in that there must be the same number of factors, levels and trials. This may be achieved by selecting the number of levels to match the number of factors.

Trial	Factor A	Factor B	Factor C	Factor D
1	1	2	3	4
2	4	1	2	3
3	3	4	1	2
4	2	3	4	1

*Successive trials 'rotate'
the levels between factors*

*There are the same number
of factors, levels and trials
(in this case, four of each)*

Fig. 16.9 Latin square

Notes

Experimentation by varying one factor at a time began with Francis Bacon, in his *experimentum crucis*. Modern statistical experiments started with R. A. Fisher's use in agricultural research during the 1920s. Since then there have been many new methods devised, and Genichi Taguchi is one of the most well-known recent contributors in this area.

Design of Experiments is a large and sometimes complex area, and this chapter has only described some basic approaches. Further details are more mathematical in nature and are thus beyond the scope of this book.

See also

Chapters: A Prioritization Matrix can be used to select factors with which to experiment. Use a Matrix Diagram to select trials. Other tools for measuring Variation include the Control Chart, Histogram, Process Capability and Scatter Diagram.

References: [Juran 79] discusses experiments in detail. [Feigenbaum 86] also discusses them. [Roy 90] and [Logothetis 92] detail both classic experiments and Taguchi's methods.

17 Failure Mode and Effects Analysis

What it's for

To identify and prioritize how items fail, and the effects of failure.

When to use it

- Use it when designing products or processes, to identify and avoid failure-prone designs.
- Use it when investigating why existing systems have failed, to help identify possible causes and remedies.
- Use it when investigating possible solutions, to help select one with an acceptable risk for the known benefit of implementing it.
- Use it when planning actions, in order to identify risks in the plan and hence identify countermeasures.

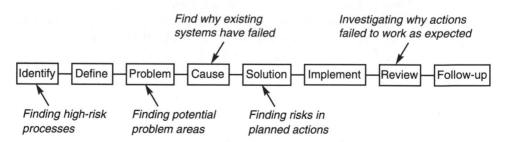

Fig. 17.1 Possible uses in improvement project framework

How to understand it

Many problems are caused by systems which fail in unexpected ways, which can result in significant costs. An example of this could be where a new roofing compound is decomposed by acid rain, with the result that the manufacturers have to pay substantial warranty costs, as well as gaining a reputation for poor products. A detailed analysis of the possible ways in which a system might fail, and the possible effects of these failures may thus save significant future costs.

Failure Mode and Effects Analysis (commonly called *FMEA*) takes the dual step of first finding out *how* an item can fail, and then finding *what effect* this failure might have. This second step thus helps to identify the importance of a failure mode, allowing identification of the key failure risks which must be addressed.

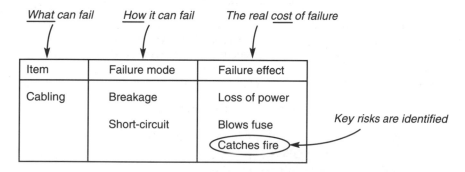

Fig. 17.2 Failure Mode and Effects Analysis

Criticality is a measure of importance that can be applied both to failure modes and to effects, allowing prioritization of remedial actions. A simple way of measuring failure mode criticality is to use the likelihood that it will occur in a given period. The criticality of a failure effect is the likelihood of that effect occurring due to *any* failure mode (see Fig. 17.3). Criticality may be further refined by also taking into account any other items which are considered to be important, such as severity of failure or chance of discovery by a customer.

Taking this extra step is performing *Failure Mode, Effects and Criticality Analysis*, or *FMECA*, although this often still referred to simply as FMEA.

A limitation of FMEA is that, although it goes into a lot of detail about the failure of individual components, it does not take combinations of failures into account. For example, the failure of a lift shaft drive may be inconvenient, but if the braking system has also failed, it could be catastrophic.

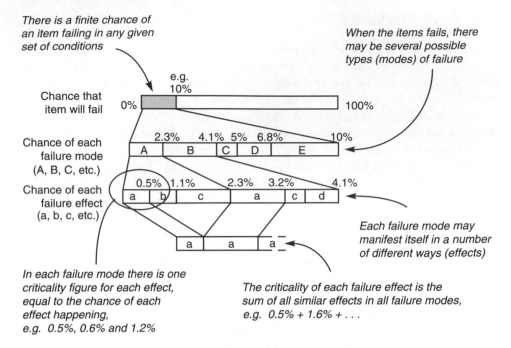

Fig. 17.3 Criticality

As with other numerical methods, figures are best derived from either actual measurement or controlled experiments. If these are not available, then estimates should be treated with appropriate caution.

Example

A developer of a word processor package received a number of complaints from its customer base about some specific features. On further investigation, it found that there were a limited number of effects that particularly annoyed customers. Working with their customers, they allocated severity ratings to these, as in Table 17.1.
An FMEA table was used to record the results of failures found in user trace logs. Only modes that resulted in the target effects were recorded. Criticality calculations were weighted with the severity ratings to take account of the customer priorities. A part of one table is shown in Fig. 17.4.
The analysis found that the mode with the highest weighted criticality score was when the disk became full. Further investigation found the actual cause was an uncurbed temporary file. The simple measure of putting limitations on the size of this file significantly reduced the defect rate.

Table 17.1 Example severity of effects

Effect	Severity
Corruption of hard disk	20
Loss of whole documents	10
Character loss	7
Printout scrambled	4

Item and (% chance of failure)	Failure mode		Effect of failure mode				
	Description	%	Description	%	Criticality $\times 10^6$	Severity	Crit. x Severity
Autosave (0.5%)	Disk full	20%	Disk corrupt	5%	50	20	1000
			Document loss	8%	80	10	800
			Character loss	12%	120	7	840
	Network drive	8%	Disk corrupt	1%	4	20	20
Print (0.2%)	Disk full	80%	Printout corrupt	20%	320	2	640
			Disk corrupt	1%	40	20	800

Fig. 17.4 Example

Other examples

- A new toaster design team uses FMEA to identify flaws in the design. This highlights ways in which the handle can stick and cause the toast to catch fire. This is prevented by adding a specific thermostatic safety release to the design.
- A boilermaker improvement team use FMEA to identify the failure modes that have caused certain pressure vessels to split. The result is the design of an effective and lasting solution.
- A secretary uses FMEA to highlight the possible undesirable effects of a room booking system not working properly, and consequently includes checks to reduce the chance of key effects of overbooking and key staff not being able to find rooms.

How to do it

1. Select the item to be analyzed. If it is a part of another item, then be clear about the boundary. For example, if the item is 'vehicle doors', it may mean passenger doors, but not the tailgate.

2. Identify the overall approach to be used. The FMEA may be a part of a larger set of failure analyses. In this case, the way that items are selected needs to be determined. Typical strategies include:
    *   *Top-down analysis,* where the system being analyzed is broken into pieces and FMEAs done on the larger items first. For example, starting with a whole vehicle and then successively breaking down into lower levels, such as doors, then catches, then screws.
    *   *Bottom-up analysis,* where the analyses of the smallest pieces are done first, followed by the higher level assemblies from which these are made. This is the reverse of top-down analysis.
    *   *Component analysis,* where the FMEAs are done on the physical parts of the system. This will typically use components specifications to determine failure levels.
    *   *Functional analysis,* where the analysis is of the intended functions and operation of the system. This is looking at failure from the product user's standpoint, rather than the engineer's, and will typically use product specifications to determine failure modes.

    Also decide whether to perform criticality analysis. This will require more effort, but will result in a numerical value being given to failure modes and effects, thus helping with prioritization of subsequent actions.

    If doing criticality analysis, determine how it will be calculated. The method below focuses just on the probability of failure modes and effects, although this can be extended to account for other important factors, as indicated in the following section on *Practical Variations*.

    Where possible, this method should utilize actual data, for example from product defect records. Otherwise define a range categories and corresponding numerical scores, then use an allocation method, such as Voting. For example, levels of 'Chance of being found in system test' being scored on a scale of 1 to 5.

3. Identify the scope of failure to be examined. The scope defines the boundaries of the examination, and may include criteria such as time period, type of user, geography of use, etc.

    For example, 'All vehicle doors failing to operate properly in final inspection and test for all shifts'.

4. Design an appropriate table to capture the right information. This will vary, depending on factors such as if and how criticality is being measured, as in Fig. 17.5.

5. Identify items which may fail and which fall into the scope defined in step 2. This can be determined by asking, '*What* can fail?' and may include individual components and any combinations, sub-assemblies, etc.

   If this list becomes unmanageably large, then either reduce the scope of the FMEA, for example by examining just the catch mechanism rather than all parts of a door, or limit the detail of examination, for example by examining the catch mechanism as a whole, but not its individual components.

6. If doing criticality analysis, determine the chance of failure for each item identified in step 5.

7. If doing criticality analysis, identify the proportion of the time during the scope described in step 2 for each item identified in step 5 to fail. For example, if the scope is a defined test, then one item may only be exercised for 10% of the test time whilst another item is exercised for 90% of the time (and consequently has more opportunity to fail).

   If all items may fail at any time, then this factor may be ignored, as it is always 100%.

8. For each item identified in step 5, list all significant failure modes. These may be found by asking, '*How* can it fail?'. For example, a hinge can seize, wear, fracture, etc. This can be simplified by identifying a standard list of failure modes for the item being examined.

9. If doing criticality analysis, identify the chance of occurrence for each failure mode identified in step 8. If all possible failure modes for an item are identified, their chances of occurrence will total 100%.

10. For each failure mode identified in step 8, determine all significant effects that may be manifested. Ask, 'What is an undesirable result of the identified failure mode?'. Again, this can be simplified by using a standard list of effects (e.g. won't close, difficult to close, stuck closed, etc.).

    Note the difference between a failure mode and failure effect; a failure mode *results in* a failure effect. For example, a broken pedal may result in a cyclist falling off.

11. If doing criticality analysis, identify the chance of occurrence of each failure effect identified in step 10. If all possible failure effects are identified, they will total 100% for each item.

12. If doing criticality analysis, calculate the criticality of each failure effect identified in step 10, by multiplying together (a) the chance of the overall item failing (from step 6), the proportion of time that the item is at risk of failure (from step 7), the chance of the failure mode occurring (from step 9) and the chance of failure effect occurring (from step 10). This is illustrated in Fig. 17.5.

13. For each mode and effect that appears in more than one line in the table, usually because they are on a standard list, sum the criticality calculations from step 12 to determine its overall criticality rating.

Chance of all possible failure modes for one item totals 100%

Chance of all possible failure effect for one failure mode need not total 100%, as effects may not always appear

Steps 5 & 6	Step 7	Step 8		Step 9	Step 10		Step 11 Step 12
		Failure mode			Effect of failure mode		Criticality
Item and (% chance of failure)	Time item may fail	Description	Chance		Description	Chance	$\times 10^6$
Door hinge (0.5%)	100%	Fractured	12%		Can't close door	11%	66
					Difficult to close	79%	474
		Fatigued	8%		Can't close door	100%	400
		Worn	80%		Difficult to close	100%	4000
Door catch (1.2%)	20%	Seized	54%		Can't close door	25%	324
					Can't open door	75%	972

Criticality = Chance of item failure x Chance of failure mode
x Chance of failure effect x Time item is at risk of failure

= 0.012 x 0.54 x 0.75 x 0.20 = 0.000972 = 972×10^6

The criticality of any mode or effect
is the sum of the criticality of its components

Criticality of mode: Door hinge fracture
= 66 + 474 = 600

Criticality of effect: Can't close door
= 66 + 400 + 324 + . . .

Fig. 17.5 FMEA table and criticality calculation

14. Examine the criticality scores and identify those failure modes and effects which will require action to be taken, and determine appropriate steps to reduce the chance of undesirable failure. Actions may include:
    - Redesigning items to make them likely to fail.
    - Adding items to handle failure of other items.
    - Adding warning systems to alert when an item fails.

Practical variations

- Focus first on a limited set of failure effects, and then work back to find the modes that cause them, so these can be addressed. This may be approached by selecting failure effects that customers would find particularly disagreeable. For example, FMEA of a computer system may focus on data loss.
- Identify a set of severity ratings for failure effects and show the criticality of each item in a separate column, as in Fig. 17.6. The sum of each column for each item then shows the severity distribution for that item.

Criticality of the severity class of each effect shown in appropriate column

Item and (% chance of failure)	Failure mode		Effect of failure mode		Criticality of effect by severity type x 10^6			
	Description	Chance	Description	Chance	V.Hi	High	Med	Low
Main stack (0.2%)	Corruption	15%	Data loss	24%	180			
			System crash	66%		495		
	Overflow	60%	Shutdown	90%			2700	
			System crash	10%		300		
	Underflow	25%	Warning	98%				1225
Total					180	795	2700	1225

Total shows severity distribution for item
e.g. 795 = ((0.2 x 15% x 66%) + (0.2 x 60% x 10%)) x 10^6

Fig. 17.6 Showing effect severity in columns

- Use a Matrix Diagram to correlate failure modes and failure effects (put items and modes in rows, put effects in columns). This will allow the connection between a large number of modes and effects to be seen in one diagram.

- MIL-STD-1629 describes two methods of FMEA. 'Method 101' covers basic qualitative FMEA, whilst 'Method 102' covers the quantitative criticality calculation. The recommended columns in the worksheet are described in Table 17.2.

Table 17.2 MIL-STD-1629 worksheet columns

Column title	Description	Method
Identification number	A number for cross-reference to other information.	Both
Item/functional identification (nomenclature)	An unique identification or description of the item being investigated.	Both
Function	The primary use or function of the item.	Both
Failure modes and causes	The failure mode of the item, also how this may be caused (useful for finding remedies).	Both
Mission phase/operational mode	When and how the item is being used when it fails.	Both
Failure effects	The detectable effects of the item failure, divided into local effects, next higher effects and end effects.	101
Failure detection method	The method of detecting the failure.	101
Compensating provisions	Other parts of the system that reduce the effect of failure (e.g. redundancy).	101
Severity class	Severity of failure effect. Typically from a set of four standard classifications.	Both
Failure probability/failure rate data source	Data source for measurements.	102
Failure rate, λ_p	The chance of the item failing during time, t.	102
Operating time, t	Proportion of test period during which the item is at risk of failure.	102
Failure mode ratio, α	The chance of the failure mode occurring during time t.	102
Failure effect probability, β	The chance of the effect occurring during time t.	102
Failure mode criticality	The criticality of the failure mode = product of the failure effect probability, failure mode ratio, failure rate and operating time, $(\lambda_p t \alpha \beta)$.	102
Item criticality	The criticality of the item = the sum of all failure mode criticalities for the item.	102
Remarks	Pertinent comments.	Both

- Weight the criticality values by multiplying them by a numeric representation of the failure effect severity. This will result in important effects standing out more clearly, enabling specific actions for these to be more easily prioritized.

  It can be useful to use a non-linear set of severity values (e.g. 1, 2, 8, 25) to reflect the common situation where serious effects are very much more important than medium or low effects.

- Weight the criticality values by multiplying them by the chance that failure will reach a point where it would be especially undesirable (e.g. reaching the customer). This recognizes that the importance of a failure may depend on where and when it is found.

Notes

FMEA is a tool that evolved from and is most commonly used in engineering reliability analysis.

See also

Chapters: Use Brainstorming, Nominal Group Technique or a Tree Diagram to find help items that may fail. Use a Matrix Diagram to relate failure modes and effects. Decision Tree, Fault Tree Analysis and Process Decision Program Chart also investigate risk.

References: [Ireson 88] and [O'Connor 91] discuss FMEA in detail within the context of reliability and the MIL-STD. [Feigenbaum 86], [King 89], [Vorley 91], [Oakland 93] and [Dale 94] take a more general view and include figures for failure severity and failure detection chance in the criticality calculation.

18 Fault Tree Analysis

What it's for

To show combinations of failures that can cause overall system failure.

When to use it

- Use it when the effect of a failure is known, to find how this might be caused by combinations of other failures.
- Use it when designing a solution, to identify ways it may fail and consequently find ways of making the solution more robust.
- Use to identify risks in a system, and consequently identify risk reduction measures.
- Use it to find failures which can cause the failure of all parts of a 'fault-tolerant' system.

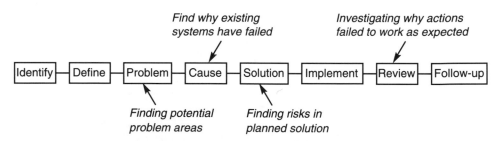

Fig. 18.1 Possible uses in improvement project framework

How to understand it

The failure of an item in a system is often caused by the failure of other items, for example where a vehicle's braking failure is caused by water in the brake cylinders, which may in turn be caused by failure of the cylinder seals.

Fault Tree Analysis, or *FTA*, provides a method of breaking down these chains of failures, with a key addition for identifying *combinations* of faults that cause other faults. Combinations of faults come in two main types: (a) where *several* items must fail together to cause another item to fail (an 'and' combination), and (b) where only *one* of a number of possible faults need happen to cause another item to fail (an 'or' combination).

The FTA diagram shows faults as a hierarchy, with two other symbols to show the 'and' and 'or' combinations, as in Fig. 18.2. These are called *gates*, as they prevent the failure event above them occurring unless their specific conditions are met.

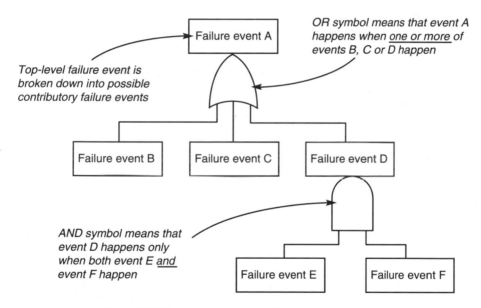

Fig. 18.2 Basic elements of Fault Tree Analysis

A third type of gate is called an *inhibit gate*, as it prevents a failure from happening unless a specific condition is met (it is effectively an 'and' of the failure and some other conditions).

In an FTA diagram, there are two main types of failure event box: *combination events*, which are the result of other events, and *basic events*, which are the start points for the chains of events above them. Basic events may be real root events or may simply not be developed further on this diagram. These and other symbols that may be used in FTA diagrams are shown in Table 18.1.

Table 18.1 FTA symbols

Symbol	Name	Description
	And gate	Event above happens only if *all* events below happen.
	Or gate	Event above happens if *one or more* of events below are met.
	Inhibit gate	Event above happens if event below happens *and* conditions described in oval happen.
	Combination event	Event that results from combination of events passing through gate below it.
	Basic event	Event that does not have any contributory events.
	Undeveloped basic event	Event that does have contributory events, but which are not shown.
	Remote basic event	Event that does have contributory events, but which are shown in another diagram.
	Transferred event	A link to another diagram or to another part of the same diagram.
	Switch	Used to include or exclude other parts of the diagram which may or may not apply in specific situations.

A common way of reducing the chance of failure of a system is to build redundancy into it, for example by having two sets of critical components running in parallel. It is possible, however, for failures to occur, which results in the fault tolerance of such systems to be negated as one failure causes all redundant parts to effectively not work. This is called *common mode failure*. For example, a motor system driven by two separate engines may fail when a common fuel line ruptures. FTA is a useful tool for discovering such failures, as it looks back down the chain of events to find possible failures in all areas.

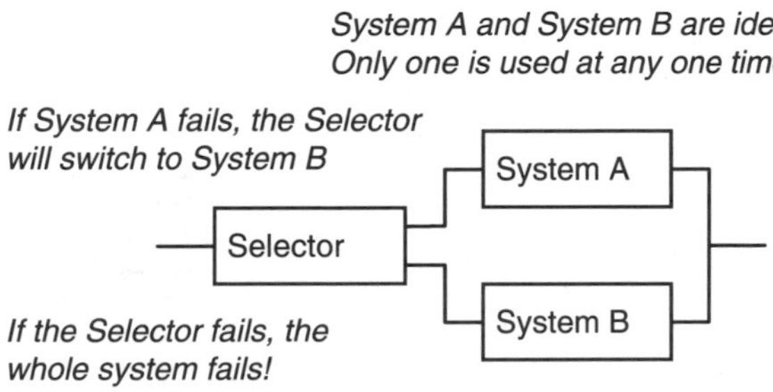

Fig. 18.3 Failure in redundant systems

Example

A company president recognized that its personnel evaluation system was not effective at motivating its employees, and charged the personnel department with improving it. As a part of the initial analysis of the existing system, they use FTA to identify the different ways that the evaluation system can fail and lead to demotivation (see Fig. 18.4).

Identified failure areas were investigated further, and the new system based on a correction of these failures. As a result, motivation increased significantly.

Other examples

- A hospital team uses FTA to identify how incorrect prescriptions may be given through combinations of events. They consequently design a system to prevent such a disaster from happening.
- An aeroplane parts manufacturer performs FTA as a standard part of the design process to identify critical faults which could cause hazardous failure. Any subsequent failures are checked against the FTA diagram to help improve the overall process.
- A quality team in a newspaper press room uses FTA to check potential failures of an improved colour registration process.

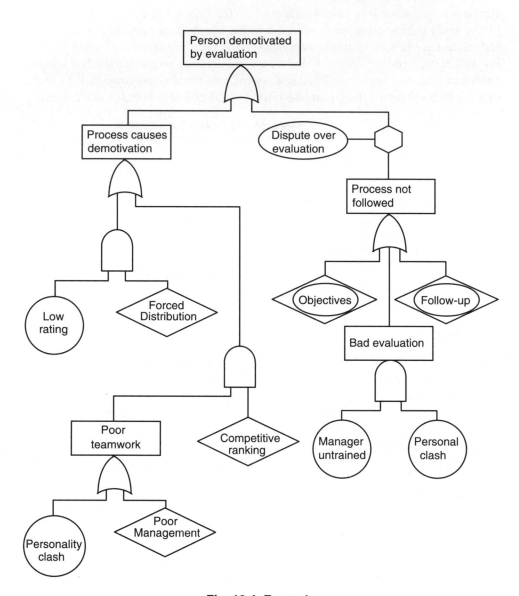

Fig. 18.4 Example

How to do it

1. Identify the failure effect to be analyzed. Typically this will be a critical effect that must be eliminated or reduced. It should be a complex failure, which may be caused by combinations of other failures, rather than a low-level failure with simple causes.

    This may be found using other tools, such as Failure Mode and Effects Analysis.

2. Write the failure effect in a box at the top-centre of the diagram area. Make this a clear phrase that describes the effect as precisely as possible, describing not only what the failure is, but how it occurs. For example, 'carburetor fails when engine reaches full temperature'.

3. List failures that may *directly* contribute to the failure described in step 2. For example, 'fuel delivery failure', 'air intake blockage', etc.

    When identifying ways in which an item may fail, try looking at the problem from different angles. For example:
    -   Excessive stresses and strains.
    -   Potential misuse and abuse.
    -   Environmental extremes.
    -   Natural variation in the system.
    -   Failure of dependent systems.
    -   Failure of related processes.

4. Divide the list of failures in the list derived in step 3 into separate groups, where all members of each group must occur together for the failure in step 2 to occur. For example, 'dirt in fuel' *and* 'partially blocked jet'. There are three possible outcomes from this:
    (a) There is one group, as all failures identified in step 3 must occur together for the failure from step 2 to happen. This is an 'and' group, so draw an 'and' gate under the failure from step 2 and connect this to boxes underneath containing the failures from step 3, as in Fig. 18.5(a).
    (b) No such groups can be found as <u>any</u> one failure from step 3 can result in the failure effect from step 2. This is an 'or' group, so draw an 'or' gate under the failure from step 2 and connect this to boxes underneath containing the failures from step 3, as in Fig. 18.5(b).
    (c) There are several groups. This is a complex grouping, so draw each group with more than one member under an 'and' gate and connect these gates to an 'or' gate under the failure effect from step 2, as shown in Fig. 18.5(c).

        It may also be worth checking whether any 'and' group actually

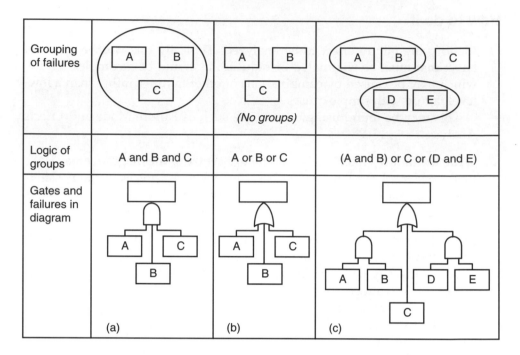

Fig. 18.5 Putting failure groupings into diagram with gates

constitutes an independent failure effect. This can be shown with an additional failure box above the 'and' gate.

There may also be additional conditions for a failure or group of failures to occur. For example, environmental or procedural conditions such as 'ambient temperature >50°C' or 'engine idling'. These may be shown with an inhibit gate, as in Fig. 18.6.

5. For each failure which has no connections below it, decide whether or not to develop this further by finding other failures which may contribute to it. If the failure is not to be developed on this diagram, draw it in an appropriate box, as in Table 18.1. Thus, if the failure cannot reasonably be developed further, put it in a circle; if it could be developed, but it is not appropriate to do this here, then use a diamond-shaped box. If the failure is to be developed, repeat step 3 to find contributory failures and appropriate gates.

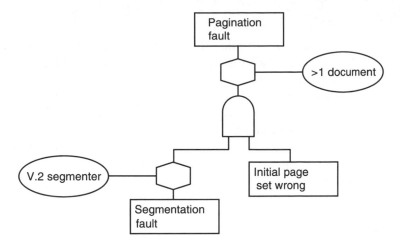

Fig. 18.6 Using the inhibit gate

6. When the diagram is complete, examine it to draw conclusions and plan for appropriate actions. For example, acting to reduce risks such as critical failures and safety hazards.

Practical variations

- Start by finding how individual items in a system can fail, and then build an FTA diagram bottom-up, to show how they might act in combinations to cause an overall system failure.
- Write the failures on 3" x 5" cards or adhesive memo notes, so they can be rearranged into the best order on the diagram.
- Make symbols easier to visually differentiate by writing 'AND' or 'OR' in them, as appropriate.

Notes

Fault Tree Analysis evolved in the aerospace industry during the 1960s. Its symbols come from electronic logic diagrams.

See also

Chapters: Use Failure Mode and Effects Analysis to identify the specific effect to be analyzed. Use Brainstorming or Nominal Group Technique to identify failures. Use Affinity Diagram to group failures. Decision Tree, Failure Mode and Effects Analysis and Process Decision Program Chart also investigate risk. Fault Tree Analysis is a variation of the Tree Diagram.

References: [Ireson 88] and [O'Connor 91] discuss Fault Tree Analysis in detail within the context of reliability. It is also discussed in [Sinha 85].

19 Flowchart

What it's for

To show the sequential steps within a process.

When to use it

- Use it when analyzing or defining a process, to detail the actions and decisions within it.
- Use it when looking for potential problem points in a process.
- Use it when investigating the performance of a process, to help identify where and how it is best measured.
- Use it as a communication or training aid, to explain or agree the detail of the process.

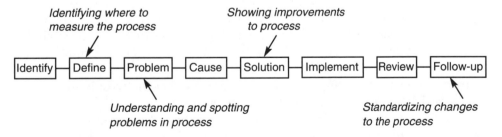

Fig. 19.1 Possible uses in improvement project framework

How to understand it

In order to improve a process, it is first necessary to understand its operation in detail. Describing this in text lacks the clarity of a pictorial diagram, where individual steps are more easily seen.

The Flowchart is a simple mapping tool that shows the sequence of actions within a process, in a form that is easy to read and communicate.

The basic element of a process is a simple action, which can be anything from striking an anvil to making a cash payment, and is represented as a box containing a description of the action. The mapping of 'what follows what' is shown with arrows between sequential action boxes, as in Fig. 19.2. This also shows the boxes for process start and end points of which there are normally one each.

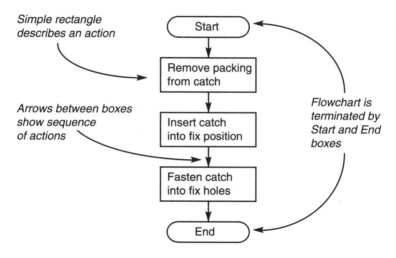

Fig. 19.2 Sequence of actions

Processes become more complex when decisions must be made on which, out of an alternative set of actions, must be taken. The decision is shown in a Flowchart as a diamond-shaped box containing a simple question to which the answer is 'yes' or 'no' as in Fig. 19.3. More complex decisions are made up of combinations of simple decision boxes.

Processes often go wrong around decisions, as either the wrong question is being asked or the wrong answer is being given.

Where boxes cannot be directly connected with lines, the separated lines are coordinated with connector boxes containing matching names. This typically occurs where lines cross onto another page, as in Fig. 19.4.

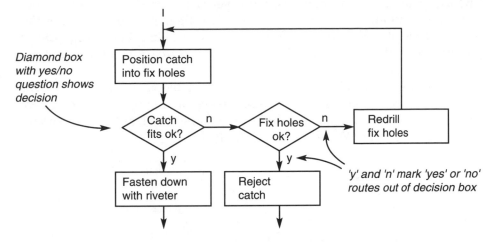

Fig. 19.3 Decisions in process

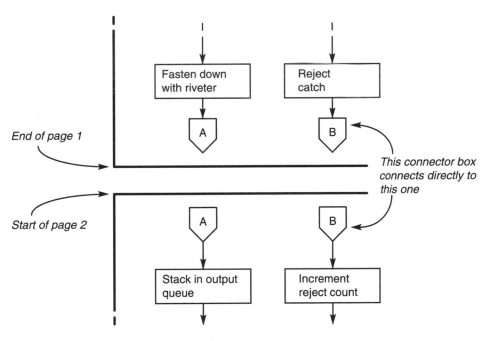

Fig. 19.4 Connector boxes

By using multiple connector boxes, it is very easy for Flowcharts to become very large, although this is usually self-defeating, as the Flowchart then becomes difficult to understand. The ideal size for a Flowchart is one page, as this gives a single visual 'chunk' that is reasonably easy to understand as a single item.

Large processes can be broken down into a hierarchical set of smaller Flowcharts by representing a lower level process as a single sub-process box. This behaves like a normal action box at the higher level, but can be 'zoomed into' to expose another Flowchart, as in Fig. 19.5.

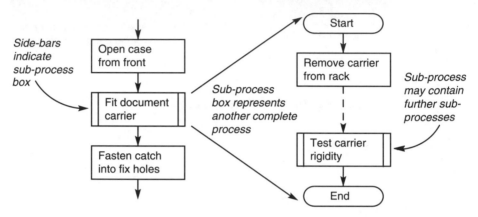

Fig. 19.5 Sub-process

An additional 'action' box that can be useful when analyzing processes is the wait box, which highlights a delay (i.e. *no* action), as in Fig. 19.6. This is a typical point where the overall cost of a process may be improved by acting, possibly on other processes, to reduce the delay.

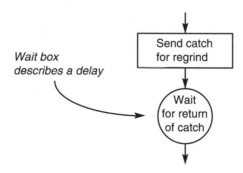

Fig. 19.6 Wait box

There are a number of different charting standards which extend this basic set of boxes. They typically include additional boxes for special types of action, such as getting input and producing output.

A confusion that may arise from different standards is that they can use the same box for different purposes or use different boxes for the same purpose. It is therefore a good idea to be clear from the beginning of any exercise on the standard to be used.

A limitation of Flowcharts is that, although they show the action sequence, they do not explicitly show the flow of information or items through the process. This may be done with other tools, such as IDEF0.

Example

A product assembly team in a gaming machine manufacturer were looking for ways of building the product more efficiently. They broke down the assembly process into a set of Flowcharts, showing how sub-assemblies were made and then built into the final product. Analysis of the reel assembly process revealed two improvements:

(a) The kit of parts was already checked by the kit assembly line, who were sometimes careless, as they knew the kit would be rechecked. The assembly line process was improved so the check here could be removed. This saved over two minutes per reel in checking, and up to fifteen minutes when the kit was faulty.

(b) Fitting the reel band after the reel had been attached to the base was awkward. Fitting the band before the reel was attached to the base was more comfortable and saved about a minute per reel.

The process Flowcharts, before and after improvement, are shown in Fig. 19.7.

Other examples
- A management team uses a Flowchart to map and agree the actions in their strategic planning process. The resulting diagram helps them to achieve a clear agreement on the actions and their sequence
- A garage mechanic uses a Flowchart to check the sequence of actions in tuning engines with a complex new system. Pinned to the garage wall, he then regularly refers to it until he has learned it by heart. He also uses it to train both existing staff and new recruits.
- A restaurant team maps the sequence of actions taken in preparing a meal in order to spot inefficiencies. The result is a significant reduction in effort.

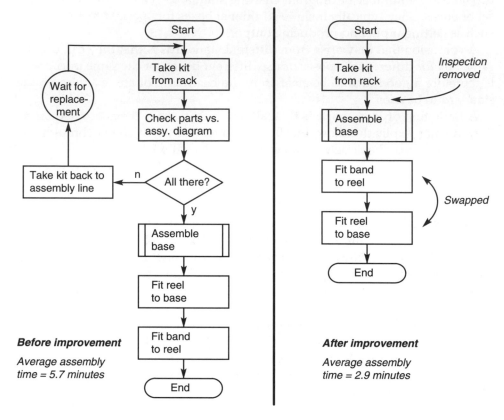

Fig. 19.7 Example

How to do it

1. Identify the process which is to be mapped. There are several ways this may be discovered:
   - It has an identifiable purpose. A good test of this is to find a realistic name for the process.
   - It has an overall owner, often the lowest level person who has responsibility for the complete process. For cross-functional processes, this is likely to be a senior manager.
   - It has identifiable customers and suppliers (these may be people or just other processes).

2. Gather the team who are to work on describing the process. These should include people who are intimately involved in all parts of the process, to ensure that it gets described as it actually happens, rather than an idealized view.

3. Agree on a standard symbol set to use, for example as in Table 19.1. Alternatively, a company standard may be available. It is important to agree a standard as there are several conflicting common uses (for example, a circle can be a delay, an operation, assistance, an on-page connector or a terminator).

Table 19.1 Typical standard Flowchart symbol set

Symbol	Name	Meaning
	Terminator	Start or end of process.
	Action	A single activity.
	Wait	A delay (a *lack* of activity).
	Decision	A yes/no decision.
	Sub-process	'Contains' another process Flowchart.
A	Connector	Connects to another similar box on another page.

4. Draw a 'start' terminator box at the top of the work area.

5. Add the first box below the start box, identifying the first action simply by asking, 'What happens first?'. Add an appropriate box around it.

   Add subsequent boxes below the previous box, identifying each action by asking, 'What happens next?'. Draw an arrow from the previous box to this one.

Points to note when building the Flowchart include:

- Keep the descriptions short and simple. Use a brief phrase rather than a complete sentence. A verb-noun phrase is often useful, saying what is being done to what. For example, 'Check customer satisfaction,' rather than, 'Investigate the level of customer satisfaction using the F3 survey system'.
- Maintain a consistent level of detail. For example, do not go from, 'Fix television' to 'Replace line output transformer' in the same Flowchart.
- Aim to keep the Flowchart within one page. This can be useful in helping to restrain the level of detail. Typically this will result in around three to twelve boxes.
- Identify and include the key decisions in the process.
- Try to use consistent directions out of decision boxes for the 'yes' and 'no' lines. This can help prevent misinterpretation by people reading the Flowchart later.
- Aim to make the main flow of the diagram flow from top to bottom, with digressions going off to the right. Branch left only for loops back up and when the right is already occupied. Generally aim for a clockwise flow, but not at the cost of clarity.
- Have only one 'end' box.

6. If the final diagram is to be used as a part of a formal system, make sure that it is uniquely identified. This may include:
   - The name of this process, plus any other unique identification, such as a number from a hierarchical numbering system.
   - An identification of the parent process (if it exists), for example by name or number.
   - The name of the person or group who drew the chart.
   - The owner of chart plus their job title.
   - The version number of the chart.
   - The date the chart was last changed.

7. Use the consequent diagram as planned. This might be one or more of:
   - Identification of measurement points. Typically this will be around critical actions such as input/output or expensive actions.
   - Identification of potential problems. Common places for these to occur are around decisions or any form of communication between people.
   - Looking for actions that are missing, wrong or unnecessary.
   - Inclusion in a quality management system as a formal description of the process.

Practical variations

- Write the actions on 3" x 5" cards or adhesive memo notes, and place them in order. This makes rearrangement easier when actions become cramped or require revision. Add arrows when the layout is stabilized.
- Where the process involves multiple people or groups, have one column for each group or person, separated by vertical dotted lines as in Fig. 19.8. Order the columns so that people who communicate are adjacent and the overall flow is still left to right.

    This is particularly useful for process improvement as problems often lie in the communications boundary between individual people. It can, however, only be used for relatively simple Flowcharts, as the width available for each person is severely limited.

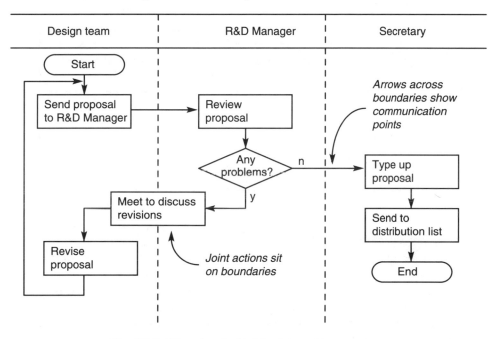

Fig. 19.8 Showing individual people or groups

- Use a more comprehensive symbol set, either to highlight critical tasks or as appropriate to the industry or application. Additional common symbols (originating from computer programming) are shown in Table 19.2.

Table 19.2 Additional Flowchart symbols

Symbol	Name	Meaning
	Input/Output	Action to get input to, or to deliver output from, process.
	Manual operation	Manual action within an otherwise automated process.
	Annotation	Comment on actions within the Flowchart.
	Document	Action or presence of document.
	Magnetic disk	Action or presence of computer disk.
	Magnetic tape	Action or presence of computer tape.
	Visual display	Display on a computer screen.

- Use horizontal dotted lines to separate distinct stages in the process, such as days or project phases.
- Annotate Flowcharts with salient notes. These can use the annotation symbol from Table 19.2 or may be simple free-form text. The general rule to apply when adding such commentary is that it should add to the understanding of the process without adding clutter.

  Annotations may be visually differentiated, for example by using a different typeface or italics.
- Show possible problems on each box with a mini-Cause-Effect Diagram on any number of boxes and arrows. This is illustrated in the section on Practical Variations in Chapter 12.
- Show the inputs and outputs to the overall process either by annotation or by using special boxes (as in Table 19.2).

  This can be extended to show the *internal* inputs and outputs, which may appear on each action box. A way of doing this is shown in Fig. 19.9.

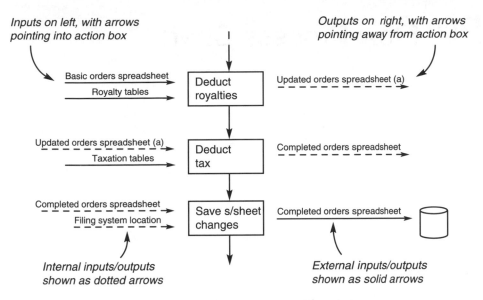

Fig. 19.9 Showing inputs and outputs

Notes

Flowcharts are often, but not always, included in descriptions of the first seven tools. They are also known as *Flow Diagrams*, *Process Deployment Flows* and *Process Flowcharts*. They are different from *Flow Process Charts*, which focus more on the *type* of action than the actual action.

The word 'Flowchart' is sometimes used to describe a wider variety of diagrams than is shown here, some of which show relationships (see Chapter 33, on the Relations Diagram) and input/output flow rather than sequential actions.

See also

Chapters: Processes may also be described with the Activity Network, Flow Process Chart, Gantt Chart, IDEF0, Relations Diagram and String Diagram. Possible problems in the Flowchart can be identified with extensions similar to the Cause-Effect Diagram.

References: The Flowchart is described in a number of books, usually briefly, including [Brassard 89], [Wadsworth 86], [Martin 85], [Sinha 85] and [Oakland 90].

20 Flow Process Chart

What it's for

To record and illustrate the sequence of actions within a process.

When to use it

- Use it when observing a physical process, to record actions as they happen and thus get an accurate description of the process.
- Use it when analyzing the steps in a process, to help identify and eliminate waste.
- Use it, rather than a Flowchart, when the process is mostly sequential, containing few decisions.

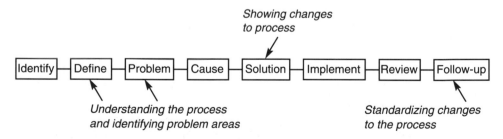

Fig. 20.1 Possible uses in improvement project framework

How to understand it

Many physical and manual processes consist of sequence of mostly simple actions, such as moving, waiting or inspecting. If these individual actions are identified, then it becomes easier to find ways of improving the process.

The Flow Process Chart records the steps in a process along a vertical line, with the action type being shown by a symbol alongside a description of the action, as in Fig. 20.2.

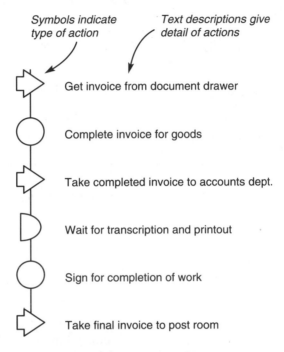

Symbols indicate type of action

Text descriptions give detail of actions

Get invoice from document drawer

Complete invoice for goods

Take completed invoice to accounts dept.

Wait for transcription and printout

Sign for completion of work

Take final invoice to post room

Fig. 20.2 Flow Process Chart

An important aspect of this type of chart is that it can be drawn *as the process happens*, for example by a person watching it. This makes it quick and easy to do and ensures that what actually happens gets recorded, rather than an idealized or abbreviated view that can come from using other process diagramming techniques.

There are three types of Flow Process Chart, depending on what is being charted: a *man-type* chart shows the actions of a person; a *material-type* chart shows what happens to a product or item; an *equipment-type* chart shows how a tool or other piece of equipment is used.

The most common symbol set used was developed by the American Society of Mechanical Engineers (ASME), and is shown in Table 20.1.

Table 20.1 ASME flow process symbols

Symbol	Title	Description
◯	Operation	A complex action or process (possibly described elsewhere), often changing something.
⇨	Transport	Movement of people or things. May be accompanied by a distance measurement.
D	Delay	Idle time of people or machines, or temporary storage of materials.
▽	Storage	Permanent storage of materials or other items.
▢	Inspection	Checking of items to ensure correct quality or quantity.

When analyzing a process, some action types become obvious candidates for improvement, such as long delays and excessive transport (which sometimes are hidden as a series of smaller actions). Individual operations may be broken down again or otherwise examined further, especially if they are difficult or costly.

Example

When a luxury biscuit manufacturer started rewarding people for improving their own processes, the people on the baking line decided to see how they could improve their process. They started in the less contentious area of materials process flow, charting how the biscuit was made, as in Fig. 20.3.

They noticed from this chart that the rejection rate of baked biscuits was very high. An easy improvement was to add an inspection just after the biscuits were moulded, as wet mix could simply be returned to the moulder. This resulted in a significant reduction in a previously high reject rate of baked biscuits. In a later improvement, the mixing and moulding processes were improved to reduce the rejection rate further.

Other examples
- A hospital surgical team uses Two-handed Flow Process Charts to analyze and help improve the efficiency of key surgical operations.
- A fork-lift driver in a builder's merchant draws a Flow Process Chart of his

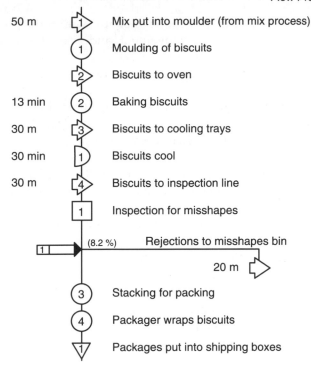

50 m — Mix put into moulder (from mix process)

Moulding of biscuits

Biscuits to oven

13 min — Baking biscuits

30 m — Biscuits to cooling trays

30 min — Biscuits cool

30 m — Biscuits to inspection line

Inspection for misshapes

(8.2 %) Rejections to misshapes bin

20 m

Stacking for packing

Packager wraps biscuits

Packages put into shipping boxes

Fig. 20.3 Example

offloading procedure. As a result, he reduces several wait and transport times.

- A sewing team in a fashion accessory manufacturer uses a Flow Process Chart to understand and improve the shoulder-bag assembly process. They supplement this by making video recordings of both the fastest and most accurate sewing machine operators, and including the best elements of each in a separate sewing chart. The resultant charts are used in training new operators.

How to do it

1. Define the objective of mapping the process, for example to find a solution to a particular problem.

2. Identify the process to be charted. It should be possible to name it, to know the start and stop points and to identify all materials, tools and other items used in it. The actual charting may be focused on one of three possible aspects of the process:

  People: Charting the actions of people within the process.

  Materials: Charting the movement and use of specific materials within the process.

  Machines: The use of machines and other tools in the process.

3. Make sure the person whose process is being charted is comfortable with the charting process being used. It is usually desirable that they are intimately involved in the whole improvement project.

4. Identify the symbol set that is to be used. Table 20.1 gives the most common set, but other symbols, such as in Table 20.2, may be used.

5. Record the steps of the process as they happen, starting at the top of the page and putting the action symbol on a vertical line with a brief description of the action to the right. Make the description complete enough to enable an unambiguous understanding of what is being done, but without being too verbose. Other points to consider include:
   - Where alternative or simultaneous actions may take place, show this by splitting the diagram into two or more vertical lines, as in Fig. 20.4, and annotate the diagram accordingly.
   - Look for consistent sized and self-contained 'chunks' of action. A chunk can be anything from inserting a screw to rebuilding a furnace, but both should not appear in the same chart! The chunk size selected will depend on the overall process being charted.
   - It is common to put numbers in each action symbol, counting each action type. Thus, the first operation circle contains a '1', the second circle (wherever it occurs) contains a '2', and so on.
   - Aim to make the process easier to read afterwards by fitting it within one page (although more may be needed if a detailed analysis is being done).

6. If recording the chart as the process is being enacted, rather than by discussion, try watching it again a few times to check that it is performed consistently. If not, use the most common approach for the main diagram, and consider doing different charts for different actions - one of them may be better than the others.

   It is also useful to review the chart with people involved, to ensure it is an accurate representation and to help gain their agreement and acceptance of any subsequent changes.

7. Use the final diagram for the objective identified in step 1.

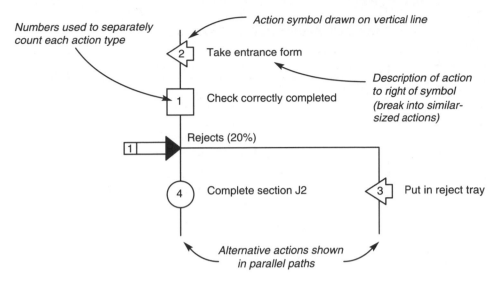

Numbers used to separately count each action type

Action symbol drawn on vertical line

2   Take entrance form

Description of action to right of symbol (break into similar-sized actions)

1   Check correctly completed

Rejects (20%)

1

4   Complete section J2

3   Put in reject tray

Alternative actions shown in parallel paths

Fig. 20.4 Building the chart

Practical variations

- Point the transport arrow left or right to indicate direction of movement, as in Fig. 20.5.
- Add information which will help the objective of using the chart. For example, if the objective is to improve efficiency, then add the time taken for each action next to the action symbol. Other information to add may include the distance travelled in a 'transport' action and the person(s) performing the action.
- Use other tools, such as the String Diagram alongside it, to help gain a fuller understanding of the process.
- Make a video recording of the process, and then draw the chart from this. This makes it easier to stop and start the video in order to record actions, which makes it particularly useful for a process with rapid changes.

   Other photographic tools include *Micromotion Photography*, which uses slow-motion film, and the *Cyclegraph* and *Chronocyclegraph*, which examine detailed hand movement by attaching a constant or intermittent light source to the hand and taking long exposure still photographs.
- An *Outline Process Chart* is an abbreviated form of Flow Process Chart, showing only the key actions (typically only operations, not transport, delays, etc.). It thus provides an overview, and can be useful for getting or giving a quick understanding of the process, especially if it is large.

Table 20.2 Additional Flow Process symbols

Symbol	Title	Description
◯ (overlaid circle in square)	Combined operation	Overlay symbols for actions which combine types. Put the main activity outside.
⊏▶⊲ ( )%	Reject	Rejection of item. Parentheses show percentage of items rejected. Line to right lead to consequent action.
Ⓒ (circle with C)	Differentiated operation	Letter shows type of operation, e.g. C = clerical, M = machine, etc.
⊥ Description ⊤	State change	Description indicates change in state, for example a liquid cooling into a solid.
⇩ (down arrow)	Alternating processes	Down-arrow indicates one of several possible actions. This can show alternative or simultaneous processes.

- Use other symbols beyond the ASME symbols, for example to show actions specific to a given industry. Other common symbols are shown in Table 20.2.
- When aiming to make a process more efficient, record the time taken for each action, then improve those that take most time.
- A *Two-Handed Process Flow Chart* individually shows the movement of each hand in a manual process, as in Fig. 20.5. It is typically used when analyzing a manual assembly process, to help make it easier to perform.
- Describe a multi-person process in the same way as a Two-Handed Flow Process Chart, with one vertical process line per person, showing simultaneous actions at the same level, and bringing them together when people work together on the same task.
- Instead of drawing the symbols for each action, use one column for each symbol and then mark the appropriate column. The change between different actions can be highlighted by drawing lines between these marks, as in Fig. 20.6.

    A standard form of this is the *OTIS Chart.* where OTIS stands for the four symbols: Operation, Transport, Inspection and Storage.

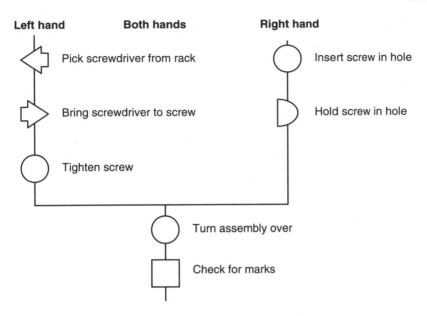

Fig. 20.5 Two-Handed Process Chart

Library selection	◯	⇨	◗	▢	▽
Find book on shelves	●—●				
Take book to checkout		●			
Take book request form		●			
Complete request form		●			
Check form is completed correctly				●	
Wait for checkout completion			●		
Put book in briefcase					●

Fig. 20.6 Using columns for action types

Notes

Flow Process Charts come from the field of Work Study, a forerunner of modern quality control.

See also

Chapters: Processes may also be described with the Activity Network, Flowchart, Gantt Chart, IDEF0, Relations Diagram and String Diagram. The String Diagram uses similar symbols.

References: Flow Process Charts are described in older books on Work Study, such as [Raybould 71] and [ILO 79], although they are often also mentioned in more modern books such as [Sinha 85] and [Oakland 93].

21 Force-Field Diagram

What it's for

To weigh up the points for and against a potential action.

When to use it

- Use it when decision making is hindered by a number of significant points for and against a decision.
- Use it when there is a lot of argument and indecision over a point, to clarify and agree the balance of disagreement.
- Use it to help identify risks to a planned action and to develop a strategy for counteracting them.
- Use it to help identify the key causes of successful or unsuccessful actions.

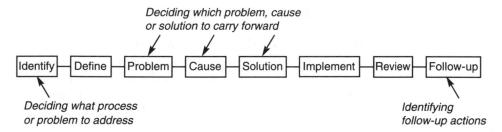

Fig. 21.1 Possible uses in improvement project framework

How to understand it

When making decisions or planning actions, there are often points against the situation as well as for it. Verbal argument can result in the wrong decisions being made as the 'winner' is often the most senior person or the one who shouts the loudest. Better decisions are made by weighing up the pros and cons in a more organized fashion.

The Force-Field Diagram uses a simple diagram to visually organize and display the arguments for and against a situation or action (see Fig. 21.2). Each argument or reason is shown as an arrow, pointing into a line, with either side of the line representing either side of the argument and the length of each arrow representing the weight or strength of the argument.

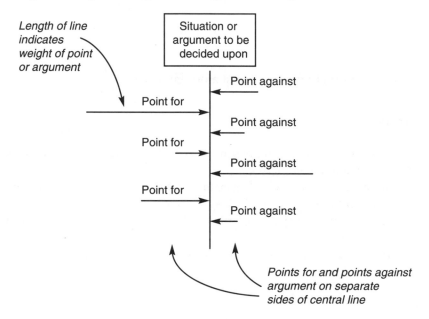

Fig. 21.2 Force-Field Diagram

The overall impression of the Force-Field Diagram is of two sets of forces pushing against one another, with the greatest overall force winning. The total force on one side is formed by the combination of both the number and weight of forces. The visual effect of the diagram can help the overall arguments for and against the situation to be weighed up and clear decisions and actions taken.

If the forces and their weight can be determined in a rigorous way, then the confidence in any subsequent decisions will be increased proportionately.

Example

One of the options for a steel works planning team looking to save future processing costs is whether to consolidate the strip mill to a single site. To help identify the forces involved, they build a Force-Field Diagram, as in Fig. 21.3.

During completion of the diagram, it was found that the most significant force was not the opposition from unions, as was expected, but the political pressure. In a time of recession and shortly before elections, the government was applying significant pressure not to close plants in areas of high unemployment. This, coupled with other consolidation costs, gave sufficient reason for this initially attractive solution to be abandoned.

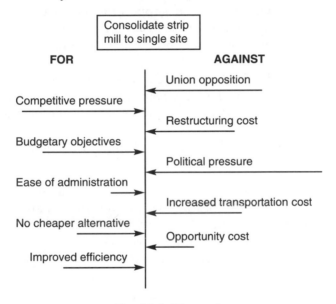

Fig. 21.3 Example

Other examples

- A supervisor disagrees with her manager's plans for their department, and uses a Force-Field Diagram to identify how the planned actions will be almost impossible to implement. In doing this she finds alternative actions which will achieve most of the original objectives, but in a far more efficient manner. When presented with this evidence, the manager readily agrees to the changes.
- A town planning team is investigating the feasibility of employing independent street cleaning crews. They use evidence from other towns to build arguments for and against the proposal, displaying these in a Force-Field Diagram.

- An assembly team in a domestic appliance manufacturer is working on reducing the number of washing machines which leak in final test. They test the idea of using silicon-bonded seals, using a Force-Field Diagram. No significant restraining forces are found, so they continue with implementing the solution.

How to do it

1. Write a statement that describes the decision or situation to be resolved. This should be a brief sentence that will make it easy to distinguish between:
   (a) *Driving* forces which will act to support the statement.
   (b) *Restraining* forces which will act against the driving forces.
   (c) Other forces, which will not affect the situation one way or another.

   Where the description is of a possible action to achieve a known objective, include both of these in the statement. For example, 'Reduce customer complaints by personally delivering and setting up all replacements'.

2. Form a team of people who, between them, will be able to identify the forces around the problem.

3. Write the statement from step 1 at the top of the work area, with a vertical line below, as in Fig. 21.4. Indicate which side will contain driving forces that will support the statement, and which side will contain restraining forces. As left to right is commonly viewed as 'forwards', it is a good idea to put forces 'for' the statement on the left so that these 'drive the problem forwards'.

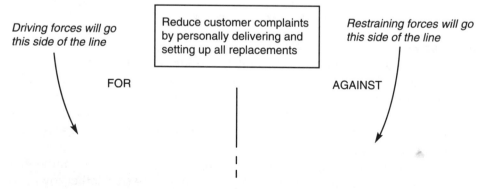

Fig. 21.4 Preparing work area

4. Identify driving and restraining forces that will act for and against the statement, writing them on the appropriate side of the central line (do not add arrows yet).

    Questions to ask to help identify the forces involved may include:
    - What must we do to make it work? What could happen to make it fail?
    - Who would help? Who would oppose it? Who would ignore it?
    - What would happen if the decision was not made or reversed?
    - What is the best and worst possible thing that could happen?
    - What will happen whatever is decided?
    - What are the costs and benefits?
    - What are the financial implications?
    - How easy or difficult will it be to implement?
    - What other forces would support or oppose identified forces?

5. Identify how to decide on the strength of each force. This includes selection of the criteria and the method of scoring.

    Criteria help to contrast the significance of each force against other forces, both on the same side and on the other side of the line. Use the objective from step 1 to help select the criteria, which might thus be 'Effect on customer satisfaction'.

    Possible scoring methods include consensus discussion, Voting, Prioritization Matrix or some other form or objective measurement. The appropriate method will depend on the severity of the problem and the available time.

6. Use the method defined in step 5 to determine the relative strength of each force identified in step 4. Draw an arrow of appropriate length under the force to show its strength, pointing into the line, as in Fig. 21.5.

7. Identify the overall force on each side. This may be clear from the diagram, or may require more discussion and summation of the forces.

8. Take appropriate action. Typical actions include:
    - Seeking to validate assumptions made about forces and their relative strengths, especially if the results are uncertain.
    - Implementing the identified action, especially where forces for the statement are overwhelming.
    - Seeking and evaluating other possible solutions, particularly where the diagram is inconclusive or where forces against are overwhelming.

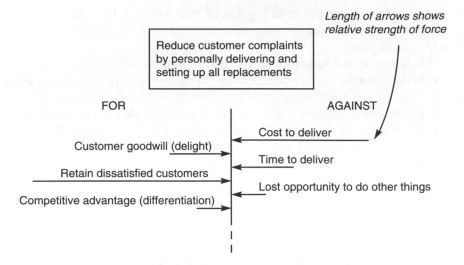

Fig. 21.5 Adding weight to each force

Practical variations

- Line length enables a variable force to be shown, but may be impractical if other variations are used which redirect the line. In this case, show the size of each force with graphical methods other than length, such as thickness, dotting, etc.
- Show the size of each force with a number. This may be derived from using tools such as a Prioritization Matrix or Voting. The total force on each side can now be easily summed.
- If some forces are clear and provable and some are based more on intuition or opinion, then mark these differently. For example, circle the well-understood forces.
- The forces can be shown pointing up and down, although this makes the horizontal text more difficult to fit, and can also give an impression of the force going down having the effect of 'gravity', giving it more weight.
- Arrows can be drawn going away from the line, to illustrate forces pulling against one another rather than pushing against one another. This may be more illustrative in some situations, for example where two groups are trying to do different things.
- If a force acts directly against a force on the other side, illustrate this by pointing the arrows against one another, as in Fig. 21.6. There will tend to be clusters of arrow heads around key decision points, which may be discussed and resolved individually.

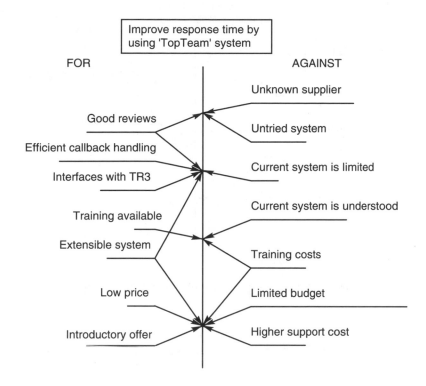

Fig. 21.6 Showing relationships between opposing forces

- Write forces on 3" x 5" cards or adhesive memo notes to allow them to be rearranged while building the diagram. This is particularly useful if showing opposing forces or hierarchies as above.
- Draw the diagram as a see-saw, with stronger forces being shown further from the fulcrum. This can be helped by first sorting forces on each side into order of strength.
- Show how forces are built up with a hierarchy, as in Fig. 21.7. Where forces in the hierarchy are given numerical force values, the number for the main force may be determined by summing its contributory forces. This is effectively combining the Cause-Effect Diagram with the Force-Field Diagram.

    This may be combined with the method shown in Fig. 21.6 to show relationships both within and between forces for and against the argument.

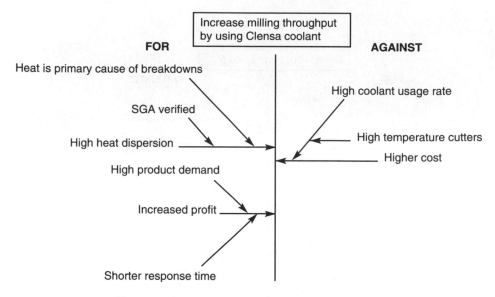

Fig. 21.7 Showing relationships in a hierarchy

- Where relations between driving and restraining forces are very intermingled and it is difficult to put them on either side of a line, build a Relations Diagram and mark the forces with positive and negative numbers.

Notes

Force-Field Diagrams are not a well-known tool, but they are used fairly widely, often appearing in company toolkits, which is a good sign of their practical value. Their use in tandem with Cause-Effect Diagrams is sometimes called *CEFFA* (for Cause-Effect diagrams with Force-Field Analysis).

See also

Chapters: Use Brainstorming or Nominal Group Technique to identify forces. Use Prioritization Matrix or Voting to identify force strength. A Force-Field Diagram can be combined with a Cause-Effect Diagram to show causal chains in forces.

References: Their use in AT&T is described in [Ackerman 87]. They are also briefly described in [Barra 83], [Oakland 93] and [Marsh 93].

22 Gantt Chart

What it's for

To show the actual time to spend in tasks.

When to use it

- Use it when doing any form of planning, to show the actual calendar time spent in each task.
- Use it when scheduling work for individuals, to control the balance between time spent during normal work hours and overtime work.
- Use it when planning work for several people, to ensure that those people who must work together are available at the same time.
- Use it for tracking progress of work against the scheduled activities.
- Use it when describing a regular process, to show who does what, and when.
- Use it to communicate the plan to other people.

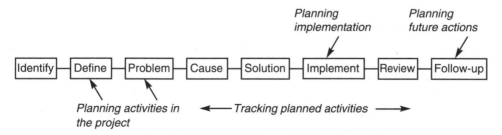

Fig. 22.1 Possible uses in improvement project framework

How to understand it

When planning for activities within a project, it can be difficult to get a clear picture of what is being done, when and by whom. Tools such as the Activity Network can be used to calculate dates, but it is still not immediately clear which tasks occur at the same time and can result in people being scheduled to work on several tasks simultaneously.

The Gantt Chart is a simple horizontal Bar Chart, where bars represent the actual calendar time which is planned for each task (see Fig. 22.2). The scale used for the time will depend on the overall size of the project and the estimation increment used.

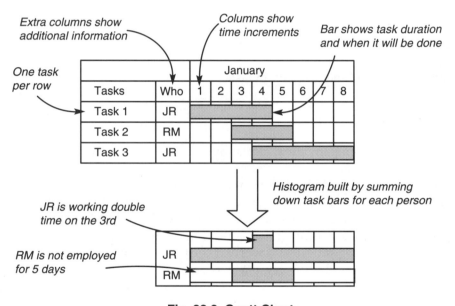

Fig. 22.2 Gantt Chart

Other information may be added to the chart, such as the resources required to complete each task (people, machines and materials). This helps the management of the task in several ways:

- Over- and under-allocation of work can be easily seen and corrected. This is commonly highlighted by summing bars down into one Histogram per person, as in Fig. 22.2.
- The interaction of people within groups can be coordinated, for example where several people are working on the same or related tasks.
- The estimation of task duration may be matched with resources allocated to it.

- Scarce resources can be allocated to the most important tasks.
- Individual holidays can be taken into account.
- Additional resource may be budgeted for, in order to reduce the project completion time or to reduce any risk of slippage or failure.

A disadvantage of the Gantt Chart is that dependencies between tasks are not shown, which can lead to tasks being ordered wrongly. This can be addressed by using an Activity Network beforehand, to calculate realistic start dates for each task. Other items from the Activity Network including slack time, tasks on the critical path, and milestones may also be displayed on the Gantt, as in Fig. 22.3.

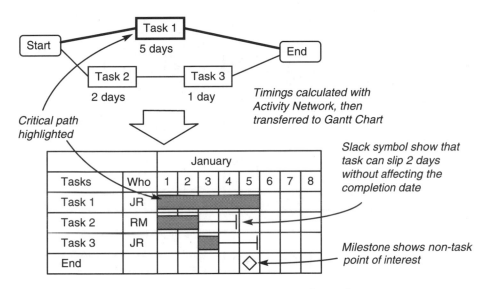

Fig. 22.3 Activity Network and Gantt Chart

Optimizing the schedule through rearranging tasks and resources is often aimed at reducing the total slack time, and may also result in a reduction in the total calendar time required to complete the project. This is called *levelling* or *load balancing*.

Tasks are often shown as a hierarchy, where the lowest level tasks (or *unit tasks*) are those which are actually worked on by someone. The higher level tasks (called *summary tasks*) serve only to 'contain' lower level tasks, helping with their identification and understanding. The way they commonly appear is shown in Fig. 22.6.

Example

A project team in a printing works had a solution to an electrical problem which required all machines to be stopped whilst a fuse box was replaced and a cable was laid into a new machine. Normally, this would have taken two days, but they used two electricians and careful optimization of the Gantt Chart to minimize slack time, as in Fig. 22.4. As a result, the work was easily completed within one day.

Key: ■ = Critical path   ◇ = Milestone |—| = Slack time

Install power to new machine			February 14th (time of day)								
Task	Who	mins	8	9	10	11	12	13	14	15	16
Power down	HS	0	◇								
Remove old fusebox	HS	40	■								
Install new fusebox	HS	80		■							
Cut cable channelling	GM	200		▨▨▨ |—|						
Fit cable channelling	HS	140				■■					
Lay new cable	HS,GM	120							■■		
Connect to fusebox	HS	40								■	
Connect to machine	GM	20								■|—|	
Power up	HS	0								◇	
Test machine	GM	60									■

HS	420	▨▨▨▨▨▨
GM	400	▨▨▨▨ ▨▨▨ ▨

Fig. 22.4 Example

Other examples

- A deliveries manager uses a Gantt Chart to show the time taken by different groups and carriers in the process of sending a package to a customer in another country. This highlights the most time-consuming steps, which then become a focus for improvement.
- A family, building their own house, uses a Gantt Chart to plan the tasks in erecting the building By careful optimization of it, they are able to reduce the original calculated building time by 25%.
- When an improvement team in a metal box manufacturer is set up to reduce the reject rate of steel boxes, they use a Gantt Chart to plan the

team's activities. They also use another chart to plan and track the implementation of the final solution.

How to do it

1. Define the requirements of the project or work to be planned. This should contain sufficient detail to enable good decisions to be made during the planning process. Defining precise requirements can be helped by identifying the constraints on the project, which typically fall into three areas:
   - *Work*, including tasks that must be completed and tasks that need not be completed. This may also include measures to determine the success of the project.
   - *Resource*, including people available, machines, tools, materials and general discretionary budget.
   - *Time*, including the calendar time by when the project must be completed, holidays and other periods when resources are not available.

2. Identify all tasks that need to be completed to meet the requirements from step 1. A common way of doing this is to perform work breakdown using a Tree Diagram.

   When breaking the work down, aim to find clearly allocable chunks, where the required skills and resources are obvious. The duration of each task should be of comparable length and be short enough to enable clear tracking. For example, in a 12 month project, it is reasonable to have tasks of around 1 week each, whilst a 4 week project may be broken down into tasks which take no more than 1 day.

   Each task should be uniquely identifiable, either from its name or an allocated code. A simple scheme is to use a coding structure based on the work breakdown structure. For example, the drawing of a a motor housing in the design phase may be coded as DE.DR.MH01.

3. For each task, identify what is required to complete it, such as specific skills and resources. This may also take into account what is known about the risks in the task. For example, it may be decided that a task with known or uncertain risks will require the involvement of a more skilled person (or even more people).

   Note that at this stage actual resources are not allocated; the information from this step is fixed, whilst actual resources may be shuffled around between tasks.

4. Perform an initial allocation of resources to tasks, taking into account the requirements from step 3 and the resources actually available.

   A tool for matching tasks and people is the Resource Allocation Matrix, as described in Chapter 37.

   It may become clear at this time or later that there are insufficient resources to complete the project within the required time-frame, necessitating the acquisition of additional resources.

   Note that there is a chicken-and-egg situation between resources, estimation and allocation. For example, a skilled person may be initially estimated to take two days to complete a task, but then is found to be over-allocated in later calculations. As a result, a less skilled person is allocated, which changes the estimation to three days, which in turn changes the overall work profile of the project. This may result in several cycles of allocation, estimation and calculation before a satisfactory solution is found.

5. Estimate the time that will be taken to complete each task, given the allocated resources. There are many ways of doing this, few of which are particularly reliable. The best method is to use data that has been collected from previous similar tasks (preferably by the same people).

6. Identify task priorities and dependencies. This typically means finding those tasks which must be completed before each task can begin (although there are sometimes more complex dependencies).

   Independent tasks, which can be performed simultaneously, may be allocated priority values, for example to ensure that higher risk tasks are done earlier.

7. Calculate the start and end dates for each task. For anything more than a simple situation, this will require the use of an Activity Network.

   A table, such as in Fig. 22.5. may be used to organize the information from steps 2 to 7.

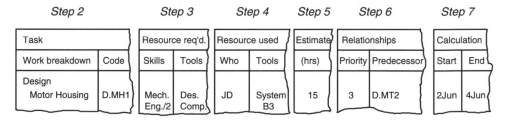

Fig. 22.5 Organizing project information

8. Identify a scale for the Gantt Chart, for example one increment on the bar may represent anything from 1 hour to 1 month. Typically, this will enable the chart to be drawn within a single page width (although using the paper in landscape, rather than portrait format will give more width). For example, if there are 30 squares available for bars, and the project is calculated to take 6 months, then it may be decided that a single square will represent all or part of a week.

9. Identify periods during which tasks may not be worked on, such as public holidays, private holidays, conferences and company events which must be attended. Mark these on the chart.

10. Draw the horizontal bars on the Gantt Chart, against each task, using the information gained in steps 2 to 9.

    At a minimum, this will include an identification of each task (name or code) plus the bar for that task. It may also include columns for additional information, typically anything from steps 2 to 8, but most usefully the names of the people who will perform the task, as in Fig. 22.6.

    The bar for each task will fill each time column (identified in step 8), even if it represents only a part of this time. For example, in Fig. 22.6, the bar for 'Design new form' occupies two full day columns, even though it may only take a part of the second day. This potential confusion can be avoided by using the same scale for effort estimates and time columns, although this may result in a large number of columns or very coarse estimates. The best approach is usually to scale the time columns to fit on the page and be careful not to get confused by any task overlap.

Information other than basic task names, such as work breakdown, codes, people, time, etc., is selected and displayed as required

When tracking, heavy vertical line shows 'now'

Task	Who	hrs	January									
			1	2	3	4	5	8	9	10	11	12
Design new form	JR	10	▓	▓								
Organise usability tests	RM	4	▓									
Do usability tests	JR, RM	14			▓	▓						
Revise form	JR	6					▓					

Fig. 22.6 Drawing the Gantt Chart

11. Investigate how well the available resources are used by summing down the time taken in each column into a Histogram for each resource, as in Fig. 22.3.

    This Histogram may then be used to perform load balancing by identifying actions to change tasks, resources, allocations and times that will enable the resources to be optimally used. For example, if a person is allocated to two tasks at one time, then either allocate one task to someone else or move it to a free period.

    After doing this load balancing, you may need to go back to step 5, repeating this process until a satisfactory chart is obtained.

12. As the project progresses, regularly re-estimate outstanding work on tasks, taking note of the accuracy of previous estimates. Thus if most tasks so far took 20% longer than originally estimated, it is probably reasonable to add 20% to outstanding tasks. Other tracking activities may include adding new tasks, changing the resources available to the project, reallocating tasks (e.g. from people who are slow to people who are quick) and recalculation of the overall schedule.

    Progress on the project can be shown by publishing the completed chart, with a vertical line to show the current date, as in Fig. 22.6. All bars and part-bars to the left of the line are completed, and all to the right are yet to be done.

Practical variations

- Colour or mark tasks on the critical path differently (typically in red), to highlight the fact that slipping these will cause the project end-date to slip.
- Sort tasks by their start date before showing them on the chart. This makes it easier to see what is scheduled at any one time, with bars generally going from top left to bottom right.
- A *Linked Bar Chart* shows the dependencies between tasks by drawing arrows between them, pointing from one task to the other tasks that follow it, as in Fig. 22.7. This combination of the Activity Network and Gantt Chart can be useful, but can also become messy if there are a large number of dependencies.
- Show the work breakdown structure on the Gantt, with different coloured or shaded bars to indicate summary tasks, as in Fig. 22.7. Other information, such as total time may also be calculated for each summary task, by summing information from other tasks that it contains.

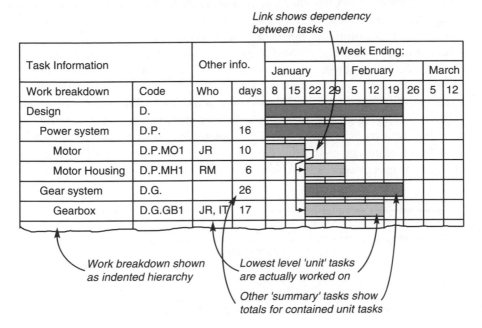

Fig. 22.7 Linked Bar Chart with work breakdown structure

- Show actual progress against plan by using two bars for each task. The first bar represents the original plan, and does not change. The other bars shows the actual time taken and reflect the latest estimates.
- Show people or other resources in the first column, instead of tasks. The actual tasks can either be shown indented from each person's name or written on the appropriate bar. This can result in a smaller diagram, with multiple bars on the same row, as in Fig. 22.8.

	January	
Who	1 2 3 4 5	8 9 10 11 12
Jane Brown	Write training	Give class
Sam Evans	Copy materials	

Fig. 22.8 Showing tasks by people

- Show slack time on the chart, as in Fig. 22.3, to indicate where tasks may slip without affecting the project end date.
- The *Delphi Method* can be used with a group of people to estimate task duration, and is described under 'Practical Variations' in Chapter 8.
- The effective progress of a project can be measured by calculating the *Project Progress Rate*, which indicates the real 'months of progress per month'. This may be calculated and plotted as in Fig. 22.9. This clearly shows if the project is ahead of schedule or is falling behind schedule.

The measure is quite scalable, for example months can be replaced by weeks or even days. It can also be applied to a single task, a complete project or even a whole set of projects.

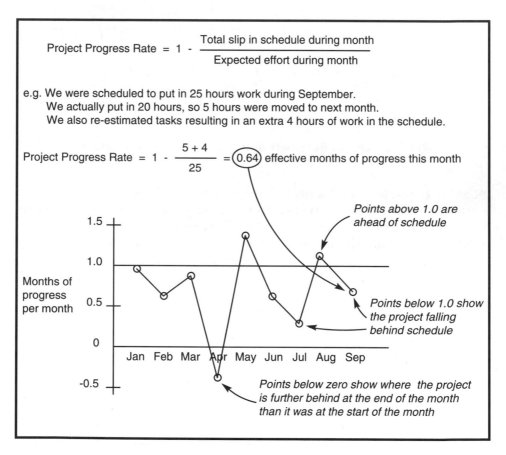

Fig. 22.9 **Calculating Project Progress Rate**

Notes

The Gantt Chart is named after its originator, Henry L. Gantt. Gantt Charts can be produced on a computer, using what are commonly called 'Project Management software'. This is particularly useful where repeated calculation of an Activity Network and subsequent levelling is to be done.

See also

Chapters: Use Brainstorming or Nominal Group Technique to help identify tasks. Use Activity Network to find task times. Use a Tree Diagram to break tasks down. Use a Histogram to show effort distribution. Gantt Charts are a special form of Bar Chart.

References: Gantt Charts are discussed in books on project management, such as [Page-Jones 85]. [Clark 52] is an old, but specialized book on the subject.

23 Histogram

What it's for

To show the frequency distribution of a set of measurements.

When to use it

- Use it to investigate the distribution of a set of measurements.
- Use it when it is suspected that there are multiple factors affecting a process, to see if this shows up in the distribution.
- Use it to help define reasonable specification limits for a process by investigating the actual distribution.
- Use it when you want to *see* the actual shape of the distribution, as opposed to calculating single figures like the mean or standard deviation.

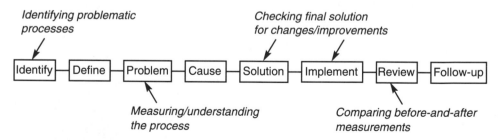

Fig. 23.1 Possible uses in improvement project framework

How to understand it

When measuring a process, it often occurs that the measurements vary within a range of values, as described in Chapter 5. By understanding *how* these measurements vary, the effects of the process and changes made to it can be better understood.

The Histogram shows the frequency distribution across a set of measurements as a set of physical bars. The width of each bar is constant and represents a fixed range of measurements (called a *cell*, *bin* or *class*). The height of each bar is proportional to the number of measurements within that cell. Each bar gives a solid visual impression of the number of measurements in it and together the bars show the distribution across the measurement range. Fig. 23.2 shows how the distribution of measurements can be seen far more clearly in the Histogram than in a table of numbers.

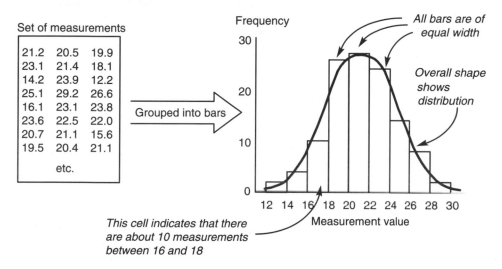

Fig. 23.2 The Histogram

In drawing the Histogram, there must be a sufficient number of measurements to be able to give a usable shape to the distribution. The number and width of the bars are also important; if the bars are too narrow, then insufficient measurements will fall into each bar to give it significant height. Similarly, if the bars are too wide, there will be too few bars to give a useful shape to the distribution.

Common Histogram shapes are shown in Table 23.1. Problems may be indicated by the distribution being naturally non-bell-shaped or by problems with the measurement. When a distribution differs from the expected shape, the underlying process should be examined to find real causes of this.

Table 23.1 Common Histogram shapes

Histogram pattern	Symptom	Possible problems
	Low with gaps	Bar range too narrow (check horizontal scale) or too few measurements (check vertical scale) or version of plateau distribution.
	High with few bars	Bar range too wide (check horizontal scale) or too few measurements (check vertical scale). Could be extreme version of truncated distribution.
	Skewed (this is positive; negative skew has tail to right)	Natural distribution (more variation in one direction - often found in item count and time distributions) or incomplete data being used.
	Exponential	Distribution is not bell-shaped (extreme version of skewed) or truncated data (could be the tail of a bell-shaped curve).
	Dual-peaked (bimodal)	Measurement is of two processes. This is very common, e.g. data from two periods, process changed mid-stream.

Table 23.1 (cont.) Common Histogram shapes

Histogram pattern	Symptom	Possible problems
	Isolated-peaked	Two processes being measured (well-separated bimodal distribution).
	Cog-toothed (or comb)	Faulty measurement, rounding error or version of plateau distribution.
	Plateau	Combination of multiple bell-shaped curves, extreme version of bimodal distribution (multiple processes) or faulty measurement.
	Edge-peaked	Modified data - often caused by shifting data that was out of specification back inside specification limits.
	Truncated	Incompletely reported data or measured after inspection has rejected items outside specification limits.

Three attributes of the Histogram are worth examining: the overall shape, the spread and the centring.

If the variation within the process is random, then the Histogram will follow a Normal (bell-shaped) curve, otherwise the shape can indicate a problem. If it is bell-shaped, then likely future values can be predicted by using the standard deviation, as described in Chapter 5. Other distribution shapes are possible, but less common. The expected shape can be determined by plotting a series of Histograms for a process that is known to be performing correctly; any significantly differing shape can trigger an investigation into the cause.

If the process has specification limits defined, then the Histogram should be centred between these limits. An off-center distribution, as in Fig. 23.3, can result in many items which are out of specification. Other measurement problems around specification limits, are shown in Table 23.1 and can be caused by a system which penalizes people for reporting measurements which are out of specification.

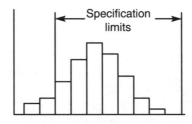

Fig. 23.3 Off-centre distribution

Example

A power engineer required a 10 ohm, 0.1% tolerance, high-power resistor. The only resistors available were 10% tolerance. To achieve the higher tolerance, he uses a series of 100 resistors each of 0.1 ohm. The summing effect was expected to average out the low tolerance, as resistors over and under 0.1 ohm balanced each other out. When the resulting resistance started overheating, the engineer measured the value of each one and plotted a Histogram, as in Fig. 23.4.

The result showed that although the resistors were within specification, their distribution was not normal and not centred on 0.1 ohm (this was probably caused by selection from an off-centre production system). The solution of a specially made resistor was significantly more expensive.

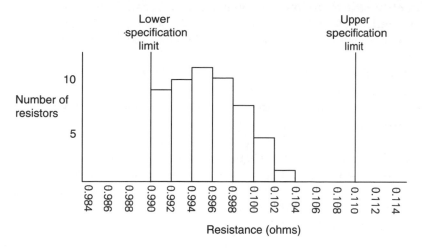

Fig. 23.4 Example

Other examples

- A poultry farmer measures the distribution of egg sizes to find if the most common sizes are also those which sell best. She then adjusts her chicken stock to change the distribution to suit their market.
- A sales department checks the distribution of orders by their value, and then analyzes the data further to determine the demographics of the high-value orders and thus improves its sales focus.
- A school checks the distribution of its examination results and streams students according to their position in the distribution. Students with marks outside the normal distribution are sent to special classes for high- or low-ability children.

How to do it

1. Identify the purpose of using a Histogram. Typically this may be one of:
   - Checking the shape against an expected distribution (typically a Normal distribution).
   - Understanding the capability of the process, particularly in terms of the spread of measurements.

2. Define what to measure. This will include identification of units, scale and tolerances. For example, 'Time taken to complete customer request, measured in seconds, to the nearest ten seconds'.

3. Identify how many measurements must be made. This should be at least 50, and preferably nearer 100. Only use less if this number of measurements is not available - and then be aware of this when evaluating results.

   If the data may be stratified (for example, by time, people or material), ensure enough measurements are taken to build a Histogram for each group. For example, if there are three groups, then take at least 150 measurements.

4. Identify the width of each Histogram bar. To do this:
   (a) Decide how many bars you wish to show on the chart. This should be sufficient to show the shape of the overall frequency distribution. A rule of thumb for this is based on the number of measurements made is shown in Table 23.2.

Table 23.2 Estimating number of bars

Number of measurements	Number of bars
Less than 50	5 to 7
50 to 100	6 to 10
100 to 250	7 to 12
Over 250	10 to 20

   (b) Identify the range of values that may be measured. This is given by the difference between the largest and the smallest probable measurement values. An expected average can help with this, as it is usually in the middle.
   (c) Determine the value range for each bar. This is given by the range of values from (b), divided by the number of bars from (a). Round this to the nearest sensible unit, arranging for any specification limits fall between bars, not within them.

   For example, 100 measurements, ranging between 10 and 50 cm are divided into 8 bars of 5 cm each. (8 bars were selected from the choice of 7 to 12 in the table as it resulted in a neat bar width of 5 cm).

5. Define the measurement process, including the design of an appropriate Check Sheet, where and when measurements are made and by whom. People taking measures should be trained as necessary.

6. Take the measurements, using the process defined in step 5. If all items are not being measured (i.e. a sample is being taken), ensure that samples are selected at random.

7. Organize the measurements to enable the Histogram bars to be sized. This can be done in a frequency table, which may be incorporated into the Check Sheet. For example as in Table 23.3.

Table 23.3 Example measurement table

Bar number	Measure from	Measure to	Total of measures
1	10.0	14.9	1
2	15.0	19.9	6
3	20.0	24.9	15
4	25.0	29.9	32
5	30.0	34.9	35
6	35.0	39.9	12
7	40.0	44.9	7
8	45.0	49.9	2

8. Draw the Histogram. Ensure the bars are clear and the diagram is appropriately labelled, including other information about the measurement, such as date and time, identification of the process being charted, etc.

6. Analyze the completed Histogram and act on your findings, for example by checking assumptions made about distribution and then changing the process accordingly.

Practical variations

- A number of different ways of using and displaying Histograms are shown in Table 23.4.

Table 23.4 Variations on Histograms

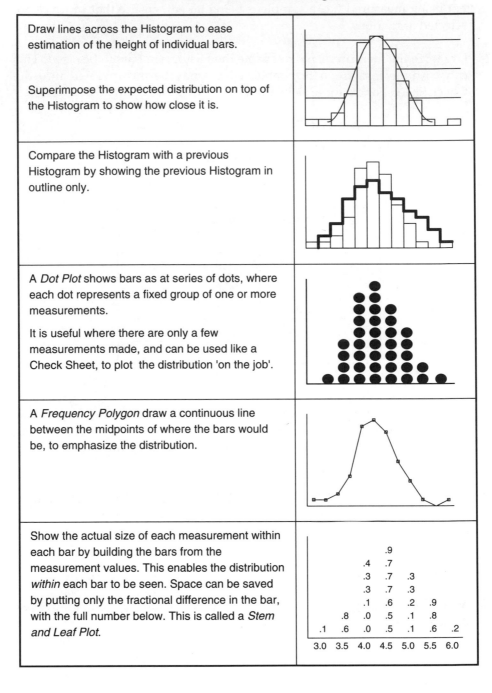

Draw lines across the Histogram to ease estimation of the height of individual bars. Superimpose the expected distribution on top of the Histogram to show how close it is.	
Compare the Histogram with a previous Histogram by showing the previous Histogram in outline only.	
A *Dot Plot* shows bars as at series of dots, where each dot represents a fixed group of one or more measurements. It is useful where there are only a few measurements made, and can be used like a Check Sheet, to plot the distribution 'on the job'.	
A *Frequency Polygon* draw a continuous line between the midpoints of where the bars would be, to emphasize the distribution.	
Show the actual size of each measurement within each bar by building the bars from the measurement values. This enables the distribution *within* each bar to be seen. Space can be saved by putting only the fractional difference in the bar, with the full number below. This is called a *Stem and Leaf Plot*.	

Stem and Leaf Plot values:

	.9				
.4	.7				
.3	.7	.3			
.3	.7	.3			
.1	.6	.2	.9		
.8	.0	.5	.1	.8	
.1	.6	.0	.5	.1	.6	.2

| 3.0 | 3.5 | 4.0 | 4.5 | 5.0 | 5.5 | 6.0 |

- Determine the number of bars by using the *Sturgess rule*, which calculates the number of bars as: $1 + 3.3 \log_{10}$ (number of measurements).
- A *Chumbo Chart* is a reusable physical device used for manual recording and Histogram display. Bars are represented by transparent tubes and coloured beads are dropped into the appropriate tube to count events.
- The frequency table used to organize Histogram data can be expanded to include a Check Sheet to record the events as they happen.
- Any Histogram can be drawn horizontally, instead of vertically. This can make labelling easier.

Notes

The Histogram was first used in 1833 by the French statistician A. M. Guerry. Histograms are a subset of (and are sometimes confused with) Bar Charts. They are one of the first seven tools.

See also

Chapters: Histograms are a special form of Bar Chart. Check Sheets can display data as a Histogram. Other tools for measuring Variation include the Control Chart, Process Capability, Scatter Diagram and Design of Experiments.

References: Histograms are covered in at least some detail by many books on quality. Books that discuss them in more detail include [Ishikawa 76], [Feigenbaum 86] and [Asaka 90], each of which have a chapter on them. [Wadsworth 86] shows a number of variations. [Grant 80], [Oakland 90] and [Brassard 89] also cover them.

24 IDEF0

What it's for

To make a detailed and clear description of a process or system.

When to use it

- Use it when formally describing a process, to ensure a detailed, clear and accurate result.
- Use it when the process is complex, and other methods would result in more complex diagrams.
- Use it when mapping a wide variety of processes, as a consistent and scalable Process Description Language (or *PDL*).
- Use it when there is time available to work on understanding and producing a complete and correct description of the process.

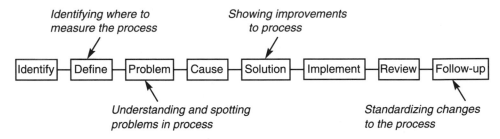

Fig. 24.1 Possible uses in improvement project framework

How to understand it

There are a number of methods available for describing processes, many of which are fairly informal, such as Block Diagrams or Flowcharts. These suffice in many circumstances but are inadequate in others, typically where the process is complex or a more rigorous approach is required. A problem which can arise when being more rigorous is that the overall understanding can be lost in the detail. The challenge is thus to find a method that is simultaneously precise and lucid at all levels.

IDEF0 (pronounced 'eye-deff-zero') provides a formal method of describing processes or systems, using several techniques to avoid the complex diagrams that could result from an attempt at a complete description using other methods.

The basic diagram element is very simple, using just one box shape to define each activity or process, as in Fig. 24.2. The four arrows around the box, whose initials give rise to the name *ICOM codes*, are:

- *Inputs*, which are the 'raw material' that gets transformed during the activity, e.g. a wire coil, outline plans.
- *Controls*, which influence or direct how the process works, e.g. safety standards, customer requirements, project plans.
- *Mechanisms*, which cause the process to operate, e.g. people, tools, machines.
- *Outputs*, which are the result of the activity and are transmitted to other processes, e.g. cut lengths of wire, final plans.

The process description starts with single box, showing the ICOM codes for the overall process. This diagram is called the 'A-0' diagram (pronounced 'A minus 0'), as in Fig. 24.3.

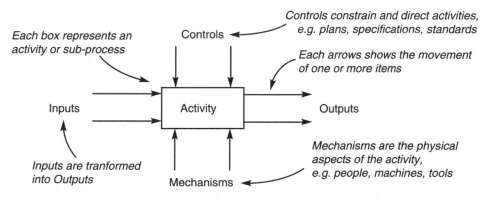

Fig. 24.2 The basic IDEF0 element

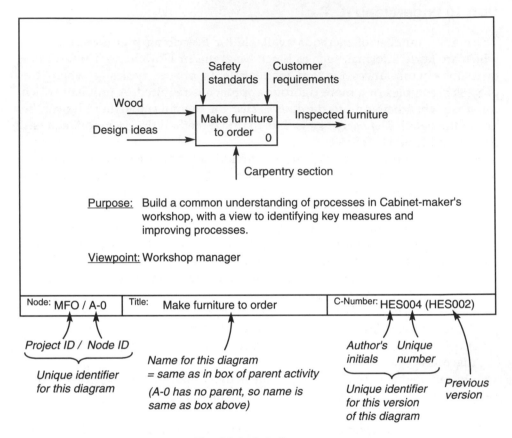

Fig. 24.3 A-0 diagram

The box (or *node*) in the A-0 diagram is then decomposed (or 'exploded' or 'zoomed') into a diagram with between three and six boxes, as in Fig. 24.4. This is called the 'A0' diagram.

This hierarchical decomposition is repeated for each box in this diagram, then for each box in the resultant diagrams and so on, until the process is fully described.

In any diagram, the boxes are generally laid out from the top left to the bottom right, in order of *dominance*, where a higher dominance box has a greater influence over a lower dominance box. Boxes are numbered in order of dominance, with the number being used to reference the box on other diagrams. Thus the first box in the A0 diagram is decomposed in diagram A1, and the third box in that diagram is decomposed as A13.

Arrows carry multiple items, and are merged or split to simplify the diagram. Names next to arrows should describe what they carry; where there are no names, the arrow contents may be deduced. Arrows which do not connect to a box at one end are those that come from or go to the parent box, from which this diagram is decomposed. These arrows are numbered to indicate which ICOM arrow they represent. Thus, C1 represents the leftmost control and I2 is the second input down on the parent box. Parentheses (a 'tunnel') at one end of an arrow indicates that this arrow does *not* appear on the parent or child diagram.

There are only five types of connection that arrows can make between boxes, as indicated in Table 24.1, which show how activities feed, enable or constrain one another. The mix of connection types in one set of diagram will indicate the overall system type. For example, a process with little feedback may indicate a lack of control.

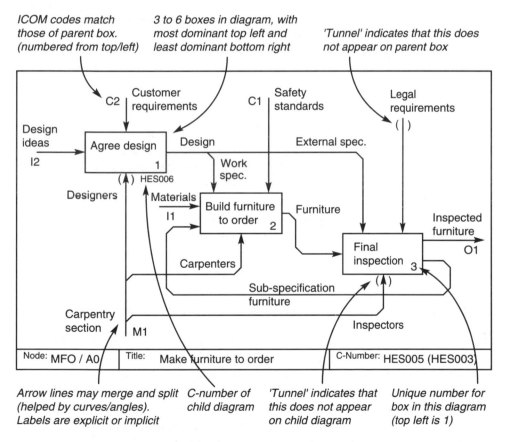

Fig. 24.4 Decomposed diagram

Table 24.1 Connections between boxes

Linkage	Type	Description
	Input connection	Output to input of lower dominance box, e.g. assembly line
	Control connection	Output to control of lower dominance box, e.g. plans, specifications
	Output mechanism	Output to mechanism of lower dominance box, e.g. setup, allocation
	Control feedback	Output to control of higher dominance box, e.g. reviews
	Input feedback	Output to input of higher dominance box, e.g. rework

One of the strengths of IDEF0 is that not only are the diagrams defined, but the *process* of how they are produced is also defined. A key part of this is that it is drawn by an IDEF0 expert (the 'author'), using the viewpoint of and with the full cooperation of a key individual within the system being diagrammed. This, along with formal authoring and reviewing cycles, helps to ensure consistent and correct detail in the final diagrams.

The completed *model* includes additional text descriptions of items in diagrams to enable the diagrams to be kept relatively light while maintaining a depth of information that can be used as required.

Example

The members of the quality management team in a furniture company selected IDEF0 as a consistent and well-defined way of describing processes for their quality management and improvement system. They decided to use a functional decomposition strategy, in which one of the major subsystems was the design and build of customized furniture. They got three people trained as IDEF0 authors, one of whom was assigned to the 'custom build' project. This author then worked with the people who used the processes which were to be documented, producing a complete IDEF0 description. Some diagrams and notes that were produced are shown in Figs 24.3 to 24.8.

One of the benefits they found from doing this was that the understanding of some of the lesser known parts of the process was significantly improved, with the result that a more consistent level of work became possible.

Several possible improvement projects were identified during the diagramming, and key ones were later implemented. The IDEF0 diagrams enabled problem areas and measurement points to be quickly identified, and were later modified to reflect actual improvements.

Other examples

- The final inspection group on a rubber goods production line identifies significant variation in shape of the final product. They use IDEF0 to selectively break down the injection process, as a part of an effort to understand what actually happens. During this, they find that the cooling process has no control of temperature gradient, which is causing the subsequent misshapes.
- A road construction company uses IDEF0 as a standard method of describing their processes, from planning through to excavation and laying, along with a set of keyed checklists. This helps them to ensure that government standards are followed and checked at all stages.

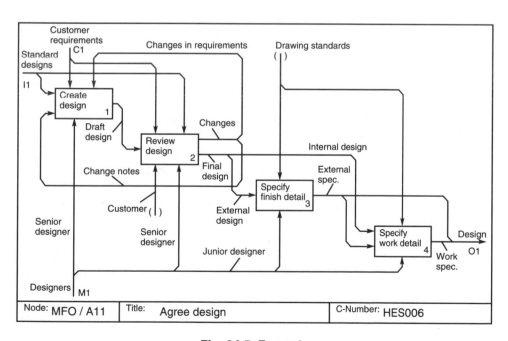

Fig. 24.5 Example

- The customer training department of a major computer manufacturer uses IDEF0 to map out the processes for development and delivery of training. They include feedback loops, which ensure that lessons learned during delivery are fed back to the development process.

How to do it

1. Identify the system or process to be described. Use a name that clearly indicates what it is, possibly adding further description of what is and what is not included.

2. Identify the purpose or objectives of describing the process. This will help to determine whether IDEF0 is an appropriate tool, and will also help when making other decisions, for example whether to decompose the system further at lower levels.

3. Decide on the viewpoint from which the process is to be described. For example, a sales manager might have a broader view of a sales process than a sales person, as the sales manager includes the clerical activities in the sales office as well as the customer-salesperson process.

   The objectives from step 2 will help with this decision. For example, if the objective is to improve the amount of direct sales, then the viewpoint of the salesperson may be most appropriate.

4. Identify the decomposition strategy to be used. This is the set of rules to use when deciding how to break down activities into sub-activities, and may depend on the type of system being described and the objectives from step 2. Possible strategies include:
   - *Functional decomposition* breaks down activities according to *what* is done, rather than *how* it is done, and is probably the most common strategy.
   - *Role decomposition* breaks down things according to *who* does what. It can be an easy and useful starting point, but is likely to constrain improvements if it is maintained.
   - *Subsystems decomposition* divides systems first by major subsystem. This is useful when these subsystems are largely independent of one another.
   - *Lifecycle decomposition* breaks down a system first by the phases of activity. Again, this is most useful when these phases are clearly defined and relatively independent.

5. Before starting to draw diagrams, gather information about the system. This may start with reading of existing documents or observing the process in action, but the most useful activity is likely to be formal interviews with selected people. This not only is the best source of information, but it will also help to gain involvement and acceptance in any later improvements. Use the following process for interviews:

- In the initial interview, aim first to agree the purpose and viewpoint, then find sufficient details to be able to draw the first two levels only (A-0 and A0).
- Before each interview, review existing information and identify the scope of what is to be identified.
- In interviews, work to acquire the most useful information, asking open questions, probing in key areas and checking the validity of assumptions.
- First, find out what is produced by and used within the process, including inputs, controls, outputs and mechanisms. This can be helped by asking questions of the process, starting with outputs (What is produced?) and work backwards (What is needed to produce this?). This will result in a list of items (often called the *data list*) that will form the arrows in the diagram.
- Next, use the data list to identify the list of activities within the process, asking *how* items are used or produced.
- Then explore how activities and data items relate to one another and how they group together. This will result in a list something like Fig. 24.6.

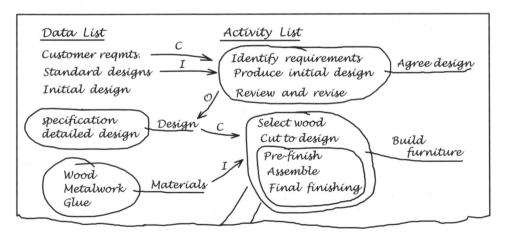

Fig. 24.6 Interview notes (part of)

6. From the information gained in step 5, draw a set of diagrams. Draw the A0 diagram first, as in Fig. 24.4, then summarize this in the A-0 diagram, as in Fig. 24.3.

   When drawing a diagram, use the following sequence of actions:
   - Use the decomposition strategy from step 4 to identify between three and six activities that will be shown on the diagram (around four is often best). It can be useful to try several different decompositions before settling on one.
   - Sort these activities into the order of dominance. The more dominant of a pair of activities is one which has the greatest influence over the other. For example 'produce plan' has higher dominance than 'build product'.
   - Place the activity boxes on the diagram, using the general layout strategy of putting most dominant activity in the top left, with subsequent activities along the diagonal, such that the least dominant activity ends up in the bottom right corner. When positioning the activities, try to think ahead to where arrows will go. Put the name of each activity in its box.
   - Draw the arrows for each data item, starting with inputs and outputs, then adding controls then mechanisms. Combine and split lines to help simplify the diagram. When the lines are drawn, write in the labels for each line, being careful that the label cannot mistakenly be confused with another item. If a label is not clearly associated with a single line, draw a short line between it and the line, as in Fig. 24.5.
   - Add parentheses ('tunnel' marks) to the end of any line which will not be shown in its parent or child diagram, as in Fig. 24.4. Tunnel items that will not add useful information elsewhere. It is common to tunnel mechanisms at higher levels, so they do not appear on lower level diagrams.
   - Identify the diagram with a node name, title and C-number, as in Fig. 24.3. It may also be useful to add other data, such as the date and the status of the diagram (e.g. initial, draft, final). Use a log, as in Fig. 24.7, to ensure that all C-numbers are unique.
   - Review the completed diagram for correctness, consistency, completeness and clarity. Check it against the purpose (step 2), viewpoint (step 3), decomposition strategy (step 4) and available information (step 5). Revise and repeat the above steps as necessary.

7. For each diagram, it is useful to write a Glossary page that further describes each data item, as in Fig. 24.8. This can contain any text that will

Initials are used with diagram numbers
to make C-numbers, e.g. ABR002

Author:	Arthur Richards			Project:	Accounting system		
Initials:	ABR			ID:	ACS		
No.	Node	Title	Date	No.	Node	Title	Date
000	A-0	Accounting system	12Jun	020	A213	Check account	21Jul
001	A0	Accounting system	13Jun	021	A214	Verify signature	21Jul
002	A-0	Accounting system	13Jun	022	A322	Input to database	23Jul

Node IDs repeat as
diagrams are redrawn

Numbers are
sequential

Fig. 24.7 C-number log

help the understanding of individual items or the overall system, although it should be kept brief, to avoid an 'information overload'.

Identify each page of the glossary with a title the same as its diagram, but with 'Gn' added to the node name, where 'n' is the page number in the glossary, and '(Glossary)' appended to the title. Use a unique C-number, adding each page to the C-number log.

Note that ICOM items from the parent diagram are not included in the glossary, as this would result in duplicate glossary entries and consequent synchronization problems.

8. Decide whether to review the pages produced so far. It is useful to review early, when the A-0 and A0 diagrams (and possibly the level below) are completed, and subsequently when significant changes have been made. If you do hold a review until all pages are completed, then this can result in significant extra effort being spent in rework.

   When holding a review, first create a *kit*, consisting of all pages requiring review, together with a cover page, and send it to appropriate contributing experts for review. The cover page details the reviewer list, the contents of the kit and what is expected of the reviewers, including when to return it and any other special instructions.

   The reviewers read the pages in the kit and write corrections, in red directly on the pages of the kit, before returning it to the author. Specific items to review include:
   - The detail of each diagram, including the title and node name, all activities and arrows, additional glossaries and other material.
   - The overall system, and how the diagrams fit together, including use

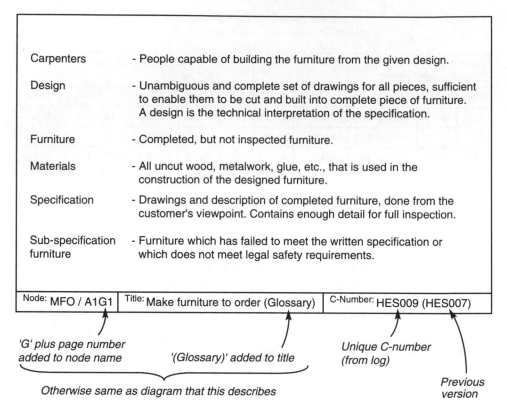

Carpenters	- People capable of building the furniture from the given design.
Design	- Unambiguous and complete set of drawings for all pieces, sufficient to enable them to be cut and built into complete piece of furniture. A design is the technical interpretation of the specification.
Furniture	- Completed, but not inspected furniture.
Materials	- All uncut wood, metalwork, glue, etc., that is used in the construction of the designed furniture.
Specification	- Drawings and description of completed furniture, done from the customer's viewpoint. Contains enough detail for full inspection.
Sub-specification furniture	- Furniture which has failed to meet the written specification or which does not meet legal safety requirements.

Node: MFO / A1G1 | Title: Make furniture to order (Glossary) | C-Number: HES009 (HES007)

'G' plus page number added to node name   *'(Glossary)' added to title*   *Unique C-number (from log)*

Previous version

Otherwise same as diagram that this describes

Fig. 24.8 A Glossary page

of the stated breakdown strategy.
- How well the stated viewpoint is represented.

The author then examines the reviewer's corrections and writes comments in blue ink (thus differentiating from the reviewer's corrections). Agreement with reviewer corrections are shown with ticks and other comments are written alongside.

The author and each reviewer then meet and discuss the comments and corrections. They agree to actual changes which the author then implements. Make sure that when an item is changed, all other diagrams affected by the change are also updated.

9. For each box which has not yet been decomposed, decide whether it is worth taking this step, or whether sufficient detail exists at this point. Considerations of whether to stop decomposition include:

- The final set of diagrams (or 'model') should contain sufficient detail to satisfy the stated purpose from step 2.
- A good point to stop is when boxes start saying 'how' instead of 'what', or where the viewpoint changes.
- Boxes should describe activities that are solid and unique functions, not trivial items nor duplicates of other boxes.

For boxes that are to be decomposed further, the above process of interview, create and review is repeated as required. Generally, the process experts should be fully involved, but they should not be worn down with too many interviews and reviews, as this is likely to cause them to become annoyed and disinterested, with consequent damage to the model and its use.

10. The final set of diagrams is then used for the purpose as described in step 2.

Practical variations

- As well as data items, glossary pages can be written for activities, especially those that are not decomposed further. Identify these as for data glossaries, but with a 'T' instead of the 'G'.
- Add description pages in the form of figures, pictures or diagrams. Identify these as for data glossaries, but with an 'F' instead of the 'G'. This can be used to show examples of completed outputs.
- Produce 'special' one-off diagrams for reviews which highlight lines and boxes for discussion. These may also have extraneous detail removed.
- Add *property labels* to activities and items to describe important properties, such as the temperature of an input to a chemical process. Show these property labels as a number in a square box, followed by the description. Connect this to the activity or item with a wavy line. Glossaries are another good place for describing properties, particularly if they are less important.
- Combine all Glossary pages into a single glossary, sorted in alphabetical order.
- *Data Flow Diagrams*, as in Fig. 24.9, are a similar tool to IDEF0, but do not show controls and mechanisms. They also recognize that some things do not travel directly between processes, but are put into storage, where they may be accessed as required by other processes. They can be useful as a simpler and possibly less formal way of describing processes or systems.
  The top-level diagram is called the *context diagram*, as it describes the

inputs to and output from the overall process. Subsequent diagrams decompose the detail of each sub-process (similar to IDEF0), with circles showing processes, parallel lines showing storage and curved arrows showing inputs and outputs.

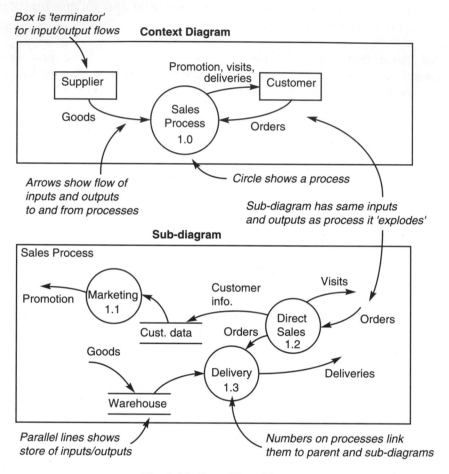

Fig. 24.9 Data Flow Diagram

Notes

IDEF0 is a subset of the *Structured Analysis and Design Technique* (or SADT), originated by Douglas Ross in the late 1960s and put into the public domain by Softech Inc. at the request of the US Department of Defense. IDEF0, is the most commonly used of a large set of IDEF specifications which are used to model various aspects of data and systems. The letters of IDEF stands for ICOM DEFinitions.

See also

Chapters: Processes may also be described with the Activity Network, Flowchart, Flow Process Chart, Gantt Chart, Relations Diagram and String Diagram. Use Survey methods in interviews. Use Affinity Diagrams to organize data list and activity list items.

References: [Marca 88] is the definitive work on IDEF0, describing it in great detail with many examples. [Martin 85] describes many other process mapping methods. [Page-Jones 80] describes Data Flow Diagrams in detail.

25 Line Graph

What it's for

To show patterns of change in a sequence of measurements.

When to use it

- Use it when an item is repeatedly measured, to show changes across time.
- Use it when measuring several different items which can be shown on the same scale, to show how they change relative to one another.
- Use it when measuring progress towards a goal, to show the relative improvement.
- Use it, rather than a Bar Chart, to show *continuous* change, rather than discrete measurements. It is also better when there are many measurements.
- Use it, rather than a Control Chart, when not measuring the degree of control of a process.

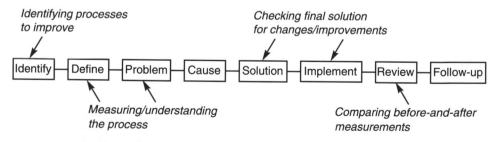

Fig. 25.1 Possible uses in improvement project framework

How to understand it

When taking measurements of a process, the result is often a simple list of numbers. Although this list may be interpreted to some degree by examination, the information contained in the numbers can often be made easier to understand by showing the numbers in a Line Graph.

The points on the graph are plotted from *pairs* of numbers in the list, with lines drawn between each pair, as in Fig. 25.2. Typically, one number in the pair is the measured item and is shown on the vertical axis, whilst the second number, shown on the horizontal axis, indicates either the time or sequence number of the measurement.

A Line Graph highlights the relative change between individual measurement points through the *slope* (or *gradient*) of the line drawn between them, as in Fig. 25.2. The change across a number of points can be seen through the overall *shape* of the graph.

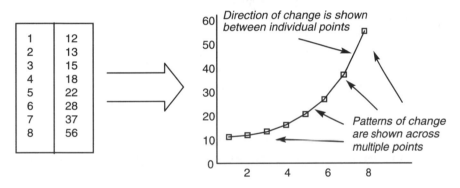

Fig. 25.2 Line Graph

When the graph is drawn, patterns of change may then be identified and interpreted. Fig. 25.3 shows some typically significant patterns:

- A *trend* shows an overall movement in one direction, which may be masked by the ups and downs of individual points. For example, where daily sales figures go up and down, but general sales slowly increase over the longer term.
- A *spike* is a short term change, which may be caused by some unusual event, such as a weak batch of yeast causing a large number of rejections in a bakery.
- A *step* is a sudden and persistent change. For example, where a silicon doping process is improved, resulting in a sharply increased yield in integrated circuit chips.

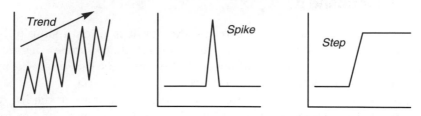

Fig. 25.3 Changes in line graphs

When a line forms a curve, then the change in slope of the curve may be significant. Decision points thus commonly occur at *maxima, minima* or *points of inflection* (where the rate of change in the slope reverses). These are shown in Fig. 25.4.

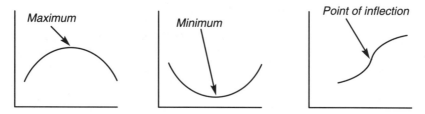

Fig. 25.4 Significant points on curves

Multiple Line Graphs, can be useful for showing multiple sets of measurements, either to save graph space or to compare measurement sets, but they become unusable where lines get confused through crossing one another. Line crossing is useful where this highlights a decision point. These are illustrated in Fig. 25.5.

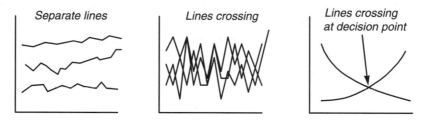

Fig. 25.5 Multiple Line Graphs

Generally, when interpreting Line Graphs, if the expected shape of the graph is known, then it becomes easier to spot significant decision points along the plotted lines.

Example

A software programming team used a Line Graph during the test phase to track unfixed defects relative to release goals (Fig. 25.6).

About half-way through the project it became evident that the goals would not be reached in time to meet the schedule. A subsequent improvement project identified that the team was spending time in low-skill testing when they could be better employed in higher skill defect fixing. An automatic testing harness was identified and installed, freeing time to fix defects. The release goals were met just in time.

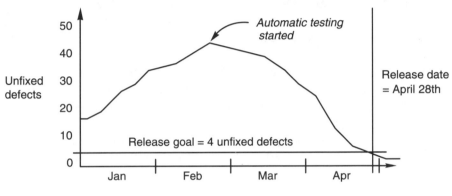

Fig. 25.6 Example

Other examples

- An accountant plots cumulative costs and revenue of a product on a line graph, identifying the break-even point where they cross. Improvement opportunities are then sought which will bring this point closer.
- A potter plots the temperature profile in her kiln during pot firing. She later correlates profiles with good and bad firings, learning how to control the temperature for an optimum pot. The result is a significant decrease in wastage. The greater reliability also allows her to fire more complex pots without the risk of losing the work done in throwing them.
- An automotive engineer hooks a set of strain gauges up to a computer and plots the stress at critical points on the body of a development vehicle during a test crash. This helps a stronger body to be designed which can also be produced using less material. The result is a saving in both money and lives.

How to do it

1. Identify the objective of the graph and what decisions may be made from its use. Typical objectives include measuring progress towards a target or variation within specified limits.

2. Decide what to measure and what lines to plot on the graph to be able to make the requisite decisions. This may include plotting additional lines such as goal or limit lines.

3. Define the axes and scales on the graph such that the line will fill the graph area without overshooting. Sometimes this cannot be done until the measurements have been made.

4. Take the measurements, recording them either directly onto the graph or into a table. If someone else is to do this, ensure they are trained and able to do it. If appropriate, do a pilot run to check that the process works.

5. Plot the points on the graph. If there are multiple lines, make sure each line can be clearly identified. Label the graph with axis titles, scales and other data, such as details of the process measured, dates, etc.

6. Interpret the graph and take appropriate action.

Practical variations

- Use point markers to emphasize the value at each point. Omit them to emphasize the overall shape of the graph.
- There are a number of common ways of showing different point markers and lines to enable them to be distinguished (Fig. 25.7). If available, colour is a very good differentiator.

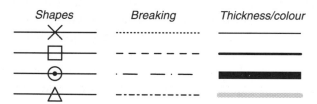

Fig. 25.7 Differentiation of point markers and lines

- Where a line varies up and down a lot, a simple way of drawing a trend line is a three-point average. In this, for each point, a new point is plotted which is the average of the previous, the current and the next point.
- In an *Area Graph*, the area beneath the line is emphasized by filling it in (often in colour). This can be used as a variation on a Stacked Bar Chart.
- A *Z-Chart* plots on one chart the current, cumulative and moving total figures for any measured value across time, as in Fig. 25.8. It is useful for showing progress in both the short and longer term. The current line shows the variation each period, whilst the moving total smooths out any seasonal variations, showing longer term progress. The cumulative line joins these and may show progress towards a goal.

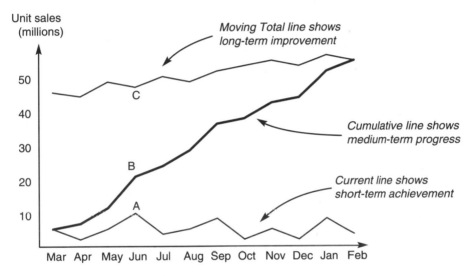

e.g. Point A: In June, 10 million units are sold this month
Point B: 22 million have been sold since March, the start of this financial year
Point C: 48 million have been sold over the last 12 months

Fig. 25.8 Z-Chart

Notes

Line Graphs which plot events over time are also called *Run Charts*. They are sometimes considered as being one of the first seven tools (often in the general category of 'graphs').

See also

Chapters: Control Charts are a specific form of Line Graph. Bar Charts are closely related, and it is sometimes difficult to decide which to use. The Scatter Diagram also plots pairs of values on an X-Y axis.

References: [Ishikawa 76] and [Asaka 90] discuss graphs in general. Other books tend to make brief reference to Run Charts. [Rose 57] and [Asaka 90] discuss Z-Charts.

26 Matrix Data Analysis Chart

What it's for

To identify clusters of related items within a larger group.

When to use it

- Use it when investigating factors which affect a number of different items, to determine common relationships.
- Use it to determine whether or not logically similar items also have similar factor effects.
- Use it to find groups of logically different items which have similar factor effects.

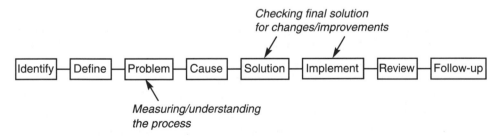

Fig. 26.1 Possible uses in improvement project framework

How to understand it

When comparing a large set of items, the complexity of the situation can make it difficult to determine how different factors relate to one another. In particular, it can be useful to find groups of items that behave in similar ways. For example, a washing powder may have different efficiencies at achieving 'softness' and 'stain removal' in garments made of acrylic, polyester, wool and various fiber mixtures. If similar affects are found in a group of fibers, then changing the powder ingredients may affect the whole group in a similar way.

The Matrix Data Analysis Chart (or *MDAC*) helps classify items by identifying two major characteristics common to all items and then plotting each item as a point on a standard x-y chart. This makes it easier to see how the individual items relate both to the characteristics and to one another, as in Fig. 26.2.

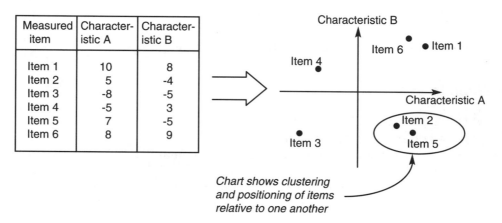

Measured item	Character-istic A	Character-istic B
Item 1	10	8
Item 2	5	-4
Item 3	-8	-5
Item 4	-5	3
Item 5	7	-5
Item 6	8	9

Chart shows clustering and positioning of items relative to one another

Fig. 26.2 Matrix Data Analysis Chart elements

Identifying the best characteristics to measure is an important task, as different sets of measurements can give very different charts. It would be useful to be able to compare many characteristics together, such as the density, color, texture, strength, etc. of cement mixtures, but we are constrained by the two dimensions available on paper. There are mathematical methods for combining multiple factors, but these are beyond the scope of this book.

A key interpretation point about an MDAC is to consider how points on the chart group together or form into *clusters* (this may be contrasted with the Scatter Diagram, which looks for linear *trends*). This interpretation is helped by highlighting significant groups of points with linear links, as illustrated in Fig. 26.3.

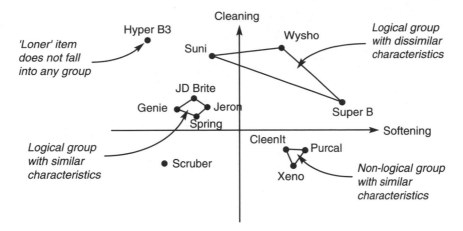

Fig. 26.3 MDAC groupings

Typical items of interest on an MDAC include:

- The behaviour of logical groups of items, which might be expected to form close clusters. For example, in a washing powder test, logical groups might be woolen items, acrylics and mixtures.
- Actual clustering on the chart which might highlight divergence from expected behaviour, and prompt new actions. For example, investigation of an unexpected cluster of different fiber types might show that they come from one manufacturer who has developed processes to give different fibers with similar specifications.

Example

A toy store was aiming to increase sales while improving the satisfaction of its customers with the toys that it sold. As a part of this, it employed a market research company to measure both the initial appeal (which related to actual purchase) and the longer term satisfaction (which related to company image) of a range of toys for boys aged 5 to 10, both being scored on a one-to-ten scale. This limited sector was chosen to prevent excessive complexity and confusion in the analysis.

These were plotted on a matrix to identify the best toys to promote and to find possible ways of improving other toys. The axes were crossed at their mid-points to form value quadrants, as illustrated in Fig. 26.4.

As a result, improved packaging and promotion was sought for the better

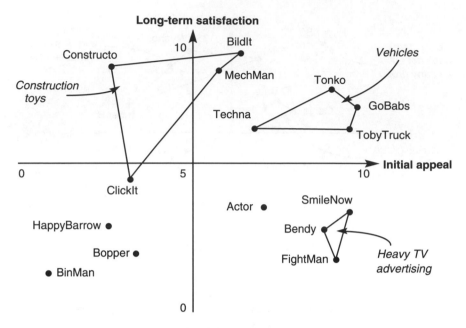

Fig. 26.4 Example

construction toys, in order to increase initial appeal, some bottom-end toys were dropped and the results of the survey were published in a form which customers could easily understand. The result was an increase in the reputation of the store as putting customer interests first, as evidenced by the increase in complimentary letters.

Other examples

- A vineyard, aiming to increase the consistency of the quality of its wines measures a 'quality rating' along with a range of different other factors, such as grape, additives, storage, etc. It then uses MDACs to isolate clusters of factors that contribute to its finest wines.
- A pharmaceutical combine examines the pain-killing drugs of its subsidiaries in terms of the cost to product and general efficacy. Products which are high cost but are not of highest efficacy are dropped. Low-cost drugs of reasonable efficacy are promoted, and high-cost drugs have a project initiated to reduce production cost.
- A production unit, looking for alternative materials to build a more durable gear casing, compares key attributes of available materials using cost and durability.

How to do it

1. Identify the items which are to be compared, and decide on the primary objective of using the Matrix Data Analysis Chart. For example, a restaurant may compare menu items with the objective of finding out what makes popular dishes.

2. Identify the measurement units for the horizontal and vertical axes of the chart. These should be two factors which are the most critical representations of the objective identified in step 1. For example, the restaurant may use a survey to find the aspects of eating that their customer most value.

3. Measure the factors identified in step 2, aiming to get realistic and unbiased values. Thus, the restaurant might take an average of customer ratings for texture and flavour of each menu item over several months.

4. Draw a chart and plot each point on it, as in Fig. 26.2. Ensure that the scale on the axes results in the points being spread over the whole chart area.

5. Look for significant clusters of points on the chart, and highlight them by linking them together into a ring, as in Fig. 26.3. The appearance and ease of interpretation are more important than the order of linkage. Groups may be either of:
   - Items that have a close logical relationship, e.g. fish dishes.
   - Items that form a close physical group on the chart.

6. Interpret the chart and act on the results. Typical activities include the investigation into and subsequent action on:
   - Why items which might be expected to group closely do not.
   - Why items unexpectedly form clusters.
   - Why individual items are not positioned where they were expected to be on the chart.

Practical variations

- When multiple measurements are made, such as texture, colour, taste, etc., a number of MDACs can be drawn and then evaluated as a group, looking for similar clusters in each chart. This can only practically be done on a limited scale, as multiple MDACs can be difficult to interpret. For example, with three measurements, A, B and C, there may be three

MDACs, A versus B, B versus C and A versus C. However, with six measurements there could be fifteen MDACs!

- Another approach when there are multiple measurements is to combine similar measurement sets. Thus if customers give similar marks to texture and colour, then they may be averaged, and the plotted characteristic now becomes 'texture and colour'.

- The vertical and horizontal axes do not have to cross at their zero points. This can be used to deliberately divide the chart into four areas, as in Fig. 26.5. If both axes represent desirable characteristics, then the top right and bottom left quadrants represent desirable and undesirable regions, respectively. The top left and bottom right quadrants, where only one characteristic is desirable, represent areas of opportunity for improvement of the other characteristic.

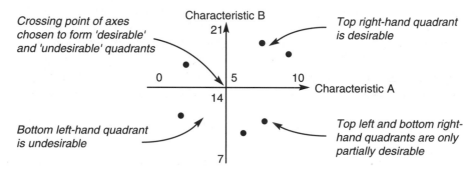

Fig. 26.5 Axes crossing to form desirable/undesirable regions

Notes

The Matrix Data Analysis Chart is one of the second seven tools according to [Mizuno 88] (although [Brassard 89] replaces it with the Prioritization Matrix). It is often abbreviated to MDAC.

The complexity of the statistical method normally associated with this diagram (*Principal Component Analysis*) has led to other books not discussing MDAC and offering an alternative 'seventh' tool. It is included here not just for completeness, but because practical use can still be made of it.

See also

Chapters: The Matrix Data Analysis Chart has similarities with the Scatter Diagram.

References: [Mizuno 88] has a chapter on MDAC. [Gitlow 90] and [Oakland 93] discuss it more briefly.

27 Matrix Diagram

What it's for

To identify the relationship between pairs of lists.

When to use it

- Use it when comparing two lists to understand the many-to-many relationship between them (it is not useful if there is a simple one-to-one relationship).
- Use it to determine the *strength* of the relationship between either single pairs of items or a single item and another complete list.
- Use it when the second list is generated as a result of the first list, to determine the success of that generation process. For example, customer requirements versus design specifications.

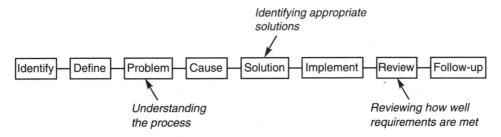

Fig. 27.1 Possible uses in improvement project framework

How to understand it

When comparing two lists, there is sometimes a simple one-to-one relationship which can be easily documented in a side-by-side table. However, when a single item from one list may be related to *several* items in the other list, then the side-by-side format does not work, as illustrated in Fig. 27.2.

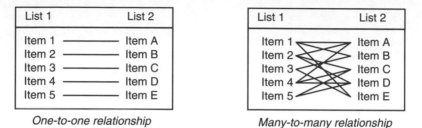

One-to-one relationship   Many-to-many relationship

Fig. 27.2 Relationships between two lists

The Matrix Diagram allows two lists to be compared by turning the second list on its side to form a matrix. Fig. 27.3 shows how the relationship between two items can now be indicated in the square or *cell* where the row and column of the two items cross.

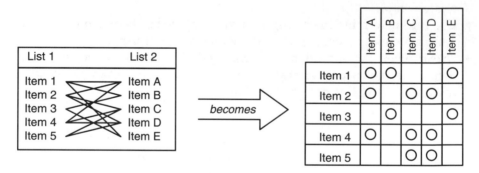

Fig. 27.3 Using a matrix to compare two lists

The matrix can be thought of as a special form of table where the cells contain a simple symbol or number, which is derived from a defined set of rules.

A common extension to matrices is to use different symbols in the matrix cells in order to show the *strength* of the relationship between pairs of items. The overall strength of the relationship between an individual item and the whole of the other list can also be determined either by visually checking the diagram or by allocating a numerical value to each symbol and summing rows and columns, as in Fig. 27.4.

The most common relationship symbols and their corresponding values are shown in Fig. 27.4. The non-linear relationship between the numeric symbol values indicates how a strong relationship is typically *much* stronger than a medium or weak relationship. Another factor that may be included in this calculation is the relative priority of each list item.

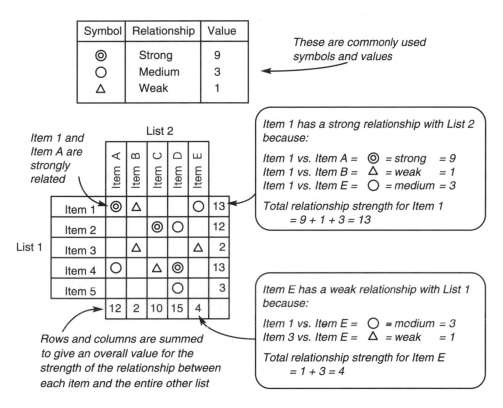

Fig. 27.4 Determining the strength of the relationships

The basic matrix shown in Fig. 27.4 is the most common matrix in use, and is called an *L-Matrix*, due to its shape. Where more than a simple comparison of two lists is required, other matrices are available, and are shown in Fig. 27.5. These also have descriptive letter names which indicate their shape.

	Item A	Item B	Item C	Item D	Item E
Item 1					
Item 2					
Item 3					
Item 4					
Item 5					

L-matrix

Compares one list against one other

			Item I			
			Item II			
			Item III			
Item a	Item b	Item c		Item A	Item B	Item C
			Item 1			
			Item 2			
			Item 3			

X-matrix

Compares four lists, each against two others, in pairs

Item I					
Item II					
Item III					
Item IV					
Item V					
	Item A	Item B	Item C	Item D	Item E
Item 1					
Item 2					
Item 3					
Item 4					
Item 5					

T-matrix

Compares one list against two others
in pairs

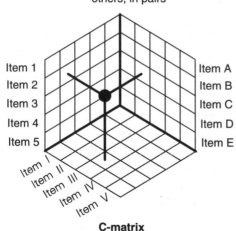

C-matrix

Compares three lists against one another, simultaneously

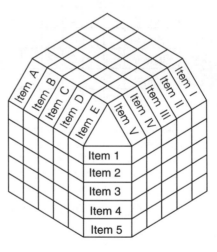

Y-matrix

Compares three lists, each against one
another, in pairs

Fig. 27.5 Types of matrix

A typical use of the Matrix Diagram to compare two lists is where the list on the left represents a problem (the 'what') and the list above represents a solution to that problem (the 'how'). For example, the first list details customer requirements for a product, whilst the second list shows how this is translated into design specifications. The relationship values now can be used to identify specific problems and other points of interest, for example:

- Rows with low totals indicate customer requirements which are not well met.
- Columns with low totals may indicate over-engineered or unnecessary design items.
- Columns with high totals indicate design items which are particularly important for meeting a number of customer requirements.

A constraint when using a Matrix Diagram is in the number of comparisons that may practically be made. A ten-by-ten matrix requires 100 comparisons, which needs a moderate effort to complete. However, a complex product might have hundreds of requirement details and a corresponding number of design specification elements, but a hundred-by-hundred matrix needs a prohibitive 10,000 comparisons to be made!

A practical use of the Matrix Diagram in a complex situation, is for focusing on the detail of critical, suspect or difficult parts of the problem, rather than trying to use it for the entire situation.

Example

A personnel department wanted to improve social activity within the company in order to increase loyalty levels. A theory was put forwards that soft-skills training contributed significantly towards this in-house socializing. The personnel manager consequently decided to use a Matrix Diagram to investigate this. The steps taken were:

- Objective: Investigate effect of soft-skills training on social activity.
- Matrix: T-matrix, with people on main stem, in-house training courses to left, attendance of social clubs to right, plus an extra column for years of service.
- Comparison: In-house training - tick for attendance within last three years; social clubs - three bands corresponding to under 30%, 30% to 70% and over 70% attendance in the same period.

The resultant matrix, as in Fig. 27.6 showed that people with higher levels of social training also tended to be more committed members of social clubs. It was also noticed that there seemed to be a particular increase in commitment

	Soft-skills courses					People in Purchasing dept.	Yrs. of service	Social clubs					
	Assertiveness	Team building	Negotiation	Listening skills	Group working			Chess	Football	Photography	Pool	Swimming	Tennis
	✓	✓				Michael Jordan	2	◎			△	△	
	✓		✓	✓		Richie Valens	5	○		○	△		
		✓				Dawn Simmons	10	△				◎	△
						Eleri Mair	4						△
				✓		Dave Morgan	3	△					
				✓	✓	Cynthia Place	5			◎			
	✓					Geraint Morgan	3	○					
	✓	✓		✓	✓	Heledd Eluned	11	◎		○	△		◎
						Gwen Uki	9	○					
		✓				Bella Bumpps	5			◎	○		

Legend

Soft-skills training

✓	Course attended

Social club attendance

◎	More than 70%
○	30% to 70%
△	Less than 30%

Measures are over past three years

Fig. 27.6 Investigating soft-skill training and social activity

after going on the team-building course. The length of service showed no particular pattern.

As a result, the training was expanded, and people were given more encouragement to attend (particularly the team-building course). This resulted in a steady increase in social activity and a reduction in attrition rates.

Other examples

- A product test team use an L-matrix to determine test effectiveness by comparing discovered defect types with named tests.
- An L-matrix is used by a marketing group to generate and validate a set of sales tools that covers all target market sectors.
- A project manager uses a T-matrix in planning, with tasks down the main stem, then resources and responsibilities for the two side lists. Everything required for one task can then be seen on one line, and reallocation then done to balance the schedule.

How to do it

1. Define the objective of using the Matrix Diagram. This may be a statement such as, 'Focus design improvements on key customer requirements', which will be used later to direct activities.

2. Recruit a team who have the time and knowledge to work on achieving the objective. Building a Matrix Diagram can take a lot more effort than some of the other diagrams described in this book, and a longer term commitment may be required.

3. Decide what needs to be compared to achieve the objective. This will result in two or more lists being identified where the investigation of their relationships will help to achieve the objective.

   This might also include identification of criteria to help decide what should and should not be included in the list. For example, if comparing insects with diseases, one criterion may be to exclude any insects which are unlikely to appear in the geographical area of study.

4. Identify the appropriate matrix to use (see Fig. 27.5). In approximate order of common use, these are:
   - The L-matrix is by far the most common diagram. If there are more than two lists, then a set of L-matrices may still be the best approach, unless the additional relationship mapping given by other matrices is required.
   - The T-matrix is useful when there are two distinct sets of questions about a core list, for example comparing school subjects against students and against teachers. An indirect relationship can be inferred between the two side lists.
   - The Y-matrix closes the loop on the T-matrix, and is useful for comparing three tightly coupled lists. It can also be used as a practical simplification of the C-matrix.
   - The X-matrix is useful for comparing two pairs of complementary lists, with each pair occupying diagonally opposite lists (as they have nothing in common and need not be compared). For example, comparing men and women against activities in athletic and intellectual pastimes, with men and women opposite.
   - The C-matrix compares three lists simultaneously, such as the people, products and processes in a factory. Being three-dimensional, it is difficult and complex to produce and draw. It becomes easier if there are few relationships to map.

5. Decide how list items are to be compared. The most common is the strong/medium/weak relationship, although there may well be circumstances where other relationships may be more appropriate. For example, when comparing a list of people against tasks, the comparison may indicate prime responsibility, influence and interest.

   This stage may also include identification of symbols to use. The most common symbols are as shown in Fig. 27.4, although any other symbol set may be chosen. Although symbols are easier to interpret visually, numbers may be preferable, particularly if a computer spreadsheet is being used.

6. Derive the lists, using guidelines from step 3. Individual items may be easily available, or may require significant effort to acquire, for example when determining key customer requirements.

   Beware of long lists resulting in large and unwieldy matrices. Initial lists may need to be trimmed down for an early focus on key areas.

7. Perform the comparison of the matrices, consistently using the rules defined in step 5. It is often preferable to aim for a relatively sparse matrix than to identify even the weakest relationship, as a symbol in every cell can result in key relationships being difficult to spot.

8. Evaluate the final matrix, looking for items of significance which will result in specific actions being carried forwards. Things to look for include:
   - Unimportant items which have few or no relationships with the other lists.
   - Key items which relate to many of the items in the other lists.
   - Patterns which strike you as odd, and which may bear further investigation.

Practical variations

- When relationships act only in one direction, for example where one item influences another, use arrows in cells to show the direction of the relationship.
- A common way of generating and organizing the lists for comparison in the matrix, particularly when a fair degree of detail is required, is to use a Tree Diagram. Space can be saved on the Matrix Diagram by removing the hierarchy links and compressing the tree elements, as in Fig. 27.7.

- The matrix may be extended in either direction to include other comparisons which use the same lists, for example to determine how well competitive products satisfy customer requirements, as in Fig. 27.7.
- Items within the same list may be compared by using a triangular half-matrix, as in Fig. 27.7. This comparison may include both positive and negative correlation to show where list items cooperate or conflict. A negative correlation occurs where the presence or increase of one item reduces the value or effect of another item – this may require trade-offs to be made between these items.

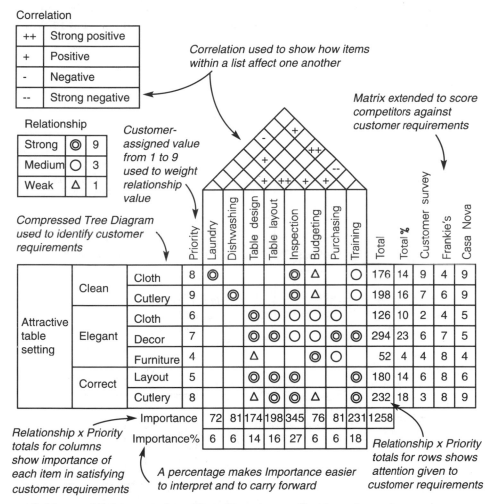

Customer requirements for table-setting versus effort in restaurant procedures

Fig. 27.7 Extensions to Matrix Diagram

- Where pairs of lists of numbers are generated, it may be feasible to show correlation between them by using a Scatter Diagram.
- In the product development process there is a sequence of transformations, such as requirements to specification, specification to design, design to fabrication, specification to tests, etc. It is easy for the customer requirements to become lost in these chains. *Quality Function Deployment* (or *QFD*) addresses this problem by using a matrix at each transformation point to map forwards what is often called the 'voice of the customer'.

This is achieved by turning the columns of one matrix into the rows of the next matrix, as in Fig. 27.8, with the importance being carried forward as priority.

Notes

The Matrix Diagram is one of the second seven tools.

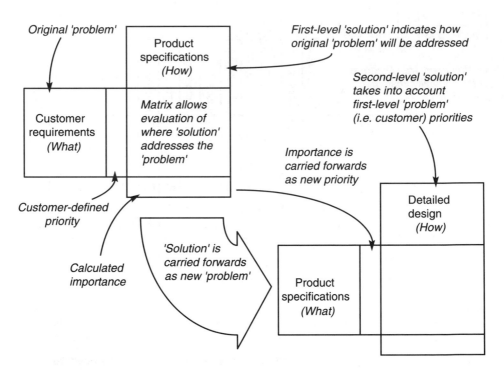

Fig. 27.8 Quality Function Deployment

See also

Chapters: Use the Tree Diagram to identify detail of lists to compare. The Matrix Diagram is a special form of Table.

References: Matrix Diagrams are described in books that detail the second seven tools. [Mizuno 88] and [Brassard 89] both have a chapter on them. [Oakland 93] and [Gitlow 90] discuss them in less detail.

28 Nominal Group Technique

What it's for

To collect and prioritize the thoughts of a group on a given topic.

When to use it

- Use it when a problem is well understood, but knowledge about it is dispersed amongst several people.
- Use it when a rapid consensus is required from a team, rather than a more detailed consideration.
- Use it when the team is stuck on an issue, for example when they disagree about something.
- Use it when the group prefers a structured style of working together.
- Use it, rather than Brainstorming, when a limited list of considered opinions is preferred to a long list of wild ideas, or when the group is not sufficiently comfortable together to be open and creative.

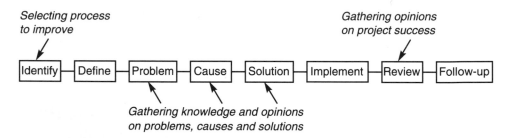

Fig. 28.1 Possible uses in improvement project framework

How to understand it

When ideas or opinions need to be gathered from within a group, Brainstorming is not always the best solution, for example where the group prefers a more structured style of working or where some group members are dominant.

The Nominal Group Technique (or *NGT*) provides a structured method of collecting and organizing the thoughts of a group. This is done in a way that prevents the originator of individual thoughts becoming known.

This anonymous gathering of ideas results in the loss of the synergistic benefits of Brainstorming, where people key off each others ideas. However, many 'Brainstorming' sessions are in fact solely used for gathering the opinions of the group, rather than the original purpose of creative idea generation. In such circumstances, NGT is a suitable tool.

NGT sessions have two clear parts. The first part involves creation and transcription of thoughts so all can see them. This part of the session is kept brief by silent writing the thoughts and constraining discussion only to clarification questions (not criticism or debate). The second part of the session is the reduction of ideas to a final selection. Again, silence is used to focus individual effort and reduce the time spent. As a result, NGT can be a very efficient method of gaining common agreement within the team.

It is the lack of interaction between the team members that gives this tool its title of 'nominal' group technique, as the team is only nominally interacting as a group.

Example

A five-man shift quality group at a coal mine was trying to improve a slow transport system for moving coal from the face to the main belt. As two of the team were known to be particularly vociferous, with another two being quiet but known thinkers, the foreman asked the site quality manager to facilitate a session that would help to identify a way to improve the system, but which would allow all shift members to contribute equally.

The quality manager started by meeting with the group to gain a common understanding of what they were trying to achieve. They agreed on a problem statement of, 'How can we find a simple way of having a low-vibration face transport system?' He then gave them seven cards each and asked them to put their seven best thoughts towards a solution, one on each card, and bring them to the next meeting.

At the following meeting, the quality manager had written the problem statement from the previous meeting on a blackboard. He started the session by checking that everyone agreed with the problem statement and had completed the seven cards. He then described the technique that they were going to use and answered a couple of questions. The group then agreed to go with the final vote that they made.

He collected the cards, shuffled them, then read them out one at a time, checking that everyone understood what the statement on each card meant. Where necessary, he helped with rewording and wrote it on a flipchart, putting a capital letter against each one.

The team were given the opportunity to add to this list by writing new ideas on more cards. Four of the people contributed ten more ideas between them.

They then voted with six votes each, ranging from six points down to one point, writing the name of the best ideas on 'ballot slips' which had the point values preprinted on them. These were handed to the quality manager, who added them up and put the final scores against the appropriate ideas.

Five ideas had high scores, but with no single idea scoring significantly more than the others in this group. To help separate out this group, they held a second ballot. This time, two complementary ideas were clearly at the top. They agreed to implement these the same week.

No-one ever said whose ideas were used, but no-one minded either, as the whole team got the credit.

Other examples
- A group of accountants working on improving a management report has a strongly structured work style, and consequently use NGT rather than Brainstorming to come up with the right format.
- A sales manager, wanting to put together a presentation for a key customer, brings together the account manager, the product marketing manager and the two key product engineers. The quality manager facilitates a session for them, where they quickly find the key product benefits over the competing products, and come up with a compelling value proposition.
- A product line team cannot agree on the best sound-proofing for a plate press, and the production manager will not pay until they agree. They get the line facilitator to run an NGT session to help uncover the real problems. This reveals that a couple of people have preferred brands and no trials have been done. After a visit to a local trade show and internal trials, they agree on a compromise system.

How to do it

1. Identify the objective of the NGT session, writing it in a clear statement or question, for example 'How can we be sure customers know about product recalls?'

   Note that if the need is to be strongly creative, it may be better to use Brainstorming rather than NGT.

2. Recruit the group members for the meeting. Between them, they should have sufficient knowledge to be able to achieve the objective described in step 1.

   If possible, get a facilitator to lead the NGT session. This is a person who has no stake in the outcome, other than to help the group meet their objective in a reasonable time-frame. In any case, ensure the meeting leader is familiar with the technique.

3. In the meeting, clearly display the objective from step 1, for example by writing it on a whiteboard, and ensure everyone understands it.

4. *Silently* and privately, the team writes down their thoughts and ideas on 3" x 5" cards. When individuals have finished, they should wait quietly for others to finish.

5. The leader collects the cards, shuffles them (to ensure individual people's ideas are not in batches), then reads them out, one at a time. If the idea is unclear, the team may discuss it, but *only* for clarification of meaning, not general debate.

   The agreed final wording is then transcribed onto a flipchart or other surface that can be easily read by the whole team. If it is agreed that the point from a card has already been transcribed, then it need not be copied again.

6. When all cards are transcribed and their meanings understood, vote on which are to be selected. A guideline for the number of votes to use is given in Table 28.1. The value of each vote is governed by the number of votes that can be cast. Thus, if there are four votes, the value of the votes are 4, 3, 2 and 1.

   Voting is done by each member of the team, silently and privately writing down votes for the listed ideas. Each vote is written on a 3" x 5" card, along with the text of the item for which the vote is being cast.

Table 28.1 Votes per person

Number of ideas on list	Number of votes per person	Value of votes
Less than 20	4	1, 2, 3 and 4
20 to 35	6	1, 2, 3, 4, 5 and 6
Over 35	8	1, 2, 3, 4, 5, 6, 7 and 8

7. The leader collects the cards, shuffles them as before and writes the value of each vote against the appropriate idea on the displayed list. The rank order of the ideas is then written against each. The final list may thus appear something like Fig. 28.2.

	Votes	Rank
- Replace machine with new Carver 342	4, 2, 2 = 8	4
- Use two Marker 40Bs instead	1, 1 = 2	
- Add new cog drive	2, 2, 1 = 7	5
- Increase service interval to two weeks	4, 1, 1 = 6	6
- Wait till end of financial year before deciding	4, 3, 2, 3 = 12	1

Fig. 28.2 Final displayed list

8. Review the results and discuss reactions to it. If there is no clear winner (for example, the top five ideas are within a few points of one another) or if there are strong objections, then a second round of voting may take place. This is done in the same way as the first voting session, but with the top ideas now transcribed again to a new sheet.

9. Act upon the final selection.

Practical variations

- Get the group to restate the original objective in their own words. This can ensure greater ownership of the problem.
- Tell the team about the objective before the meeting, so they can spend more time thinking about ideas. They can then bring completed cards to the meeting. This is likely to result in more and better ideas.
- Use adhesive memo notes, so the ideas can be posted up on a vertical surface such as a whiteboard. When doing this, ensure they are written with broad-tipped marker pens so they can be read from anywhere in the room. This saves the duplication of writing cards that are not changed by the discussion. It also enables them to be organized using other tools, such as the Affinity Diagram or Tree Diagram.
- Whilst the cards are being discussed, allow the meeting participants to write new cards, then repeat the process, collecting, shuffling and discussing these. This allows an element of the synergy of Brainstorming to be used.
- When writing cards, prioritize them with a number or letter (of pre-agreed meaning). In the discussion stage, the leader then reads out the top priority items first.
- A non-anonymous version is that, instead of the leader reading cards in the discussion stage, each person in turn reads out one of their own cards. Individuals may also read out their votes, rather than give them to the leader to read.
- If there are a large number of items on the list (typically over 50), reduce this number before voting. For example, combine ideas or allow team members to withdraw their own ideas.
- Number the ideas on the displayed list. This enables votes to be cast without the whole idea having to be rewritten. Take care on voting slips to differentiate between idea numbers and vote values.
- Use various other methods of Voting.
- The team walks to the list of ideas and marks their votes on them themselves. This is quicker, but less anonymous.

Notes

Nominal Group Technique is a tool that appears surprisingly often in literature on problem solving. It is commonly abbreviated to NGT.

See also

Chapters: Voting is used for selection. Voting results can be displayed in a Pareto Chart. The Nominal Group Technique method of collecting thoughts can be used in most situations where the creativity of Brainstorming is used, which is as an input to many other tools. Surveys are another data collection method, used for gaining information from diverse groups.

References: Although this is a widely referenced tool, there are varying descriptions of its actual use. [Barra 83], [Ackerman 87], [Brassard 89], [Scholtes 88] and [Oakland 93] all describe it differently.

29 Pareto Chart

What it's for

To show the relative importance of a set of measurements.

When to use it

- Use it when selecting the most important things on which to focus, thus differentiating between the 'vital few' and the 'trivial many'.
- Use it after improving a process, to show the relative change in a measured item.
- Use it when sorting a set of measurements, to emphasize their relative sizes visually.
- Use it, rather than a Bar Chart or Pie Chart to show the relative priority of a set of numeric measurements.

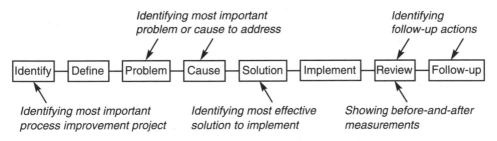

Fig. 29.1 Possible uses in improvement project framework

How to understand it

Given a set of recurring problems, it is unlikely that each problem will occur the same number of times in any one period. In fact, it is common that a few problems will occur far more often than the rest put together. This unequal distribution occurs in many situations and can be used to single out the 'vital few' from the 'trivial many'.

The Pareto Chart is simply a Bar Chart in which the bars sorted into size order, with the highest bar on the left, as in Fig. 29.2.

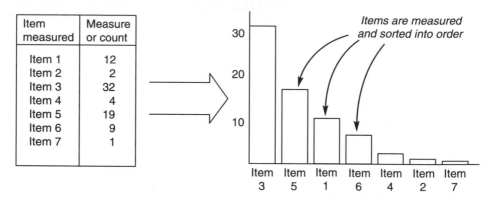

Item measured	Measure or count
Item 1	12
Item 2	2
Item 3	32
Item 4	4
Item 5	19
Item 6	9
Item 7	1

Items are measured and sorted into order

Fig. 29.2 Pareto Chart

This not only shows the *absolute* priority of each bar, through its position in the chart, but also its *relative* priority, through its height as compared with the other bars.

As the Pareto Chart is often used for decision making, it is an important parts of building a Pareto Chart to identify the right item to measure and show on the chart, as different measures may well result in the bars be ordered quite differently.

In a stable process, the order of the bars may be expected to remain constant. Thus, if the order of the bars changes with successive measurements, this may indicate an unstable process (or an insufficient number of measurements). Improvements (i.e. changes in the process) will often result in the order of the bars changing. If the improvements are maintained, the new bar order will remain stable.

Pareto Charts may have different overall 'shapes' as shown in Table 29.1. The 'spiky' Pareto Chart is the most useful, as it enables an easy selection of items to carry forwards for further action.

Table 29.1 Shapes of Pareto Chart

Shape of chart	Description	Interpretation
	Plateau	All bars are of comparable height. No clear selection of items.
	Convex	A number of bars on the left are of similar height. It is easier to reject those on the right than select from those on the left.
	Concave or spiky	One or two bars are significantly higher than the rest (often making up 80% or more of the total). This is the ideal shape for selecting the vital few items for further action.

Example

A purchasing department often wasted time going back to managers who gave them order forms which could not be used for some reason or another. So they recorded the problems over one month and plotted a Pareto Chart. A clear majority of problems were due to missing information. To narrow down the cause, they did a survey of managers, asking why they missed out information. The replies fell into four categories, which were plotted in a second Pareto Chart (see Fig. 29.3).

As a result, they produced two order forms. One suited most purposes, and was very clear and simple. The other was more complex, but was needed by only a few people.

Other examples

- A team in a glass manufacturer use a Pareto Chart to sort classifications of reject window glass. A Cause-Effect Diagram is then used to identify causes of the highest bar.

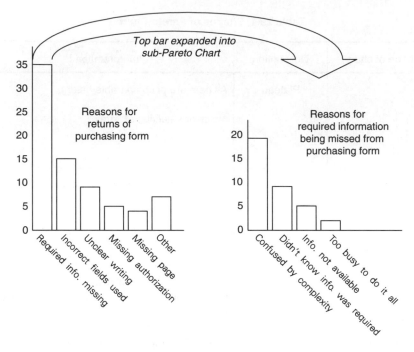

Fig. 29.3 Example

- A publisher draws a Pareto Chart of errors found in published books and uses this to produce an ordered checklist to help proofreaders.
- A sales team use a Pareto Chart to identify the techniques which result in large orders being placed with minimum sales effort.

How to do it

1. Identify the group of items that are to be charted and consequently sorted. This should be a complete and single group, for example, 'Sales of product line 32'.

   Break down the group into actual items to be measured. It can be useful to do this in several different ways plotting several charts, in order to find the most spiky chart and thus the most significant grouping. For example, product sales may be broken down by industry, geographic area and turnover, with a Pareto Chart being drawn for each.

   If possible, aim not to have too many items in each group (about seven is a good maximum), or else bars will be too low to be of use. Thus, when breaking down by industry, you might use major groupings such as 'chemical' and 'medical' rather than finer groups such as 'acids' and 'polymers'. If a group is found to be significant, then it can be broken down further, as in Fig. 29.3.

2. Identify the unit of measurement. All items on the chart must be measurable in this unit. Common units include frequency, cost and size.

   Use a measure which best reflects the key objective. For example, if the aim is to reduce cost, then measure the total failure cost of each defect type rather than the number of defects. Fig. 29.4 shows how using a different measurement unit can significantly change the Pareto ordering.

3. Determine the sample size or period during which measurements will be made. This should be enough to ensure that the final chart will have bars of varying height, sufficient to compare them. A test of this is that increasing the number of measurements should not change the order or relative height of the bars (unless the process is unstable).

   If the measurement unit is a simple frequency, aim for a total of 50 or more measurements.

   In any repeat measurement, keep constant any variables which might distort the figures. This includes the sample size or measurement period, along with anything else which might affect the result, such as people, materials, etc. If this cannot be done, then recognize it and take it into account when interpreting the final chart.

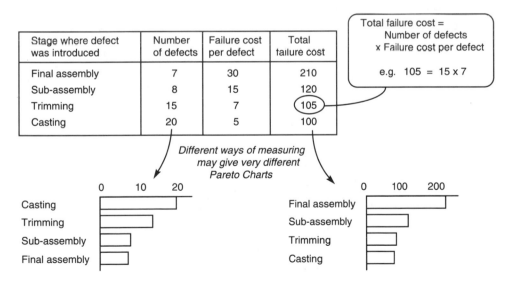

Fig. 29.4 **Effects of measuring different items**

4. Measure the items, for example using a Check Sheet, as in Fig. 29.5. Ensure that people doing the measuring are able to do it correctly, training them as necessary.

5. Sort them into size order, putting the largest measure first. If there are more than about six items, and the smaller measures are significantly smaller than others, then these can be added together to form an 'others' group (placed at the end of the list, whatever its size), as in Fig. 29.3.

6. Plot these in vertical bars, with the largest bar on the left, as in Fig. 29.5.

Step 1: Items to measure	Step 4: Measure	Step 5: Sort by size	
Work item	Time spent (min.)	Total time (min.)	Order by size
Data capture	6, 12, 14, 6	38	4
Analysis	60, 20	80	2
Review	10	10	6
Plotting graphs	20, 40	60	3
Preparing presentation	10, 25, 25, 50, 55	165	1
Presenting results	20	20	5

Fig. 29.5 Building Pareto Chart

7. Interpret the results and act accordingly. If there is no clear highest bar, then it may be worth producing another Pareto Chart using a different set of measured items. If there are one or two bars which are clearly higher, then these may be carried forwards for further analysis and action (possibly with another Pareto Chart).

Common sense should always be used during interpretations, as the highest bars do not always represent the best action items. For example, in producing a report, 'analysis' may be a high-value activity, so the aim may be to increase this at the expense of other activities. There may also be other selection criteria to take into account, such as the time and cost of corrective actions.

Practical variations

- A common addition is a cumulative line, which adds the height of each bar in turn. A right-hand scale can be used to show the cumulative line as a percentage of the total of all measurements, as in Fig. 29.6.
- Take the 80/20 rule literally, and draw a line across from the 80% mark to the cumulative line and then down into the bars, as in Fig. 29.6. Select all bars which are completely or partially to the left of this line. This gives a simple rule-based selection procedure.

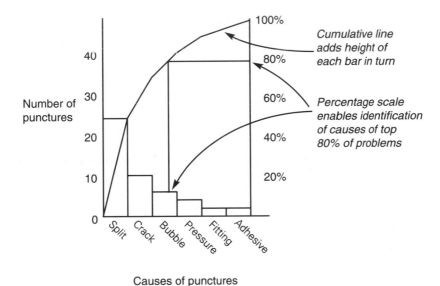

Fig. 29.6 Pareto Chart with cumulative line and 80% line

- When a cumulative line is used, the bars may be omitted. This line is sometimes called a *Pareto curve*.
- Turn chart on its side, to allow horizontal text for bar labels. This is particularly useful when the labels are long, as in Fig. 29.7.
- Draw scale lines across the chart to help estimate the values on each bar, as in Fig. 29.7.
- Add numbers to bars to show exact values. Either put them inside the bar or on top of the bar, as in Fig. 29.7.

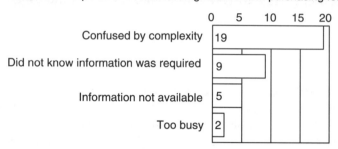

Reasons for required information being missed from purchasing form

Fig. 29.7 Horizontal Pareto Chart with scale lines and numbered bars

- In *ABC Analysis,* the cumulative figures are divided not only at 20%, but also at 50%. This gives three areas (A, B and C) which are expected to contain 80%, 15% and 5% of the problems, respectively.
- Compare the current Pareto Chart figures with a previous set of measurements using either a *Pareto Pyramid* or a *Paired Pareto Chart*, as in Fig. 29.8.

Notes

Vilfredo Pareto was an 18th century Italian economist, who observed that about 80% of the wealth of the country was owned by about 20% of the population and that this pattern repeated itself within the wealthy group (thus very few people were very wealthy).

J. M. Juran called the generalization of this uneven distribution the 'Pareto Principle', which is also sometimes called the '80/20 Rule'. *Pareto Analysis* is the act of using this principle.

Pareto Charts are one of the first seven tools.

Pareto Pyramid

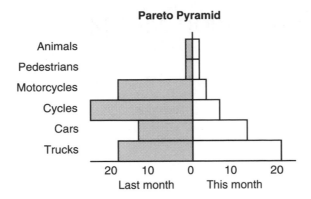

Paired Pareto Chart

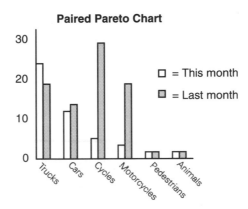

**Fig. 29.8 Comparing current and previous
Pareto Charts**

See also

Chapters: The Pareto Chart is a special form of Bar Chart. It can be used to display the results from a Check Sheet, Prioritization Matrix and Voting. Key problems discovered can be carried forwards for use in a Cause-Effect Diagram or Relations Diagram.

References: Many books on quality discuss Pareto Charts to some extent. [Ishikawa 76] and [Asaka 90] each have a chapter on them. [Oakland 90] and [Brassard 89] also cover them in some detail. [Wadsworth 86] discusses some variations. [Juran 88] discusses general applications of the Pareto Principle.

30 Prioritization Matrix

What it's for

To sort a list of items into an order of importance.

When to use it

- Use it to prioritize complex or unclear issues, where there are multiple criteria for deciding importance.
- Use it when there is data available to help score criteria and issues.
- Use it to help select items to be actioned from a larger list of possible items.
- When used with a group, it will help to gain agreement on priorities and key issues.
- Use it, rather than simple Voting, when the extra effort that is required to find a more confident selection is considered to be worthwhile.

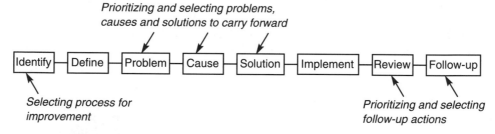

Fig. 30.1 Possible uses in improvement project framework

How to understand it

Deciding what is really important from a list of issues can be very difficult, especially if there is no objective data available and the people involved have a difference of opinion about which should be acted upon first. For example, when customers are asking for a list of product enhancements, how do you decide which to implement?

The Prioritization Matrix provides a way of sorting a diverse set of items into an order of importance. It also enables their *relative* importance to be identified by deriving a numerical value of the importance of each item. Thus an item with a score of 223 is clearly far more important than one with a score of 23, but is not much more important than one with a score of 219.

In order that the items can be compared with one another in this way, each item is scored against each of a set of key criteria, and the scores for each item are then summed. For example, a potential solution of 'Use high grade materials' will get a high score on the criterion of, 'Low cost of maintenance', but will get low score on 'Low cost of materials'.

A good criterion reflects key goals and enables objective measurements to be made. Thus 'material cost' is measurable and reflects a business profit goal, whilst 'simplicity' may not reflect any goals and be difficult to score.

When there are multiple criteria, it may also be important to take into account the fact that some criteria are more important than others. This can be implemented by allocating *weighting* values to each criteria, as in Fig. 30.2.

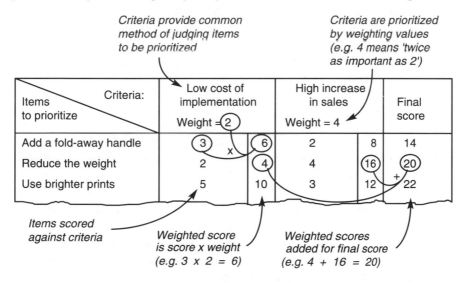

Fig. 30.2 Prioritization Matrix elements

Example

The personnel department of a major manufacturer had a number of problems highlighted in a company motivation survey. They decided to work as a team on improving the survey score. To select aspects on which to focus, they decided to use a Prioritization Matrix with the top eight motivational problems and three selection criteria.

They discussed and agreed on distributing 100 weighting points between the criteria. Scoring of problems was done differently for each criterion, but then converted to a percentage before multiplying by the weight. This scheme resulted in final scores that were also percentage figures. Scoring of problems against criteria was done as follows:

- For the criterion of 'We are able to influence', the ability of the personnel department to effect a real change was discussed, and 100 points distributed between problems.
- For the criterion of 'Many people have problem', the actual number of people mentioning this problem in the survey was used and then converted to a percentage.
- For the criterion of 'Likely survey improvement', the improvement in the survey score in these areas if this problem was fully addressed was used and then converted to a percentage.

Fig. 30.3 shows the Prioritization Matrix. Pay and work overload, as the highest scoring motivational problems, were selected for carrying forward for further investigation. As a result of consequent work in the project, the pay structure for certain grades was revised and training on job scheduling was introduced. In the following year, the survey improved in these areas by 2 and 3 points, respectively.

Other examples

- In a project to increase revenue, a sales team finds a direct correlation between the time spent in front of customers and sales totals. They identify multiple causes which prevent them from getting in front of the customer, and consequently use a Prioritization Matrix to help identify the causes which have the most effect on 'customer-facing' time. As this is a critical item, they employ the Full Analytical Criteria method and spend time gathering actual data for use in the matrix.
- An automobile manufacturer's stores manager uses a Prioritization Matrix to help decide which items to put closer to the store's counter. Criteria include 'weight' and 'request frequency'.

Prioritization criteria: / Motivation problems	We are able to influence Weight = 20		Many people have problem Weight = 30		Likely survey improvement Weight = 50		Final score
Unhelpful management	25%	5.0	21 = 11%	3.2	2 = 9%	4.6	12.8
Insufficient pay	19%	3.8	29 = 15%	4.5	4 = 18%	9.1	17.4
Work overload	6%	1.2	36 = 18%	5.5	5 = 23%	11.4	18.1
Unclear objectives	20%	4.0	23 = 12%	3.5	3 = 14%	6.8	14.4
Inadequate tools	8%	1.6	45 = 23%	6.9	3 = 14%	6.8	15.3
Poor food in canteen	4%	0.8	21 = 11%	3.2	2 = 9%	4.6	8.6
Uncooperative workmates	13%	2.6	10 = 5%	1.5	2 = 9%	4.6	8.7
Untidy workplace	5%	1.0	10 = 5%	1.5	1 = 5%	2.3	4.8
Totals			195		22		100

Fig. 30.3 Example

- A small taxi company wants to identify a way of deciding whether to accept calls. The owner and a group of his senior drivers brainstorm a list of possible criteria, writing them down on cards, then used a Bubble Sort to find the priority order, using the criteria of 'secure' and 'profitable'.

How to do it

1. Identify the overall objective. For example, 'Increase the profitability of the umbrella product line'.

2. Gather the people who are to work on the problem. They should, between them, understand the problem area and how items on the list may be judged.

3. Produce the list of items to be prioritized. This may be done using other tools, such as Brainstorming or Surveys.

4. Identify a list of criteria which may be used to judge how well each item on the list from step 3 serves the objective from step 1. This may be a fairly long list, but is reduced in steps 5 and 6.
   Approaches to identifying criteria may include:
   - Analyze the statement of objectives (e.g. What are the components of profit?).

- Identify practical constraints (e.g. How easy is it to do?).
- Consider the benefits, costs and risks.
- Aim for criteria that can be measured objectively and easily, rather than subjectively or with difficulty.

Word the criteria such that it is clear that agreeing with them is desirable. Thus use 'Low cost of ownership', rather than 'Ownership cost'.

5. Allocate a weighting number to each criterion to show their relative importance in achieving the overall objective. Thus a criterion with a number of 4 is twice as important as one with a number of 2.

   When allocating numbers in a group, if consensus cannot be reached, give each person the same number of points to spread amongst the criteria or use some other Voting method.

6. Select the actual criteria to use against the list items to be prioritized. This may be done by:
   - Rejecting criteria which have an importance number which is much lower than others.
   - Reducing the number of criteria to a small and manageable number, typically around three, by selecting those with the highest importance number.

7. Define how the list items from step 3 will be scored against each of the criteria identified in step 6.
   Approaches to consider include:
   - Have a limited set of possible score values, with associated text to describe what they mean. Thus a score of 4 may mean 'item strongly supports the criterion'.
   - Use a Voting system, as in step 5, where each person has a fixed number of points to distribute across items.
   - Use negative scores for negative effects. An example is where the criterion is 'reduces manufacturing cost', but the list item actually *increases* manufacturing cost.
   - Use a percentage scale either for direct scoring or to convert the final score into a percentage. This makes it easier to deduce information, for example if one item has a score of 64%, it is clear that all other scores against this criterion total only 36%.

8. Score each item against each criterion, using the method identified in step 7, as in Fig. 30.4.

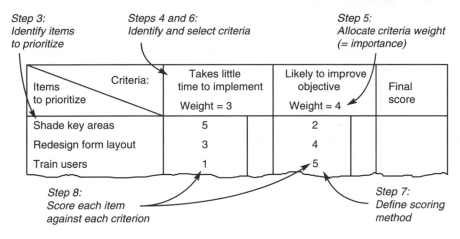

Fig. 30.4 Scoring list items against criteria

If actual numerical values are available for these comparisons, translate the values into the same score range as identified in step 7. For example, if actual costs are available, but the scoring system uses a total of 100, then divide each cost by the total of all costs and multiply by 100.

9. Multiply each score from step 8 by the number allocated to the appropriate criterion in step 5 to get the weighted score for each item against each criterion, as in Fig. 30.5.

10. For each item, add up all of the weighted scores from step 8. This gives the final prioritizing score for each item, as in Fig. 30.5. The scores may left as they are or converted to percentage values.

Items to prioritize / Criteria:	Takes little time to implement Weight = 3		Likely to improve objective Weight = 4		Final score
Shade key areas	5 x	15	2	8	23
Redesign form layout	3	9	3	12	21
Train users	1	3	4	16	19

Step 9:
Calculate weighted scores for each item and criteria as Score x Weight e.g. 15 = 5 x 3

Step 10:
Calculate overall priority score for each item as sum of weighted scores e.g. 19 = 3 + 16

Fig. 30.5 Weighting scores for final priority number

11. The final list of prioritized items may be made clearer for communication and decision making by sorting it into priority order and displaying it in a Pareto Chart.

Practical variations

- In the *Full Analytical Criteria Method*, the allocation of weighting and scoring numbers is done through comparing each item against all others by using a standard scoring scheme. This requires a matrix to be calculated for both (a) allocating weights for criteria against the objective, as in step 5, and (b) comparing the list of items against *each* criterion, as in step 8. Thus, with three criteria, four matrices must be used (one for weighting the criteria and one for scoring *each* list against the criteria). The detail in this method makes it useful for critical applications, but it is probably too time-consuming for most normal situations.

  The process is illustrated in Fig. 30.6, and is described below:

  (a) Draw a square matrix, with items both in rows down the left and also in columns along the top.

  (b) In each square, compare the row item against the column item, using the following scoring scheme:

10	= Row item is much more important than column item
5	= Row item is more important than column item
1	= Row item is equally important to column item
0.2	= Row item is less important than column item
0.1	= Row item is much less important than column item.

  Squares may be done in diagonally opposite pairs, as if A versus B scores 5 then B versus A must score 0.2. Note that as with other scoring schemes, use of real data will give much better results than subjective guesses.

  (c) Add up the numbers in each row and convert to a percentage by dividing each one by the total of all row totals.

  This final figure is now used for the weight (when comparing criteria against the basic objective) or score (when comparing all items against one criterion).

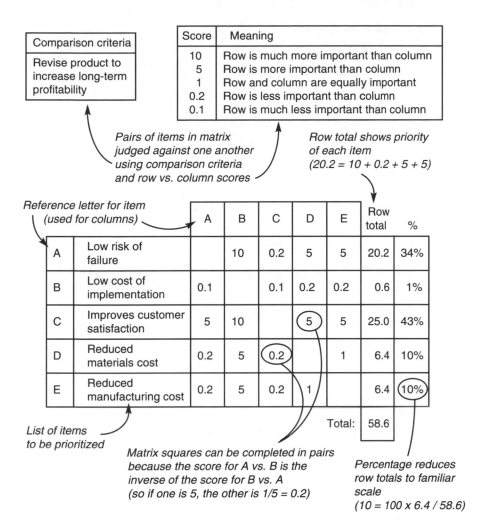

Comparison criteria

Revise product to increase long-term profitability

Score	Meaning
10	Row is much more important than column
5	Row is more important than column
1	Row and column are equally important
0.2	Row is less important than column
0.1	Row is much less important than column

Pairs of items in matrix judged against one another using comparison criteria and row vs. column scores

Row total shows priority of each item (20.2 = 10 + 0.2 + 5 + 5)

Reference letter for item (used for columns)

		A	B	C	D	E	Row total	%
A	Low risk of failure		10	0.2	5	5	20.2	34%
B	Low cost of implementation	0.1		0.1	0.2	0.2	0.6	1%
C	Improves customer satisfaction	5	10		5	5	25.0	43%
D	Reduced materials cost	0.2	5	0.2		1	6.4	10%
E	Reduced manufacturing cost	0.2	5	0.2	1		6.4	10%
						Total:	58.6	

List of items to be prioritized

Matrix squares can be completed in pairs because the score for A vs. B is the inverse of the score for B vs. A (so if one is 5, the other is 1/5 = 0.2)

Percentage reduces row totals to familiar scale (10 = 100 x 6.4 / 58.6)

Fig. 30.6 Full Analytical Criteria matrix

- *Paired Comparison* provides a simple way of prioritizing a list of items when there is a single ranking criterion, as in Fig. 30.7. As each pairwise comparison selects the more important item in the pair rather than giving a score, the result is a prioritized list, but without relative priority shown in a score figure.

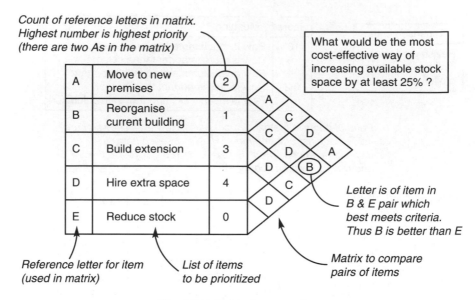

Fig. 30.7 Paired comparison

- Another variation of paired comparison is the *Bubble Sort*. This is a quick and easy method which can be performed as follows:

  (a) Write each item to be prioritized on a 3" x 5" card, then place the cards one above another in a vertical column.

  (b) Compare the top two cards to determine which is the most important. If the lower card is more important, then exchange the positions of the cards. This will result in the more important card being positioned above the less important card.

  (c) Repeat this pairwise comparison and exchange for the second and third card, then third and fourth card and so on until the bottom of the column is reached.

  (d) If any cards have been moved during steps (b) and (c), repeat the process for the whole column, starting again with the top two cards, as in step (b).

  (e) Keep repeating the overall process until no cards are exchanged during a complete pass through the column. The cards are now in priority order.

Notes

Priority matrices are sometimes described as one of the second seven tools.

See also

Chapters: Use Brainstorming, Nominal Group Technique or Surveys to identify issues and criteria. Problems selected by it may be further investigated with a Cause-Effect Diagram or Relations Diagram. Voting gives a simpler but less certain method of selection. The results of a Prioritization Matrix can be displayed in a Pareto Chart.

References: [Brassard 89] describes Prioritization Matrices in detail. [Francis 90] discusses weighted decision-making methods.

31 Process Capability

What it's for

To determine the ability of a process to meet specification limits.

When to use it

- Use it when setting up a process, to ensure it can meet its specification limits.
- Use it when setting specification limits, to ensure they are neither too wide nor too narrow.
- Use it when investigating a process that is not meeting its specification limits.
- Use it only when the process is stable and has a Normal distribution.

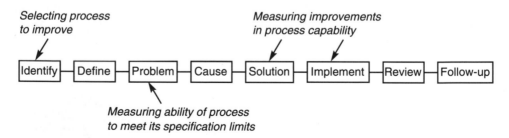

Fig. 31.1 **Possible uses in improvement project framework**

How to understand it

Any process will have variation in its output, as discussed in Chapter 5, and it is common for specification limits to be defined such that if the measured output of the process exceeds the specified limits, the process is deemed to have failed. The term 'specification limits' is most commonly used for the dimensions of a manufactured item, but can be used in any process. Thus, for example, the specification limits for the time a telesales operator may take to answer a customer call may be between zero and five seconds.

The results of most processes will vary around a central value, as described in Chapter 5, and the 'capability' of the process is defined as the spread of results around this value, with high capability occurring when process results group closely around it. Thus a process that can be used to produce parts to within 0.001 mm of a target value is more capable than one which can only produce them to within 0.015 mm.

The most common measure of this spread is standard deviation, and 'Process Capability' may be defined as the range between three standard deviations either side of the average.

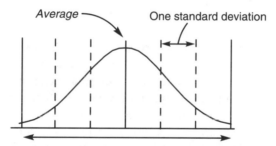

Process is capable of achieving results which are consistently
within three standard deviations either side of the average

Fig. 31.2 Process Capability

Specifications are often defined separately from the process that is being measured and without a great deal of consideration of how easily the process can meet them. This can result in either many failures and rejects or effectively redundant specifications, as the variation in the process fits badly or well within the specified limits, as in Fig. 31.3.

Specification limits and Process Capability thus need to be considered together. The limits still cannot be too tight as if calibration is done under ideal conditions, process distribution may subsequently drift or spread, for example as a result of wear in a machine tool.

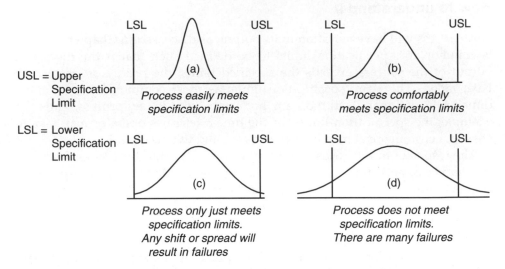

USL = Upper Specification Limit

LSL = Lower Specification Limit

Fig. 31.3 Capability of process to meet specification limits

A common Process Capability measure, Cp (often called a Process Capability Index), indicates how well the process distribution fits within its specification limits, and is simply the ratio of the specification width to the variation width, as in Fig. 31.4. Thus, in Fig. 31.3, processes (a) and (b) have Cp greater than one, (c) is equal to one and (d) is less than one.

The problem with Cp is that it does not take account of how well the process distribution is centred within its limits, which can result in a process with both a low Cp and many rejects. The solution to this is a second measure, Cpk, which measures a similar ratio, but considers only the variation half that is closest to the specification limits, as in Fig. 31.4. Thus Cp and Cpk, taken together, give a measure of both the potential and centring of the process distribution within the specification limits.

Process Capability measures are only as good as the data used, and there is plenty of opportunity for misinterpretation. In particular, Process Capability measurement is based on three important assumptions which are thus preconditions for valid calculations:

1. The process is in a state of statistical control, and there are no special causes of variation. The implication of this is that before Cp and Cpk can be measured, special causes must be found and eliminated. This may be done using the Control Chart over a period of time long enough to give confidence that this has been successfully completed.

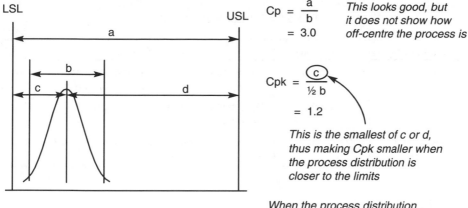

Fig. 31.4 Cp and Cpk

2. The process distribution is bell-shaped or 'Normal', which allows the width of the distribution to be calculated as six times the standard deviation (as discussed in Chapter 5). In practice, there are many situations where the distribution is not normal, and in Process Capability measurement the Central Limit Theorem does not act to normalize this, as it does when using a Control Chart.

3. The measured data is representative of the process. This means that it should be a randomly selected and large sample, taken over a long period. Samples taken over a short period can suffer from a limited range of changes in either external seasonal effects or internal process variables, such as humidity or tool wear.

When interpreting values of Cpk, there are three significant regions which may be considered, and a general rule is given in Table 31.1. The value of 3 as a 'total confidence' limit may be lowered if measurements are taken as the average of sample batches. This commonly happens when Cpk is measured using the same data used to plot the Control Chart (e.g. the confidence limit reduces to 2 for the common sample size of 4).

In the broader sense, studying Process Capability is more than just measuring Cp and Cpk; it involves understanding the statistical performance and operational working of the process. Most importantly, it means understanding what causes variation within the process, under what conditions, and how these variables interact. The purpose of doing this is to enable confident process improvement that steadily reduces variation.

Table 31.1 Interpreting Cpk

Value of Cpk	Capability	Action
Less than 1	Incapable	Improve by reducing common causes of variation in process variables. Use 100% inspection.
Between 1 and 3	Capable	Do nothing or some process improvement. Dependent on sample size.
Greater than 3	Very capable	Do nothing or reduce specification limits. No inspection necessary.

Example

A company producing kitchen worktops, specified the length of one range at 120 cm ± 0.25 cm. As a normal part of production monitoring, Control Charts were kept for such specified measures and all output was inspected against specification limits. A request from the sales team for tighter limits prompted the question of whether the limits could be reduced to ± 0.1 cm, as this could result in significant orders from a new customer who preferred not to shave worktops to fit.

The production supervisor used the Control Chart data to draw a Histogram and check for Normal distribution, then calculate Cpk, across samples from a week's work, as in Fig. 31.5. This showed that the process was currently so capable that inspection could be dropped and the new limits still met. This turned out to be as a result of old specification limits coupled with several recent process improvements.

As a result, the new orders were achieved and savings were also made on inspection costs.

Other examples
- A sales completion team, aiming to reduce the shipment time of urgent orders, studies the process, including plotting control charts and using them identifying variables and eliminating common causes of variation. They then measure the Process Capability and use the results to set delivery targets for each of a set of geographical areas. Knowing their capability, they then guarantee delivery times to customers.
- A lathe operator doing an ongoing process improvement of his work learns the variables involved and how to measure them. He then uses a Control Chart to help stabilize the process. Work pieces are still sometimes failing specification limits, so he uses a Process Capability index measure

Worktop length Process Capability

X1	X2	X3	X4	Average	Range
120.03	120.02	120.01	120.01	120.0175	0.02
120.01	120	120.03	119.98	120.005	0.05
120.02	120.01	120	120	120.0075	0.02
120	120.03	120.04	120.01	120.02	0.04
120.01	120.02	120.02	119.99	120.01	0.03
120.01	119.98	120.01	120	120	0.03
120	120.01	120.02	119.99	120.005	0.03
120	120	120.02	120	120.005	0.02
120.03	120.02	119.99	120.02	120.015	0.04
120.01	120.01	120.01	119.99	120.005	0.02
120.03	120.02	120.01	120	120.015	0.03
120.02	119.99	120	120.01	120.005	0.03
120.01	120.01	120	120.03	120.0125	0.03
120	120.03	119.97	119.98	119.995	0.06
120.01	119.99	120	119.98	119.995	0.03
120.01	120	120	120	120.0025	0.01
120.01	120	120.02	120.01	120.01	0.02
120	119.99	119.99	120.02	120	0.03
119.99	120.03	120	120.01	120.0075	0.04
120.02	119.98	119.99	120.01	120	0.04
120.01	120.02	119.99	120	120.005	0.03
119.98	120.02	119.99	119.99	119.995	0.04
120	120.01	120.02	120.02	120.0125	0.02
120.01	120.04	119.98	119.99	120.005	0.06
120.03	120.01	120	120.01	120.0125	0.03
			Total	3000.163	0.8
			Average	120.0065	0.032

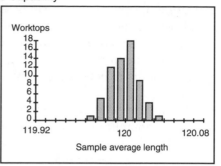

	Current limits	Proposed limits
LSL	119.5	119.9
USL	120.5	120.1
s	0.0155	0.0155
Cp	10.723	2.144
Cpk(USL)	10.863	2.284
Cpk(LSL)	10.584	2.005

Fig. 31.5 Example

to identify how capable the overall process is of meeting limits. He finds that the process is centred, but only just capable. Further process improvements help to improve this situation.

- An auctioneer studies the pricing variation on different categories of cars, and uses a Process Capability study to help determine pricing limits. She then uses this data to start bidding prices and advise potential sellers.

How to do it

1. Identify the objectives of measuring the Process Capability. Typical reasons include:
    - Prioritization of process improvement projects.
    - Investigation of causes of specification limit failure.
    - Setting realistic specification limits for process.
    - Determining results of improvements made.

2. Define the process that is to be investigated. Typically this will encompass all actions and variables that will affect the item to be measured and which may be changed. For example, if measuring the elasticity of a rubber cord, both the moulding and curing processes may be included in the study, when both are believed to contain variables that affect the elasticity.

3. Identify the actual measure to make. This is usually easy to find, as it has specification limits already defined.

   Also define the process of measurement in order that measurements may be consistently made. This may include such activities as verification of measurement equipment accuracy, training of people doing the measurement, etc.

4. Take sample measures of the process at random times over a period which is long enough for all variables within the process to travel through their full range of possible values. Also take enough measurements to enable this range to be identifiable, as detailed in step 5.

   The measurements should be made under normal working conditions, because if machines and other items in the process are set up specially for measurements to be made, the result will only show the capability of the process under 'best case' conditions.

5. Verify that the process is in a 'state of statistical control', with no special causes of variation. This can be performed by plotting Control Charts and checking for significant trends or points outside the control limits. If special causes are found, they must be eliminated before Process Capability indices can be measured.

   Make this as accurate as possible by using Average and Range (X-bar, R) Control Charts, plotting at least 25 points, for example with 100 measurements and a sample size of 4. If so many measurements are not possible, use Individuals and Moving Range (X, MR) Control Charts with at least 31 measurements.

5. Verify that the process has a Normal (bell-shaped) distribution, for example by plotting a Histogram and inspecting its shape.

6. Calculate the Capability Indices, using the same data used for drawing the Control Charts, as in Fig. 31.6.

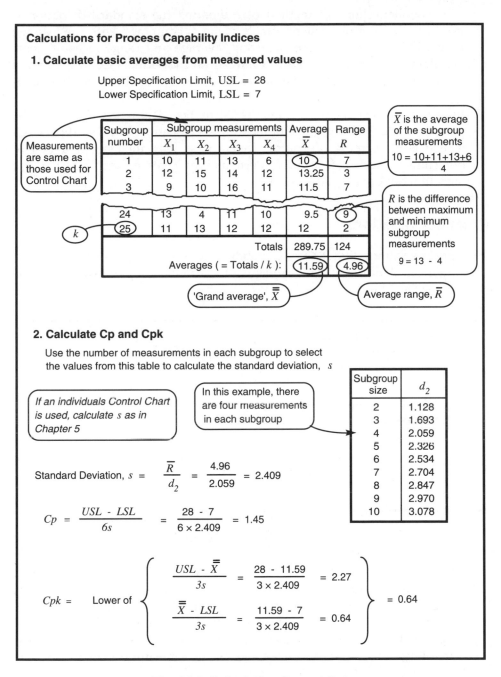

Calculations for Process Capability Indices

1. Calculate basic averages from measured values

Upper Specification Limit, USL = 28
Lower Specification Limit, LSL = 7

$\bar{X}$ is the average of the subgroup measurements

$10 = \dfrac{10+11+13+6}{4}$

Measurements are same as those used for Control Chart

Subgroup number	Subgroup measurements				Average $\bar{X}$	Range R
	X_1	X_2	X_3	X_4		
1	10	11	13	6	10	7
2	12	15	14	12	13.25	3
3	9	10	16	11	11.5	7
24	13	4	11	10	9.5	9
25	11	13	12	12	12	2
Totals					289.75	124
Averages (= Totals / k):					11.59	4.96

k

R is the difference between maximum and minimum subgroup measurements

$9 = 13 - 4$

'Grand average', $\bar{\bar{X}}$

Average range, $\bar{R}$

2. Calculate Cp and Cpk

Use the number of measurements in each subgroup to select the values from this table to calculate the standard deviation, s

If an individuals Control Chart is used, calculate s as in Chapter 5

In this example, there are four measurements in each subgroup

Subgroup size	d_2
2	1.128
3	1.693
4	2.059
5	2.326
6	2.534
7	2.704
8	2.847
9	2.970
10	3.078

Standard Deviation, $s = \dfrac{\bar{R}}{d_2} = \dfrac{4.96}{2.059} = 2.409$

$Cp = \dfrac{USL - LSL}{6s} = \dfrac{28 - 7}{6 \times 2.409} = 1.45$

$$Cpk = \text{Lower of} \begin{cases} \dfrac{USL - \bar{\bar{X}}}{3s} = \dfrac{28 - 11.59}{3 \times 2.409} = 2.27 \\[3mm] \dfrac{\bar{\bar{X}} - LSL}{3s} = \dfrac{11.59 - 7}{3 \times 2.409} = 0.64 \end{cases} = 0.64$$

Fig. 31.6 Calculating Cp and Cpk

A common short-cut method of estimating the standard deviation is used in this example, where a table value is combined with the average range. This is useful where subgroup, average and range measurements are already made for a Control Chart. If an Individuals Control Chart is used, then the standard deviation can be calculated as shown in Chapter 5.

7. Interpret and act on the results. Thus, in Fig. 31.6, Cp shows that the process is reasonably capable of meeting specification, but Cpk shows that it also is performing off-centre. The process may then be examined to determine whether it can be permanently centred and whether the variation can be reduced some more.

Practical variations

- Cpm is an alternative Process Capability index which gives a measure in a single calculation. Fig. 31.7 shows how to calculate Cpm, using the same data as Fig. 31.6.

$$\left.\begin{array}{l} \text{Upper Specification Limit}, USL = 28 \\ \text{Lower Specification Limit}, LSL = 7 \\ \text{Standard Deviation}, s = 2.409 \\ \text{Average}, \overline{\overline{X}} = 11.59 \end{array}\right\} \text{From Fig. 31.5}$$

$$T = \text{Target value (usually mid-way between LSL and USL)} = \frac{28 - 7}{2} = 10.5$$

$$t = \sqrt{s^2 + (\overline{\overline{X}} - T)^2} = \sqrt{2.409^2 + (11.59 - 10.5)^2} = 2.644$$

$$Cpm = \frac{USL - LSL}{6t} = \frac{28 - 7}{6 \times 2.644} = 1.32$$

Fig. 31.7 Calculating Cpm

- Set up an optimum environment before measuring the Process Capability, rather than measuring under normal working conditions. For example, use new tools, most skilled people, graded materials, slower execution, etc. This will give a measure of the *potential* of the process. The difference between this and the measure taken from the normal working Process Capability will give some indication of the possible improvement that may be made.

Notes

The investigation of a process and its capability is often called a *Process Capability Study*, or *PCS*.

See also

Chapters: Other tools for measuring Variation that can be used in a Process Capability study include the Control Chart, Histogram, Scatter Diagram and Design of Experiments.

References: [Oakland 90] details Process Capability calculations. [Juran 88] discusses its applications in the context of process management. It is also referenced in [Deming 82], [Feigenbaum 83], [Owen 93] and [Logothetis 93].

32 Process Decision Program Chart

What it's for

To identify potential problems and countermeasures in a plan.

When to use it

- Use it when making plans, to help identify potential risks to their successful completion.
- When risks are identified, use it to help identify and select from a set of possible countermeasures.
- Also use it to help plan ways of avoiding and eliminating identified risks.
- It is of best value when risks are non-obvious, such as in unfamiliar situations or in complex plans, and when the consequences of failure are serious.

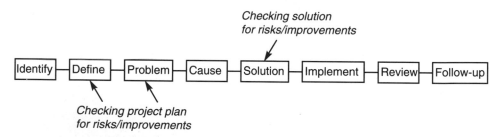

Fig. 32.1 Possible uses in improvement project framework

How to understand it

Any plan is a statement of what is expected to happen, although as many planners will agree, the best laid plans of mice and men seldom happen exactly as expected. There are two approaches to coping with this problem: firefighting or risk management.

Firefighting is an approach that is taken surprisingly often. The manager spends most of his or her time coping with the unexpected, issuing orders, changing plans and slipping schedules. It can give a false sense of heroism as immediate dangers are averted by dramatic last-minute actions.

On the other hand, risk management involves looking ahead at the planning stage for potential future problems. The most difficult part of this activity is often the actual identification of risks. The Process Decision Program Chart (commonly abbreviated to the less unwieldy *PDPC*) provides a simple method to help in identifying both risks and countermeasures.

Quite simply, if the plan is displayed diagrammatically (typically in a Tree Diagram), then identified risks and countermeasures are added in subsequent boxes, as in Fig. 32.2. This may appear to be quite trivial, but as with many other tools, the construction and thought involved is as important as the final diagram.

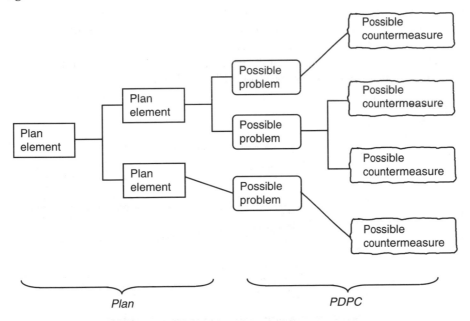

Fig. 32.2 PDPC elements appended to plan

The simplicity and flexibility of the PDPC can result in very different diagrams, with various levels of detail and different symbols and boxes used to indicate specific items. The common theme is the identification of risk and how it might be handled.

Two of the most common elements of risk are cost and time, for example where there is a risk in a busy schedule of key equipment being unavailable and consequent time loss and additional expense being incurred in hiring replacement machines. A possible resolution of this risk is to hire standby equipment, which may be selected if this cost is considered to be lower than the cost of missing a committed completion date.

There are three possible routes that may be taken for coping with identified risks: risk avoidance, risk reduction and contingency planning. The chosen approach in each case may affect actions during the construction of the PDPC, as indicated in Fig. 32.3.

Risk avoidance means not taking an action that will result in an identified risk. Typically this route involves finding alternative actions. In sensitive cases, where the consequences of the risk occurring are be catastrophic and there is no acceptable alternative, risk avoidance could result in the whole plan being abandoned.

Risk reduction means taking some action that will reduce, but not eliminate, the identified risk. It may involve additional actions, such as extra testing to reduce the risk of failure of the final product. Typically this results in a trade-off of additional cost against reduced risk.

Contingency planning does not reduce the chance of the identified risk occurring. Instead, it involves making additional plans, so that if the risk does occur you will be prepared and able to control the situation with the minimum cost and disruption.

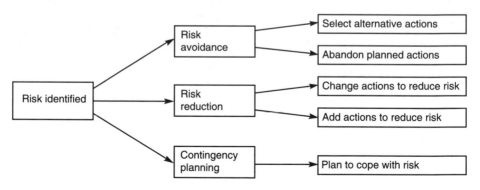

Fig. 32.3 Possible risk management routes

Example

A dress production team at a clothes manufacturer was improving the cutting-out process in order to minimize material wastage. They decided to use PDPC on the work breakdown structure to identify potential problems and ways of avoiding them.

As the most expensive element is the material itself, they defined a significant risk as, 'Anything that might cause the cut cloth to be ruined', and viable countermeasures as, 'Anything that will reduce the risk, and which costs less than 100 pieces of cloth'.

The resulting PDPC is shown in Fig. 32.4. As a result of this, the cutting was tested on cheaper material, resulting in the material clamp being redesigned to

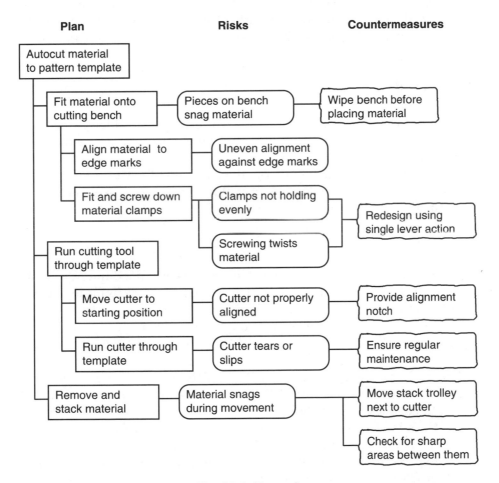

Fig. 32.4 Example

prevent drag, a start notch provided for the cutter and the general area being inspected for sharp corners to minimize snag problems. The cutting operator was involved in the PDPC process and the subsequent tests, resulting in her fully understanding the process. The final cutting process thereafter ran very smoothly with very little error.

Other examples

- A structural engineering project manager uses it to help find problems in a plan for constructing a road bridge.
- A kitchen hygiene improvement team uses PDPC to check for possible areas where infection could come into contact with consumable foodstuffs. An individual sub-project is then spawned for all identified danger areas.
- A mailroom project to improve delivery times uses it to help check the proposed solution, checking in particular that it will not have any side-effects that might upset other processes.

How to do it

1. Identify the objective of using PDPC. For example, 'To identify risks in a specific area of a plan, and to identify countermeasures where the cost of the risk occurring is greater than a certain figure'.

   Ensure that the situation merits the use of PDPC. This will usually be when risks are either unknown or may have serious consequences if they occur.

   The plan should be available and complete, unless the PDPC activity is being used as an integral part of the planning process.

2. Identify the areas of the plan which need to be examined in order to meet the objectives. If it is a large plan, then attempting to examine all elements of it will result in a practical limitation on the effort that can be put into each element. It is usually better to use PDPC only on the higher risk areas of the plan.

3. Gather the people to work on the PDPC. Between them, they should have as wide a view as possible of the situation, so that diverse risks may be identified. These may include:
   - High-level managers who can see the 'big picture' and relationships with other people and events.
   - Experts in specific elements of the plan who can see potential problems with planned actions.

- People experienced in planning and using PDPC, who may have discovered other problems in similar situations.

4. Identify the criteria for making decisions during construction of the PDPC. These include:
   - How to identify a risk (step 5). For example, 'Something that has a significant effect on the schedule completion time'.
   - How to select risks that need countermeasures to be identified (step 6). For example, 'The top 10% of identified risks and also those for which simple countermeasures are obvious'.
   - How to identify countermeasures (step 7). For example, 'A measure that has a good chance of reducing the identified risk'.
   - How to select countermeasures to implement (step 8). For example, 'Those which cost less than the savings they would make if they were implemented'.

   Factors to consider when identifying selection criteria include:
   - *Time*. How much time would a risk cost? Is it on the critical path of the schedule? How much time could countermeasures save?
   - *Cost*. What would be the overall cost of a risk occurring? What would be the cost of a countermeasure? Would it be worth it?
   - *Control*. How much control do you have for preventing the risk? What control would you have should it occur? How could you change that?
   - *Information*. How much do you know about the risk? What warning would you have of its impending occurrence?

5. For each plan element to be considered, identify potential problems that could occur. Ask, 'What if ...', using Brainstorming techniques to identify a broad range of risks. This can be helped by using a checklist of questions to ask.

   These risks can either be written down in a separate list or on 3" x 5" cards that can be moved about during step 6. Cards are particularly useful if larger numbers of risks are being identified or if the PDPC is being done as a part of a planning session which is also using cards.

6. For the risks identified in step 5, decide which ones should be carried forward onto the PDPC. These will be examined in more detail when determining countermeasures in step 8. This may be carried out by Voting, Prioritization Matrix or some other method for selecting items.

   To keep the PDPC manageable, select only a few risks per plan element (typically three or less).

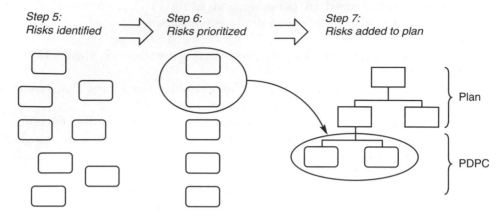

Fig. 32.5 Adding risks to plan

7. Put the identified risks on the plan, using shaped boxes or some other method to enable these risks to be clearly differentiated from then plan elements. Steps 5 to 7 are illustrated in Fig. 32.5.

8. For each risk now on the PDPC, identify possible countermeasures in a similar manner to the identification of risks in step 5, but now asking, 'How can this risk be reduced?'. Look for methods of eliminating, reducing or handling the risk (see Fig. 32.3).

9. In a similar manner to step 6, prioritize these countermeasures and select those which are to be carried forward to the PDPC, using the criteria determined in step 4.

10. In the same way as step 7, add the selected countermeasures to the plan under the appropriate risk item. Steps 8 to 10 are illustrated in Fig. 32.6.

11. Carry out or otherwise prepare the selected countermeasures, ensuring that any changes to the plan are fully resourced and are treated thereafter as normal plan elements. Actions here might include:
    *   Changing the plan, e.g. to remove or replace high risk elements.
    *   Adding new elements to the plan, e.g. verification activities.
    *   Preparing contingency plans which will only be executed should specific risks occur.

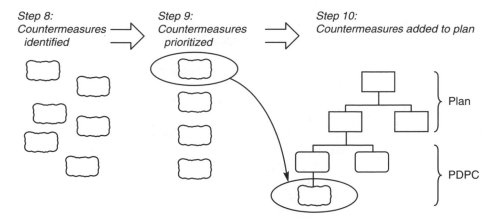

Fig. 32.6 Adding countermeasures to plan

Practical variations

- PDPC elements may be informally added to any plan or other appropriate diagram (such as a Flowchart), simply by drawing directly on the plan as risks are identified. This is simpler than the above process, but may identify fewer risks and countermeasures. Which approach to take should be selected on the importance of identifying and handling any critical risks.
- Instead of identifying risks and countermeasures, the objective can be reversed with PDPC being used to identify opportunities and ways of increasing the chance of these 'side benefits' occurring.
- The countermeasures to be implemented can be identified after they have been added to the PDPC. This is usually shown by putting a 'O' next to accepted countermeasures, and 'X' next to rejected ones, as shown in Fig. 32.7.
- If the plan is displayed in a text hierarchy, then the PDPC can be implemented in the same style, using two lower levels, as in Fig. 32.7. The PDPC elements can be made to show up more by using a different style to the plan elements (e.g. italics).

```
      2.0  Milling of casting master
           2.1  Put design detail into computer
                2.1.1  Miskeyed detail
 O                2.1.1.1  Use same computer format as design software
 X                2.1.1.2  Key twice for verification
           2.2  Produce machine control tape
           2.3  Mount tape
           2.4  Clamp raw casting block into milling machine
                2.4.1  Wrong material
 X                2.4.1.1  Spectral analysis
 O                2.4.1.2  Visual check in process notes
                2.4.2  Wrongly clamped
 O                2.4.2.1  Train operator
           2.5  Run machine to compete milling
```

Key: *O = Selected countermeasure*
        X = Rejected countermeasure (too expensive, difficult, etc.)

Fig. 32.7 PDPC in plan which uses text hierarchy

- A simple method of quantifying and comparing a set of identified risks is to calculate the *Risk Exposure* (or *Risk Impact*). This is simply the probability of the risk occurring multiplied by the cost, should the risk occur, as illustrated in Fig. 32.8. This can be used even where exact figures are not known, provided that reasonable comparative estimates can be made.

    This method uses probability-times-cost to give an effective 'actual value'. It can be understood by considering how the return on a series of bets of $200 at odds of 100 to 1 would be the same as a series of bets of $20 at odds of 10 to 1 (each method will average ($200 x 0.01) = ($20 x 0.1) = $2 return per bet).

- A simple quantitative way of selecting from a set of identified countermeasures is to calculate and compare the *Risk Reduction Leverage*. This is the reduction in risk exposure divided by the cost of implementing the countermeasure, as shown in Fig. 32.8. As with Risk Exposure, if exact figures are not known, comparative estimates can still make this a useful method.

Risk Exposure, RE

Risk Exposure calculates the effective current cost of a risk, and can be used to prioritize risks that require countermeasures.

Risk Exposure, RE = Probability of risk occurring × Total loss if risk occurs

$$RE \ = \ 2\% \ \times \ 80K \ = \ \frac{2}{100} \ \times \ 80000 \ = \ 1600$$

Risk	Probability of occurring	Total loss if it occurs	Risk Exposure
Product recall situation	2%	80K	1600
Significant product rejection	0.1%	1000K	1000
Competitive strike	10%	25K	2500

Highest Risk Exposure indicates most serious risk

Risk Reduction Leverage, RRL

Risk Reduction Leverage calculates a value for the 'return on investment' for a countermeasure and can thus be used to prioritize possible countermeasures.

Risk Reduction Leverage of a countermeasure, RRL = $\dfrac{Reduction\ in\ Risk\ Exposure}{Cost\ of\ the\ countermeasure}$

$$RRL \ = \ \frac{2500 \ - \ 150}{40000} \ = \ 0.059$$

Risk		Probability of occurring	Total loss if it occurs	Risk Exposure	
Competitive strike		10%	25K	2500	
Countermeasure	Total cost	New risk probability	New total loss	New RE	RRL
Advertising campaign	40K	3%	5K	150	0.059
Price promotions	30K	5%	10K	500	0.067
Simultaneous launch	10K	8%	15K	1200	0.13

Highest RRL indicates most cost-effective countermeasure

Fig. 32.8 Calculations for quantifying risk and countermeasure

Notes

The Process Decision Program Chart is one of the second seven tools.

See also

Chapters: Use Brainstorming or Nominal Group Technique to identify risks. Decision Trees, Failure Mode and Effects Analysis and Fault Tree Analysis also investigate risk.

References: PDPC is discussed by most books that cover the second seven tools. [Brassard 89], [Mizuno 88] and [Gitlow 90] cover it in detail. [Oakland 93] discuss it in the context of the second seven tools. [Boehm 90] discusses many other concepts and practices about risk.

33 Relations Diagram

What it's for

To clarify and understand complex relationships.

When to use it

- Use it when analyzing complex situations where there are multiple interrelated issues.
- Use it where the current problem is perceived as being a symptom of a more important underlying problem.
- It is also useful in building consensus within groups.
- It is commonly used to map cause-effect relationships, but also can be used to map any other type of relationship.
- Use it, rather than an Affinity Diagram, when there are logical, rather than subjective, relationships.
- Use it, rather than a Cause-Effect Diagram, when causes are non-hierarchic or when there are complex issues.

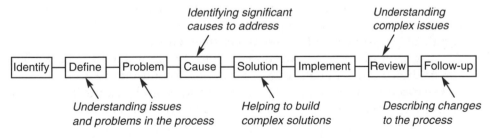

Fig. 33.1 Possible uses in improvement project framework

How to understand it

In many problem situations, there are multiple complex relationships between the different elements of the problem, which cannot be organized into familiar structures such as hierarchies or matrices. The Relations Diagram addresses these situations by showing relationships between items with a network of boxes and arrows, as in Fig. 33.2.

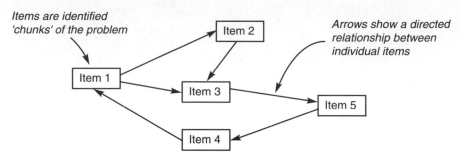

Fig. 33.2 Relations Diagram

The most common use of the Relations Diagram is to show the relationship between one or more problems and their causes, although it can also be used to show any complex relationship between problem elements, such as information flow within a process.

The cause-effect Relations Diagram contains one or more effects and multiple causes, with arrows pointing from cause to effect. The network of arrows is built up as multiple causes interrelate. The result can be considered as a complex Cause-Effect Diagram, as in Fig. 33.3. Note how causes are visually differentiated from effects.

Several useful points may be identified when interpreting a cause-effect Relations Diagram:

- Arrows flowing only away from a cause indicate a *root cause*. Eliminating root causes can result in subsequent causes also being eliminated, giving a significant improvement for a relatively small effort.
- A cause with multiple arrows flowing into it indicates a *bottleneck*. This can be difficult to eliminate, due to the multiple contributory causes.
- A *key cause* is one which is selected to be addressed by future action. Key causes may be highlighted in some way, such as double circling.

A good cause-effect Relations Diagram has a balance of causes and relationships that describes the problem clearly and completely, without going into obscuring detail or being vague and brief.

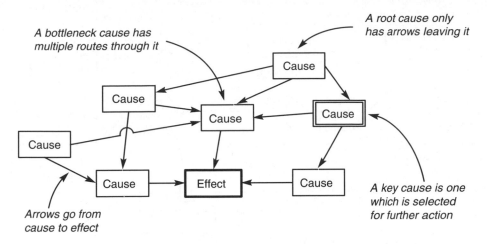

A bottleneck cause has multiple routes through it

A root cause only has arrows leaving it

Arrows go from cause to effect

A key cause is one which is selected for further action

33.3 Components of cause-effect Relations Diagram

Example

The design department of a company which produces industrial cabinets were continually irritated by the production department, who kept modifying their designs. The production department, on the other hand, considered the design department to have their 'heads in the clouds' when it came down to real production issues. To understand this problem, two members from each department met to try and find the key causes of this problem and how they could address it. Initially they could not agree, and so decided to use a cause-effect Relations Diagram to try and work from their two problems in towards common causes that could be addressed. They defined the problems as (a) production make bad changes to design, and (b) designs are impractical to build.

In the next meeting, they put the problem cards on either side of the work area and started Brainstorming possible causes, working in towards one another. Initially, each department naturally focused on their grievance area. However, working together, keying off each other's thoughts they soon started to find common areas. Their mutual understanding further improved when they started to add causal links, and they were surprised how easily they agreed on the final key causes. Their diagram is shown in Fig. 33.4.

As result, a cross-functional task force developed a product lifecycle to involve all departments. This included cross-functional meetings and training requirements.

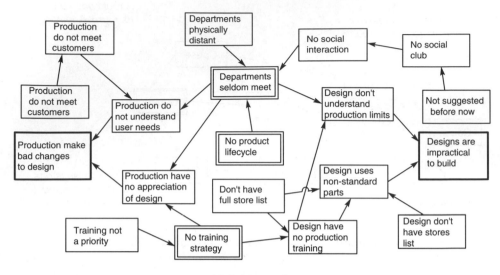

33.5 Example

Other examples

- A firm of consulting engineers uses a Relations Diagram to ensure that all eventualities are covered in an investigation report into the laying of a new cross-country gas pipeline.
- A library manager uses a State Diagram to help identify what happens as an outstanding book report progresses from a late return to legislative action.
- A production engineer uses a Block Diagram to show how the machines, materials and processes interrelate and improving the flow of metal flanges through a plating process.

How to do it

1. Form a team of between four and seven people to work on the problem. The ideal team has a close working knowledge of the problem area (to be able to identify why things happen) and between them can cover all potential topics.

2. Identify the type of relationship to be mapped, and how this is to be displayed. A useful way of doing this is to identify a simple question which, when answered, will enable related items to be identified. For example, 'What must be done before this item?'. Encourage a common

approach in the meeting by displaying this question clearly.

The most common Relations Diagram is a map of the interrelationship between the causes of one or more problems, in which case the question is, 'What *directly* causes this item?'. Some other possible relationships are discussed under *Practical Variations*, below.

3. Define each problem clearly, writing it as a complete, but brief, sentence on a 3" x 5" card. This may come from a key issue identified through the use of another tool. There may be more than one such problem statement.

    Mark the problem cards to differentiate them from other cards, for example with a bold border.

4. Produce the set of items to be related in the diagram. There are several approaches that may be taken here:
    * Use the identified relationship and question from step 2 with a Brainstorming or Nominal Group Technique session.
    * Use items that have been already generated from other tools, such as an Affinity Diagram, Cause-Effect Diagram or Tree Diagram.
    * Data can also be collected in other ways, such as with Surveys. Where data represents what someone has said, retain the exact wording so that the associated feeling is not lost.

Write each item on a 3" x 5" card, distinguishing item cards from problem cards, for example by writing problem cards with heavier printing or adding a box around the text. Aim for around 15 to 50 cards. Less may indicate a problem which may not benefit from using this tool, whilst more becomes difficult to handle.

5. If Brainstorming was used in step 4, then put the item cards randomly in a 'parking area' where they may be transferred to the main 'organization area' (see Fig. 33.6). If other methods were used, then they may already be in an order which is worth keeping (such as Affinity groups).

    Putting cards into a random order before selecting them destroys any prior patterns and encourages more creative and original thought when reorganizing them in step 7.

6. Determine where to place the problem description card(s) from step 3 in the organization area. This should give sufficient space for the other cards to be placed in step 7.

    Thus, if there is one problem and many apparent interrelationships between item cards, place the problem card centrally. If it looks like there are long chains of relationships, with some being remotely connected with the problem, put the problem card on the right. If there are multiple problems with many shared item cards, space the problem cards out around the edge of the area.

The organization area needs to be large enough to easily contain all cards, spaced out sufficiently to draw in arrows between them (in step 9).

7. Select a card in the organization area and look for a card in the parking area which answers the question identified in step 2. For a cause-effect Relations Diagram this will be a card which is a direct cause of a problem card.

    Move this to the organization area, as in Fig. 33.6, placing it near the appropriate problem card, leaving space to draw an arrow between the two cards (do not draw any arrows now, as cards may be moved). This may require some discussion, but avoid lengthy argument as this may make the session overly long.

    Repeat this step, selecting and placing cards near the problem cards, until all cards with a direct relationship have been moved.

8. For each card laid in step 7, repeat the process of searching for cards in the parking area that are directly related to it, then placing this new card nearby. When placing cards, also look for links to or from other cards in the organization area and position the card accordingly.

    You may have to pause occasionally to move cards on the organization area, to make space for new cards or show newly discovered relationships. In these cases, be careful to preserve the relative positioning of cards.

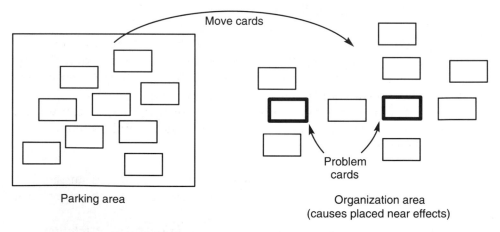

Fig. 33.6 Laying out Relations Diagram

During this process, additional new cards may be written as new relationships are noticed.

9. Review the layout with the team and use the question from step 2 to help draw arrows between cards on the diagram as relationships are agreed. Draw the arrows going from causes to effects, as in Fig. 33.7. Avoid confusion where lines cross by using a 'hump-back' bridge.

   Beware of adding arrows for weak relationships, as this can result in the important link being hidden in a mass of arrows. If in doubt, draw in the main links first, and only add lesser links as long as the diagram remains intelligible. Also avoid two-way arrows; where the relationship is bidirectional, place the arrowhead to show the most significant direction.

10. Identify and mark key items that are to be addressed further, such as with shading or emboldening. For example, when using a cause-effect Relations Diagram, actions might include:
    - Addressing cause cards with most arrows entering and leaving them may be an easy way to have significant effect.
    - Addressing causes with arrows leaving them may contribute to resolving a number of subsequent causes.
    - Addressing causes that have multiple arrows entering them may unblock bottlenecks.
    - Addressing causes that have no arrows entering them may fix root causes.

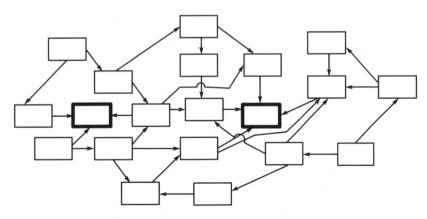

Fig. 33.7 Adding arrows to Relations Diagram

11. Treat this diagram as a first draft. Check that assumed causes are actual causes. Review it for other changes, marking up changes on the copies.

    If the diagram may be read by people who do not understand the symbols, add a key.

12. Review the marked changes, update the document accordingly and repeat the review as necessary. Plan and implement concrete actions to address key items.

Practical variations

- Use adhesive memo notes instead of cards. These stay where they are put, and can be used to sort the notes vertically, on a whiteboard or flipchart. Their disadvantage is that they are not as durable as card.
- If cards are used, stop them from moving by attaching them to the organization area, either with reusable adhesive pads or by using a pinboard.
- Instead of using cards, draw the diagram directly. This can result in a less tidy first diagram, particularly in a complex, uncertain situation, but requires less resource. It can be helped by first writing the causes as a list, then crossing them off as they are added to the diagram.
- Display a list of items that may help the team to identify causes. These may be taken from (and even displayed as) the Cause-Effect Diagram. For example, manpower, machines, methods, materials, (the '4 Ms') money, management, plans, customers. These may be broken down further into specific items, such as individual roles, machines, etc.
- Indicate differing confidence cards in relationships. For example, where there is a mixture of measured, unmeasured and speculative relationships, show the difference by circling those which are measured and underlining those which are unmeasured.
- Start with a *desired* effect, and determine what must be done to cause it by asking the question: 'What must be done to make this happen?'.
- Use the diagram to determine what *may* be caused by a planned action, using the question: 'What could happen as a result of this?'
- Use different shaped boxes to indicate different items, as in Fig. 33.8.
- Show groups of related items by putting dotted lines around them.
- Include items, other than problems and causes, which affect the problem, such as documents.
- Use it to show the relationships between *any* items. For example, the boxes may be people, and the arrows indicate where one person influences

another's decisions.

- Use it to show relations between items within a process, as in Fig. 33.8. This is an informal way of mapping processes which is often called a *Block Diagram*. The question may thus be: 'What happens next?'.

A typical use is for understanding the top level of a process. Each process in this diagram may then be detailed further ('zoomed into' or 'exploded') in subsequent diagrams. Typically these will be more Block Diagrams or Flowcharts.

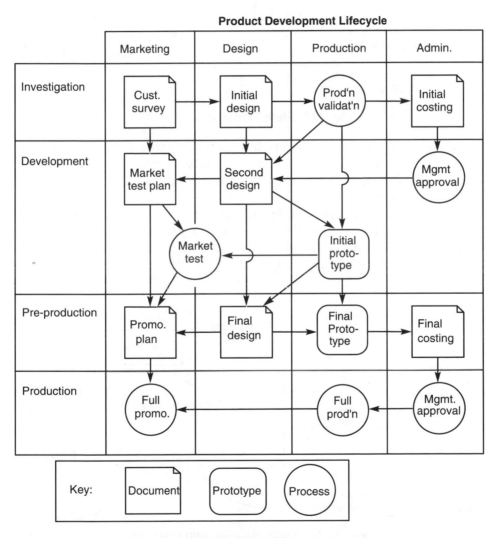

Fig. 33.8 Block Diagram

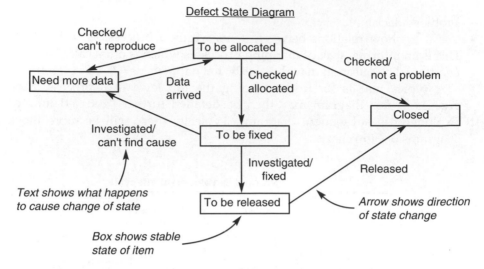

Fig. 33.9 State Transition Diagram

- A *State Transition Diagram* (or *Finite State Diagram*) is used to describe a type of process where an item passes between a number of stable 'states', as in Fig. 33.9. It is useful for describing specific parts of processes which take this form.

  The relationship between items is in terms of the stimulus that causes the change in state and the action that is taken after the stimulus is recognized, in order to complete the state change.

- An *Entity-Relationship Diagram* shows the relationship between individual items, including the *cardinality* of each relationship (i.e. how many of each item may exist), as in Fig. 33.10.

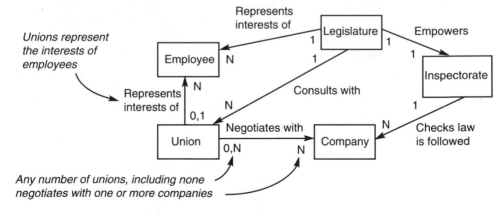

Fig. 33.10 Entity-Relationship Diagram

- A *Mind Map* or *Spider Diagram* (as in Fig. 33.11) is an informal diagram which can be used in individual thinking or Brainstorming to help build and relate individual items. This starts with the main problem in the middle of the page, and has related items spread around it and connected with lines and arrows.

  There are few formal rules, as the objective is to assist in thinking, and it may be adapted to suit the individual, for example by using annotations, doodles, shapes and colour to express elements of the problem and emboldening, dotting or drawing wavy arrows to indicate the certainty of links.

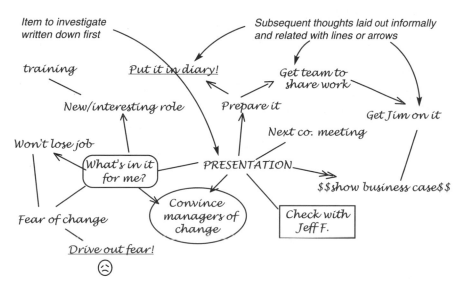

Fig. 33.11 Mind Map

Notes

The Relations Diagram is one of the second seven tools. It is also known as an *Interrelationship Digraph*.

See also

Chapters: Use Brainstorming, Nominal Group Technique or Surveys to identify individual items. The Activity Network also uses a network. Processes may also be described with the Activity

Network, Flowchart, Flow Process Chart, Gantt Chart, IDEF0 and String Diagram. The Cause-Effect Diagram is a more common way of finding possible problem causes, but assumes a tree structure.

References: [Mizuno 88] has a chapter on it, showing many variations on its use. [Brassard 89], [Asaka 90] and [Gitlow 90] give details of its use. [Oakland 93] briefly describes it in relation to the other second seven tools. [Buzan 89] describes Mind Maps. [Martin 85] describes the State Transition Diagram and Entity Relationship Diagram.

34 Scatter Diagram

What it's for

To show the type and degree of any causal relationship between two factors.

When to use it

- Use it when it is suspected that the variation of two items is connected in some way, to show any actual correlation between the two.
- Use it when it is suspected that one item may be causing another, to build evidence for the connection between the two.
- Use it only when both items being measured can be measured together, in pairs.

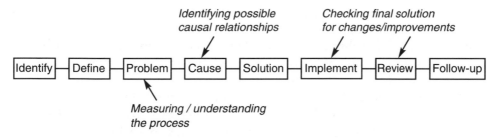

Fig. 34.1 Possible uses in improvement project framework

How to understand it

When investigating problems, typically when searching for their causes, it may be suspected that two items are related in some way. For example, it may be suspected that the number of accidents at work is related to the amount of overtime that people are working.

The Scatter Diagram helps to identify the existence of a measurable relationship between two such items by measuring them in pairs and plotting them on a graph, as in Fig. 34.2. This visually shows the *correlation* between the two sets of measurements.

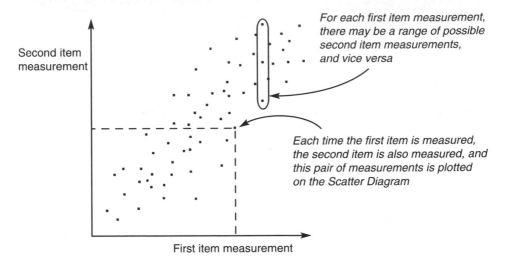

Fig. 34.2 Scatter Diagram

If the points plotted on the Scatter Diagram are randomly scattered, with no discernible pattern, then this indicates that the two sets of measurements have no correlation and cannot be said to be related in any way. If, however, the points form a pattern of some kind, then this shows the type of relationship between the two measurement sets.

A Scatter Diagram shows correlation between two items for three reasons:
(a) There is a cause and effect relationship between the two measured items, where one is causing the other (at least in part).
(b) The two measured items are both caused by a third item. For example, a Scatter Diagram which shows a correlation between cracks and transparency of glass utensils because changes in both are caused by changes in furnace temperature.
(c) Complete coincidence. It is possible to find high correlation of unrelated items, such as the number of ants crossing a path and newspaper sales.

Scatter Diagrams may thus be used to give evidence for a cause and effect relationship, but they alone do not prove it. Usually, it also requires a good understanding of the system being measured, and may required additional experiments. 'Cause' and 'effect' are thus quoted in this chapter to indicate that although they may be suspected of having this relationship, it is not certain.

When evaluating a Scatter Diagram, both the *degree* and *type* of correlation should be considered. The visible differences in Scatter Diagrams for these are shown in Tables 34.1 and 34.2.

Where there is a cause-effect relationship, the degree of scatter in the diagram may be affected by several factors (as illustrated in Fig. 34.3):

- The *proximity* of the cause and effect. There is better chance of a high correlation if the cause is directly connected to the effect than if it is at the end of a chain of causes. Thus a root cause may not have a clear relationship with the end effect.
- *Multiple causes* of the effect. When measuring one cause, other causes are making the effect vary in an unrelated way. Other causes may also be having a greater effect, swamping the actual effect of the cause in question.
- Natural *variation* in the system. The effect may not react in the same way each time, even to a close major cause.

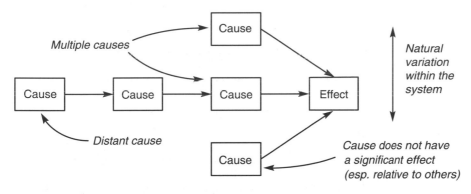

Fig 34.3 Reasons for low correlation of cause and effect

There is no one clear degree of correlation above which a clear relationship can be said to exist. Instead, as the degree of correlation increases, the probability of that relationship also increases.

If there is sufficient correlation, then the shape of the Scatter Diagram will indicate the type of correlation (see Table 34.2). The most common shape is a straight line, either sloping up (*positive correlation*) or sloping down (*negative correlation*).

Table 34.1 Degrees of correlation

Scatter Diagram	Degree of correlation	Interpretation
	None	No relationship can be seen. The 'effect' is not related to the 'cause' in any way.
	Low	A vague relationship is seen. The 'cause' *may* affect the 'effect', but only distantly. There are either more immediate causes to be found or there is significant variation in the 'effect'.
	High	The points are grouped into a clear linear shape. It is probable that the 'cause' is directly related to the 'effect'. Hence, any change in 'cause' will result in a reasonably predictable change in 'effect'.
	Perfect	All points lie on a line (which is usually straight). Given any 'cause' value, the corresponding 'effect' value can be predicted with complete certainty.

Table 34.2 Types of correlation

Scatter Diagram	Type of correlation	Interpretation
	Positive	Straight line, sloping up from left to right. Increasing the value of the 'cause' results in a proportionate increase in the value of the 'effect'.
	Negative	Straight line, sloping down from left to right. Increasing the value of the 'cause' results in a proportionate decrease in the value of the 'effect'.
	Curved	Various curves, typically U- or S-shaped. Changing the value of the 'cause' results in the 'effect' changing differently, depending on the position on the curve.
	Part-linear	Part of the diagram is a straight line (sloping up or down). May be due to breakdown or overload of 'effect', or is a curve with a part that approximates to a straight line (which may be treated as such).

Points which appear well outside a visible trend region may be due to special causes of variation, and should be investigated as such.

In addition to visual interpretation, several calculations may be made around Scatter Diagrams. The calculations covered here are for linear correlation; curves require a level of mathematics that is beyond the scope of this book.

- The *correlation coefficient* gives a numerical value to the degree of correlation. This will vary from -1, which indicates perfect negative correlation, through 0, which indicates no correlation at all, to +1, which indicates perfect positive correlation. Thus the closer the value is to plus or minus 1, the better the correlation. In a perfect correlation, all points lie on a straight line.
- A *regression line* forms the 'best fit' or 'average' of the plotted points. It is equivalent to the mean of a distribution (see Chapter 5).
- The *standard error* is equivalent to the standard deviation of a distribution (see Chapter 5) in the way that it indicates the spread of possible 'effect' values for any one 'cause' value.

Calculated figures are useful for putting a numerical value on improvements, with 'before' and 'after' values. They may also be used to estimate the range of likely 'effect' values from given 'cause' values (assuming a causal relationship is proven). Fig. 34.4 shows how the regression line and the standard error can be used to estimate possible 'effect' values from a given single 'cause' value.

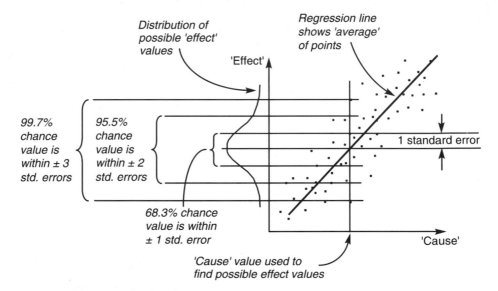

Fig 34.4 Regression line and standard error

Example

A town planning team, during an investigation of road accidents, identified a number of possible causes. Three main causes were suspected: the speed of the vehicles, the traffic density and the local weather conditions. As there was no clear evidence available to support any of these hypotheses, they decided to measure them, and used Scatter Diagrams to check whether the link between any of the causes was strong enough to take further action.

In order to get sufficient measures, they made daily measures for two months, using local road sensors and reports from the ambulance service. Scatter Diagrams were drawn for each possible cause against the accident count. The results enabled the following conclusion to be made:

- There was a low, positive correlation with traffic density.
- There was an inconclusive correlation with road conditions.
- There was a high, positive correlation with traffic speed, with accidents dropping off more sharply under 30 mph.

As a consequence, more traffic speed control measures were installed, including signs and surfaces. This resulted in a measurable decrease in accidents.

Other examples

- A baker suspects that the standing time of the dough is affecting the way it rises. A Scatter Diagram of rise time against measured bread density shows a fair correlation on an inverse U-shaped distribution. He thus uses the time at the highest point on the curve to get the best chance of well-risen bread.
- It is suspected that press temperature is causing rejects in a plastic forming process. A Scatter Diagram shows a high positive correlation, prompting a redesign of the press, including the use of more heat-resistant materials. This results in a significant reduction in the number of rejected pieces.
- A personnel department plots salary against the results of a motivation survey. The result is a weak negative correlation. A second Scatter Diagram, plotting time in company against motivation, gives a higher correlation. A motivation program is targeted accordingly and results in a steady increase in the score given to motivation in the company's next personnel survey.

Road condition index	Average speed (mph)	Traffic density (veh/min)	Accidents in day
1	28.4	13.4	11
1	37.6	4.3	13
0	39.4	14.3	17
7	19.6	4.4	3
1	31.0	6.8	13
5	16.2	6.1	4

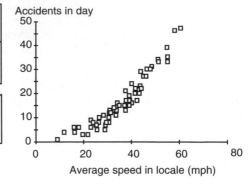

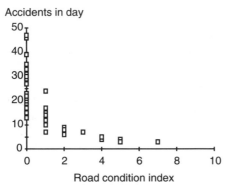

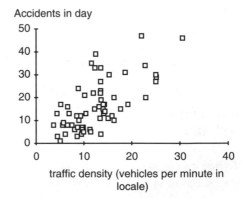

Fig. 34.5 Example

How to do it

1. Determine the two items that you wish to compare. One may be identified as the suspected cause and the other as the suspected effect. This may come from the use of other tools, such as a Cause-Effect Diagram or Relations Diagram.

2. Identify the measurements to be taken. Both must be variables (i.e. measurable on a continuous scale) and it must be possible to measure both at the same time.

   Make the measurements as specific as possible in order to reduce variation and increase the chance of a higher correlation. For example, measurements from a single supplier's materials may be better than measuring all supplied materials.

3. Make 50 to 100 pairs of measurements. When doing this, aim to keep all other variables as steady as possible, as they could interfere with the final figures.

   Be *very* careful when measuring human behaviour, as the very act of measurement can cause the measured people to change their behaviour, especially if they suspect they may lose out in some way.

4. Plot the measured pairs on the Scatter Diagram. Design the axes and scales on the diagram to give the maximum visual spread of points. This may involve using different scales and making the axes cross at non-zero values (as in Fig. 34.6).

   If investigating a possible cause-effect relationship, plot the suspected cause on the x-axis (horizontal) and the suspected effect on the y-axis (vertical).

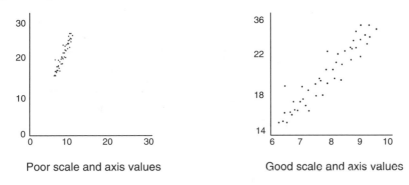

Poor scale and axis values   Good scale and axis values

Fig 34.6 Different axis scale and crossing point

5. If the correlation is high, a regression ('average') line may be drawn through the plotted points, to emphasize the trend. This may be calculated as in Fig. 34.7 or estimated by eye (this should be made clear to any future readers of the diagram).

6. If the correlation is reasonably linear, then a correlation coefficient may be calculated, as in Fig. 34.7.

7. Interpret the diagram and act accordingly. This may be to identify improvements or to enable estimation of future effect values. If it is the latter, the standard error may be calculated, as in Fig. 34.7.

   When using a Scatter Diagram to estimate future effect values, only estimate within the known range of correlation, as the shape may change outside that range.

Calculations with Scatter Diagrams

The correlation coeffficient, the standard error and the equation of the regression line can all be easily calculated from five basic elements.

1. Calculate basic elements from cause and effect numbers

Pairs of measured values

Measure number	x	y	xy	x^2	y^2
1	2	3	6	4	9
2	0	1	0	0	1
3	12	12	144	144	144

60	7	8	56	49	64
(61)	4	5	20	16	25
Totals:	(192)	(232)	(1126)	(1170)	(1334)

n $\sum x$ $\sum y$ $\sum xy$ $\sum x^2$ $\sum y^2$

2. Calculate interim values from basic elements

The interim values are three numbers that will be used in the final calculation:

$$a = \frac{n\sum xy - \sum x \sum y}{n\sum x^2 - (\sum x)^2} = \frac{61 \times 1126 - 192 \times 232}{61 \times 1170 - 192^2} = 0.70$$

$$b = \frac{n\sum xy - \sum x \sum y}{n\sum y^2 - (\sum y)^2} = \frac{61 \times 1126 - 192 \times 232}{61 \times 1134 - 232^2} = 0.88$$

$$c = \frac{\sum y - a\sum x}{n} = \frac{232 - 0.70 \times 192}{61} = 1.60$$

(Continued...)

Fig. 34.7 Calculations with Scatter Diagrams

Calculations with Scatter Diagrams (continued)

3. Calculate required items

Correlation coefficient, r

$$r = \sqrt{a\,b} = \sqrt{0.70 \times 0.88} = 0.78 \text{ (positive correlation)}$$

If a and b are both positive, then the correlation is positive, otherwise it is negative.

Standard error, s

$$s = \sqrt{\frac{\sum y^2 - \sum cy - a\sum xy}{n}} = \sqrt{\frac{1334 - 1.60 \times 232 - 0.70 \times 1126}{61}}$$

$$= 1.69$$

Regression line

Regression line has equation: $y = ax + c = 0.70\,x + 1.60$

Only draw line between lowest and highest points in linear range.

	Cause, x	Effect, $y = 0.70\,x + 1.60$
Lowest value	1	0.70 x 1 + 1.60 = 2.30
Highest value	10	0.70 x 10 + 1.60 = 8.60

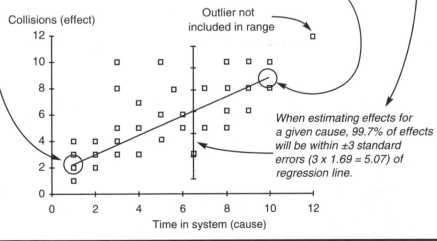

Collisions (effect)

Outlier not included in range

When estimating effects for a given cause, 99.7% of effects will be within ±3 standard errors (3 x 1.69 = 5.07) of regression line.

Time in system (cause)

Fig. 34.8 Calculations with Scatter Diagrams (continued)

Practical variations

- If points on the Scatter Diagram coincide with other points, the fact that one point is actually two or more may be highlighted by emboldening them or by using concentric circles.
- If measurements are difficult to obtain, as few as 30 measurement pairs can be used.
- Use a *Correlation Table* when multiple coincidental points are measured, typically when there are a limited number of possible positions. This is effectively a cross between a Scatter Diagram and a Check Sheet, where each x-y position is represented by a box in which multiple points can be indicated.

	Totals	24	18	16	17	14	16	105
	> 3	/			//	//	///	8
	2.5 - 3	//	/	//	///	///	////	15
Time to serve	2 - 2.4	₶ ////	///	////	₶ //	₶	///	31
one customer	1.5 - 1.9	////	₶ //	₶ /	///	//	///	25
(min)	1 - 1.4	////	///	///	//	/	//	15
	0.5 - 0.9	///	//	/		/	/	8
	0 - 0.4	/	//					3
		1 - 3	4 - 6	7 - 9	10 - 12	13 - 15	>15	Totals
				Customers in checkout queue				

Fig 34.9 Correlation Table

- Separate measurement sets may be shown on the same Scatter Diagram, which may be distinguished from one another by using different shaped markers for each set of points. A typical use is where one variable is being changed, for example to show measurements of material from several different suppliers.
- Where non-linear correlation appears, rough estimates may be made using them by dividing them into approximately linear sections and calculating the regression line and standard error as above.

Notes

Scatter Diagrams are one of the first seven tools. Computer spreadsheets are a useful tool for plotting them. Scatter Diagrams are also known as *Scattergrams* or *Scatterplots.*

See also

Chapters: Other tools for measuring Variation include the Control Chart, Histogram, Process Capability and Design of Experiments. It can be used after a Cause-Effect Diagram or Relations Diagram, to help verify possible key causes. The Scatter Diagram has similarities to the Matrix Data Analysis Chart.

References: [Ishikawa 76] and [Asaka 90] each have a chapter on Scatter Diagrams. Other books discuss them in varying detail, including [Oakland 90], [Sinha 85] and [Wadsworth 86]. The calculations are covered in detail in statistical texts, including [Hamburg 70].

35 String Diagram

What it's for

To investigate the physical movement in a process.

When to use it

- Use it when analyzing a manual or physical process that involves significant physical movement, in order to make movements easier and quicker. Movements may be of people, materials or machines.
- Use it when designing the layout of a work area, to identify the optimum positioning of machines and furniture.

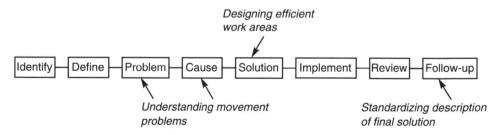

Fig. 35.1 Possible uses in improvement project framework

How to understand it

The placement of equipment and furniture in work areas is often done randomly and sequentially, rather than with any sense of what positioning will make the work easier. The result is that subsequent work requires much more moving about than is necessary. A part of the problem is that when designing a work area, it can be difficult to 'see' what movement will be necessary.

The String Diagram is a simple tool for analyzing and designing work spaces such that movement can be minimized. The basic diagram simply consists of a map of the work area, with the actual movements drawn on top, as in Fig. 35.2.

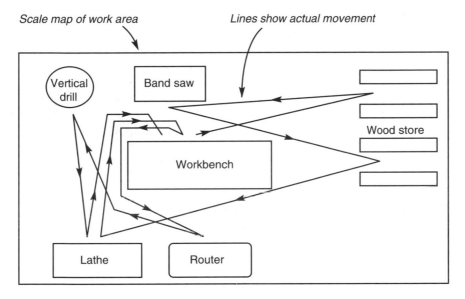

Fig. 35.2 String Diagram

It is common to also indicate type of actions being done at each point. This is typically done using the same symbol set that is used in the Flow Process Chart.

When analyzing the diagram, both the positioning of equipment and the sequencing and detail of actions may be considered. A simple revision of the process may enable the distance moved to be significantly reduced (this may well be preferable to moving heavy equipment around).

Example

A metal worker became fed up with walking what seemed to be half-way around the machine room just to build a metal box. With help from the works facilitator, he measured the distance he traveled to build one box, using a pinboard and scale map of his workshop area, as in Fig. 35.3. Using this, he simply moved the machines into a U-shape. the result was an easier and faster process, which also used less floor space.

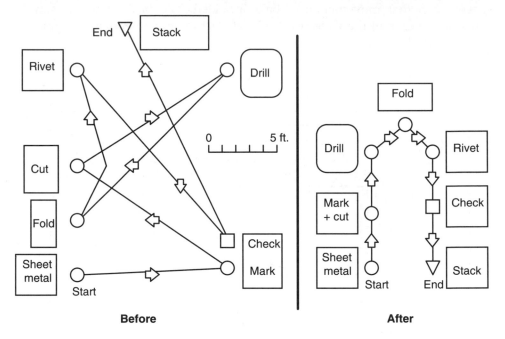

Fig. 35.3 Example

Other examples

- A self-service restaurant team measures the route taken by customers around the food counters and also identifies the most popular meals that they are building. They rearrange the counters and food to enable a logical progression for the most common meals. They also include complementary and high-margin food in this line, which helps to increase the profitability of the restaurant.

- A traffic planning department uses a helicopter to spot the routes taken by a sample of vehicles passing through the town, plotting the lines on a street map. Common destinations and routes are now easily identified (along with short-cuts taken through residential areas). As a result, some roads are widened, others are blocked and signs erected. The result is a much smoother traffic flow.
- A maintenance team measures the route taken by engineers making routine checks on key equipment throughout the plant, plotting it on a site plan. They are then able to plot a much shorter route to each of the same machines.

How to do it

1. Identify the process to be analyzed. This will be one which involves a significant amount of movement by people, materials or both.

2. Produce a scale map of the work area, not including machines, but including items that cannot easily be moved, such as power points, air lines, etc. This may be available from the site office.

3. Add all machines, furniture and other equipment to the diagram. If possible, do this in a way that will allow these to be moved, for example by using shaped pieces of card that can be pinned to the work area map from step 2.

4. Identify the points in the process where actions take place and mark the positions of these on the map with map pins.

   Where there are different action types, these can be differentiated by marking or pinning down paper action symbols (typically the same as those used in the Flow Process Chart).

5. Tie the end of a piece of string to the pin where the process starts, and then wrap it around each pin in turn, following the movement around the process, as in Fig. 35.4. Tie the string off at the last position (which may be the start point, if the person returns there).

6. Mark the string at the start and finish points, using a pen. Remove the string and measure between the penmarks, using the map scale. This will give the total distance travelled during the process.

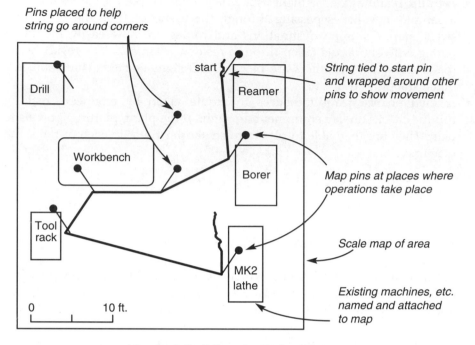

Fig. 35.4 Building the String Diagram

7. Rearrange the movable items on the map, aiming to reduce the total distance as measured in step 6. It may be appropriate to change what is done during the process at the same time. For example, some operations may be combined or eliminated. Strategies for deciding layouts include:
   - *Mobility.* Rearrange items and movements around fixed or immovable items, such as heavy machines.
   - *Function.* Put machines or people together that perform the same function. This is useful when varying loads may be shared between machines.
   - *Product.* Put machines or people together that make the same product. This works well when each machine is used for only one product.

8. Repeat steps 4 to 6, to get a new total distance travelled. Using the same piece of string will make it easy to see how much shorter this is.

9. Check that it is feasible to move equipment as planned in step 7, then do so. Measure the final process in practice to check that improvements are as expected.

Practical variations

- Do a Flow Process Chart first, then follow up with a String Diagram. This helps clarify the actions in the process, making the String Diagram easier to complete. It also results in a more complete analysis.
- Draw the map and 'string' on a single sheet of paper. This requires less resources, and gives a result that can be easily copied, although it is less flexible for redesigning.
- Do multiple plots on the same diagram, for example where one person does the same process in a different way, or where multiple people or items are involved.
- Use coloured pins to indicate different action types or different plots done on the same map.
- Use coloured string to show different plots.
- If it is significant, add the time taken for each movement.
- Annotate the diagram with pertinent notes to help interpretation, for example by giving notes on what is being done at each point, and why.
- A *Topological Movement Chart* represents locations as small circles and movement as lines between them. The distance is written next to each line, as in Fig. 35.5. This is particularly useful for movement between remote sites, such as travel between buildings or towns.

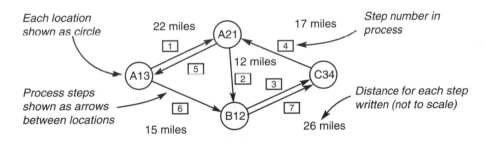

Fig. 35.5 Topological Movement Chart

- A *Travel Chart* is useful where there are multiple (and possibly irregular) movement between places. It is a variation on the Check Sheet, indicating movements from and to any combination of a given set of locations, as in Fig. 35.6.

Count of occurrence / Distance between places

Visits in 1 week

To

		Accounts	Goods in	Stores	Production	Total Visits	Total Distance
From	Accounts		III 112	II 120	ℍℍ III 90	13	1296
	Goods In	ℍℍ 112		15	IIII 18	9	632
	Stores	I 120	II 15		12	3	150
	Production	II 90	III 18	ℍℍ II 12		12	318
Total	Visits	8	8	9	12	37	
	Distance	860	420	324	792		2396

Fig. 35.6 Travel Chart

Notes

The String Diagram originated in the field of Work Study.

See also

Chapters: Processes may also be described with the Activity Network, Flowchart, Flow Process Chart, Gantt Chart, IDEF0 and Relations Diagram. The Travel Chart described above is a variation of the Check Sheet.

References: String Diagrams are well described in older books on Work Study, such as [Raybould 71] and [ILO 79], although they are often also mentioned in more modern books such as [Sinha 85] and [Oakland 93].

36 Surveys

What it's for

To gather information from people.

When to use it

- Use it when information that is required is held by an identifiable and dispersed group of people.
- Use it to help decision-making, by turning disparate qualitative data into useful quantitative information.
- Use it only when the time and effort are available to complete the survey.
- Use it, rather than Brainstorming or Nominal Group Technique to gather *real* data about what a diverse group of people think (rather than an opinion of what they think).

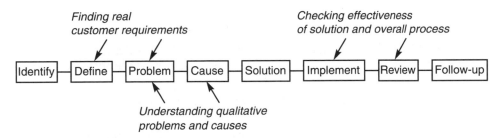

Fig. 36.1 Possible uses in improvement project framework

How to understand it

In many situations, information required about a problem is held by a broad group of people, such as female customers or company engineers. Simply asking them about the problem without any thought of how their replies will be used is likely to lead to wrong conclusions and bad decisions. Good decisions require careful data collection and analysis.

'Surveys' is a general term for a number of methods of collecting data from people, which includes questioning them individually and collectively, in person, over the telephone or on paper. The decision of what type of survey to use is driven by such factors as the accessibility of the people and the response required. For example, in-depth personal interviews can give much useful information, but may be impractical when there are many people to ask.

There are two main approaches to surveys, *interviews* and *questionnaires*, as contrasted in Table 36.1. Interviews involve one or more interviewers asking questions of one or more respondents, whilst a questionnaire contains written questions and answers. The most noticeable difference is that with a questionnaire, the person asking the questions and the respondent answering them may never meet.

Table 36.1 Interviews vs. Questionnaires

Interviews	Questionnaires
Two-way. Can ensure interviewee understands questions and vice versa.	One-way. Comments cannot be queried.
Flexible. Can be changed on the fly to follow interesting information.	Fixed. Questions cannot be changed.
Interviewer does the writing, as well as questioning.	Respondent does the writing.
May gather a large amount of information in one interview.	Gathers limited information.
Best for open, in-depth questions, exploring ideas and feelings.	Best for closed, structured questions, checking facts and opinions.
Personal. Can be awkward when asking sensitive questions.	Impersonal. Replies may be anonymous.
Can only be used with limited number of respondents.	Can be used with many respondents.
Predictable number of respondents.	Unpredictable number of respondents - can often be lower than expected.
Tends to give qualitative data. Can be difficult to analyze.	Mostly quantitative data. Ease of analysis depends on questionnaire design.

A problem with asking people questions is that not only will different people answer differently, but changes in the wording, sequence and environment of questions are likely to result in different responses from the same person. The design of a questionnaire and the execution of an interview must therefore be done with great care.

The two main types of questions that can be asked in surveys, *closed* questions and *open* questions are contrasted in Table 36.2.

Where there is a large population to question, it is often impractical to survey everyone and care must be taken to select a random sample. As with other tools that use sampling, a non-random selection can give biased results.

The opinion that people hold is often heavily influenced by their professional or social peer group. If the results of a survey of a wide group are just summed or averaged, then these differences may be lost. It is thus important to recognize and differentiate between clustering of results, either by questions asked in the survey, or, if different questions need to be asked, by separately surveying recognized groups.

Surveys often require a significant amount of effort in preparation, execution and analysis. However, this is often the best method of acquiring the information needed to make reliable decisions.

Table 36.2 Closed and Open questions

Closed questions	Open questions
Narrow focus, aiming to find specific detail.	Broad focus, aiming to explore general area.
Start with: Which, What, Where, When, How many, How much.	Start with: Why, How, Tell me about.
Short reply, often one word (e.g. yes, no, ten, screws).	Long reply, often of uncertain length.
Limited set of possible replies, often given in multiple-choice questions.	Wide variety of possible replies.
Good for quantitative (numeric) data for use in Pareto Charts, etc.	Good for qualitative data, for general understanding.
Control is with person asking questions.	Control is with person being questioned.
Can miss important points. Can be leading question.	Can drift off the point. Can be insensitive.
Can be used to 'set the scene' for open question.	Can be used to capture points missed with closed question.

| Particularly useful in questionnaires. | Particularly useful in interviews. |

Example

The doctors' committee in a medical practice wanted to improve their rapport with patients. They considered asking them directly, but concluded that many patients would be too shy to criticize to their face someone they viewed as an authority figure. Consequently, they decided to use an anonymous questionnaire, which patients would be asked to complete when their treatment was finished.

They identified the main focus areas as patient-doctor interaction during both diagnosis and treatment, and designed the questionnaire accordingly. The questionnaire was then piloted with a sample of patients, reviewed and revised. One of the changes was to keep the average completion time down to two minutes. A part of the final questionnaire is shown in Fig. 36.2.

The scheme was then introduced for the planned two-month period, with all patients asked to complete the questionnaire after each treatment. A quiet part of the waiting room was set aside for the purpose, with a table, pencils and post-box for the completed questionnaires.

An early effect of the survey was the definition of an interactive diagnosis process, including specific discussions with the patients about their feelings towards the illness. A surprise result of the improvements was an increase in the success rate of treatments.

Pettingdon Practice Doctor-Patient Survey

Thank you for taking part in this survey. At Pettingdon Practice, we want to give the best care to all of our patients and thus need you to tell us how well we are doing.

Please tick one box in each of the questions below, and add any further comments in the space provided, then and put the completed paper in the box on the wall.

Thank you for your time and consideration,

The doctors and staff of Pettingdon Practice

---

1. When you saw the doctor, how easy did you find it to discuss your problem or illness?

   [ ] Very easy   [ ] Quite easy   [ ] Quite difficult   [ ] Very difficult

2. When the doctor examined you, did he/she discuss any related previous problems?

   [ ] Yes   [ ] No   [ ] No related previous problems

   If your answer was 'No', did you feel able to remind him/her about this?

Fig. 36.2 Example

Other examples

- A restaurant manager surveys staff and customers, aiming to improve customer satisfaction. He find a strong correlation between satisfied customers and happy staff, and so initiates a motivation scheme which results in a happier restaurant, and increased business.
- Members of a press team in a shoe manufacturer are uncertain about the effectiveness of an idea they have for a new steam press. They conduct tandem interviews with machine suppliers and with specialists within their own company, to determine the technical feasibility of implementing the idea. As a result, they abandon an idea which otherwise could have taken much effort in developing for no eventual results.
- After suggestions by a local newspaper that parents are dissatisfied with a school, the headmaster organizes a telephone survey of a random sample of 100 parents. He finds that there is no strong dissatisfaction with the academic standard, but there is a significant feeling that there is insufficient communication between the staff and parents. He gets this result published in the following week's paper and organizes a parent-teacher team to improve communication.

How to do it

1. Identify the objective of the survey. For example, 'To gain ideas for a new machine shop layout'. This can be helped by determining what decisions or actions might occur as result of the survey. It can also be useful for identifying non-objectives, such as 'Not to select machines'. Also ensure objectives are not ambiguous. For example, if investigating employee satisfaction, be clear about the meaning of both 'employee' (All employees? Including managers?) and 'satisfaction' (What does it mean? What does it not mean?).

2. Identify the target group of people to be surveyed. This will be one or more groups of people who have information or opinions which will contribute to achieving the survey objective. Note that sometimes it is polite or politic to survey people who will not directly contribute.

3. Select the type of survey to use. This will be an interview or questionnaire, as compared in Table 36.1.

   When using an interview, consider the strategy that might be used. This may include one or several of the following approaches:
   - A *structured interview* follows a strictly defined format, aiming to answer a predefined question set. It may be little more than an assisted questionnaire.

- In an *informal interview*, there will still be predefined questions, but these are used only as a guide for the interviewer, who may decide whether or not to use them. This approach is more flexible, but is more difficult to handle as it is easier to become side-tracked.
- A *telephone survey* enables the interviewing of people who are geographically remote, such as customers or suppliers. It is usually fairly short and therefore needs a more structured format to capture the requisite information.
- A *tandem interview* uses two interviewers, typically with one person questioning and the other recording. This can make interviews quicker and capture more useful information.
- A *group interview* or *focus group* involves multiple interviewees. It is useful for gaining group consensus and using synergy to create new ideas, but may need careful control as it can degenerate into a free-for-all.

4. Plan the detail of the survey, and ensure that sufficient resources and people are available to perform it. This includes designing and distributing questionnaires, conducting interviews and collating and analyzing results.

   Be aware of the time that will be required. For example, a phone survey may require two to three weeks, whilst a mail survey is likely to take at least two months before all responses are returned and collated.

   Where appropriate, get permission to conduct the survey, indicating the expected start time and duration required. Also find out if the people have been recently surveyed on other topics as an otherwise helpful person could turn out to be irritated by 'yet more questions'.

5. Select the questions that are to be asked. This is particularly important for a questionnaire, as the questions cannot be interactively explained.

   Use the objectives from step 1 to identify the key questions that must be answered, then design actual questions that will elicit useful responses. This may require several questions to get a complete answer. In an interview this can be done by starting with an open question, then following up with probing questions to capture requisite detail. The reverse is applicable to a questionnaire, which may start with several closed questions and follow up with an open question that captures other points the respondent may wish to make.

   For example, if aiming to determine the effectiveness of a suggestion scheme, an interviewer may start with, 'What do you think of the new suggestion scheme?' and then follow up responses with such as, 'Why do you believe that?' and, 'What feedback did you get to your suggestion?'. By contrast, a questionnaire might start with several closed questions, such as, 'How many suggestions have you made during the last six months?'. and close with, 'Do you have any further comments you would like to make about the suggestion scheme''. Open and closed questions are contrasted in Table 36.2.

Ensure interviewees know about a subject before questioning more deeply. Thus in the previous paragraph, you might start with, 'Did you attend the presentation on the new suggestion scheme?'.

Be careful with sensitive questions. One way of handling this is to depersonalize the question, for example, 'Do you think the evaluation process is fair?'.

Questions may be identified and organized by using tools such as Brainstorming and the Affinity Diagram. It can be useful to put the final question set into a Tree Diagram to help check that a complete and coherent question set has been found. Make use of available expertise in the question topic during design and review of the question set.

Multiple-choice questions are particularly useful in questionnaires, as they are quick and easy to answer and give specific data that is easy to analyze. Types of multiple choice questions are illustrated in Fig. 36.3.

Avoid any questions which are either likely to give false information or which may upset or annoy the interviewee. These include:

- Ambiguous questions that may be interpreted differently by different people. The vagueness of many words makes this an easy trap into which many fall. For example, 'Are you often satisfied?' ('often' and 'satisfied' are ambiguous, and thus require more definition). Slang and jargon words are another way to confuse.
- Asking for details that people are unlikely to know or which may have been forgotten. 'Which brand of cereal did you eat this time last year?'.
- Complex or negative questions, such as, 'If these people are not found guilty, should they be prevented from visiting people who do not want to see them?'.
- Leading or coercing questions, such as, 'We find most people like it. You do like it don't you?'. Question sequencing can also lead, for example where two questions about the benefits of a particular product are followed by a query about 'Your preferred product'.
- Multiple questions, such as, "Which do you like, how, when and why do you like it, and how did you come to this opinion?'
- Discrimination or antagonism. 'Aha, so you're the little woman. You probably won't understand this question ... '.
- Emotionally charged words, such as 'stealing' or 'redundancy'.

Multiple Choice Questions

A. *Selection* questions, where a single selection must be chosen:

```
Have you ever written an article for the company magazine?
[ ] Yes
[ ] No
```

B. *Inventory* or *checklist* questions, where multiple items may be ticked:

```
Which type of computer applications do you regularly use?
(please tick all that apply)

[ ] Wordprocessor
[ ] Spreadsheet
[ ] Presentation graphics
[ ] Electronic Mail
[ ] Others  . . . . . . . . . . . . . . . . . . . . . . . .
           . . . . . . . . . . . . . . . . . . . . . . . .
```

C. *Ranking* questions, where given items are put into order:

```
These issues were identified by the works committee as
requiring work. Please number them in order of importance to
you for fixing.

Use 1 for the most important down to 4 for the least important.

[ ] Noise from adjacent office
[ ] Occasional failure of power supply
[ ] No parking lines in car park
[ ] Insufficient lighting over copier
```

D. *Rating* questions, where items are scored on a given scale:

```
Please indicate your agreement with the following statements by
circling the appropriate letters.

SA = Strongly Agree   A = Agree   N = Neither agree nor
disagree
D = Disagree          SD = Strongly Disagree

I am satisfied with the pay review scheme     SA  A  N  D  SD
The suggestion scheme is effective            SA  A  N  D  SD
...

Please circle a point along the scale to indicate how easy you
find the event recorder to operate.

    Very easy  *....*....*....*....*....*  Very difficult
```

Fig. 36.3 Types of Multiple Choice Question

6. Build the questions into a complete questionnaire or interview guide that can be used in the survey.

   Start by thanking the respondent for helping and then give a brief explanation of the purpose of the survey. This will help the respondent feel comfortable with the questions and may assist them in giving appropriate answers.

   Give instructions on how to complete the survey, either for the interviewer or questionnaire respondent. Instructions may include:
   - How to fill in answers (writing, ticking, circling, etc.), possibly with examples. Repeat this, at least in summary, on all pages where it applies.
   - Where to go if questions may be skipped.
   - The date by when the survey should be completed.
   - The person to whom the completed survey should be sent.

   Lay out the questions, making sure there is enough room for answers. Make sure that each question and its answer space fits completely on one page.

7. Review the final question set against the objectives, checking that responses will allow the objectives to be fully met. Look for missing, incorrect or unnecessary questions.

8. Perform a pilot test with volunteers to ensure it is understandable, that it elicits the right sort of response and can be completed within an acceptable time period. This can also be used to try out different questions or options, for example to determine how consistently they are answered.

9. Execute the survey, as planned. Consideration of the following points will help it to be successful.

   A questionnaire simply requires sending to the distribution list. If appropriate, include a stamped, addressed envelope for the reply (never expect respondents to pay for the return postage!). If delivering them to known people, a personal request can help to encourage replies.

   Interviews require significant work at this stage, and effort should be put into making them as consistent as possible. Use a standard approach, such as:
   - Ensure the person is relaxed enough to answer honestly and freely. If possible, use a quiet, comfortable and confidential room. It can help if the interviewer is socially similar to the interviewee, for example having similar clothing and hairstyle.

- Introduce yourself and explain why they are being surveyed. This can use closed, factual statements and questions that are easy to answer. For example, 'We have been working on ways to ensure people can work well together. Have you read about the new team management policy?'.
- Start exploring of the area of interest with open questions, such as 'How do you feel about this policy?'. Use body language (nodding, grunts, etc.) to encourage the person to keep talking. Watch their body language, spotting signals and conflicts (e.g. saying yes, but avoiding eye contact).
- Spot specific points of value and probe for more details: 'Can you tell me more about ... '. Differentiate between facts, opinions and feelings. Be careful when talking about areas of personal sensitivity, and only probe there if it is essential.
- Summarize and test understanding with tentative statements: 'It seems as if your prefer ... '.
- Conclude with a closed question: 'So you definitely prefer a structured approach?'.
- Repeat the above steps for each of the areas of interest.

10. Analyze the survey data to give a usable set of information from which decisions can be made and the objective from step 1 be met.

    When doing this analysis, if there are gaps in the information, avoid guessing what the respondent might have said. Treat gaps simply as missing information or go back and ask more questions.

Practical variations

- Use a tape recorder in an interview. Ask the interviewee for permission to do this, as some people may be uncomfortable with it.
- Encourage questionnaire respondents to reply by offering a prize. This can also be a small gift for everyone, or entry into a draw for a bigger prize. This can be used for unsolicited interviews, such as in consumer tests.
- Surveys can also include other required actions, such as tasting new foods, watching videos or looking at pictures. Typically these actions are followed up with appropriate questions (often about preference).
- Use a shaded background on questionnaires, leaving white only those areas that are to be written on. This makes it very easy to see where a response is required.

Notes

The roots of modern surveys come largely from marketing, where they are used for identifying customer opinions, needs and expectations.

See also

Chapters: Use Brainstorming and Nominal Group Technique to help identify questions. Use Affinity Diagram, Relations Diagram and Tree Diagram to identify questions and build the question structure. The results of questionnaires may be analyzed and displayed in numerical analysis tools, such as the Prioritization Matrix, Pareto Chart and Histogram.

References: Surveys are often discussed in marketing books, such as [Kotler 88], but are covered detail by specialized books, such as [Hoinville 78], [Fink 85] and [Oppenheim 92]. [Pease 81] and [Pease 85] cover body and verbal communication in detail. [Argyle 83] and [Shaw 81] discuss interpersonal psychology.

37 Tables

What it's for

To organize and relate multiple pieces of information.

When to use it

- Use it when gathering information, to help prompt for a complete set of data.
- Use it when information is disorganized, to help collate and understand it.
- Use it for summarizing information to make it easier to present and understand.
- Use specific table tools as frameworks for particular tasks, either to organize existing information or to prompt for specific categories of information.

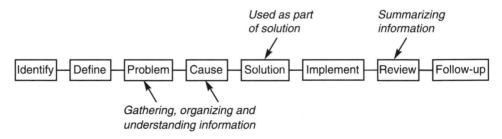

Fig. 37.1 Possible uses in improvement project framework

How to understand it

When working with problems, it is common either to have little information and little idea of what information is needed, or to have plenty of information which is fragmented and disorganized.

A simple table can help in either of these cases. For situations with little information, the table can provide prompts for the information to collect, and provides an organizing framework for situations with much information.

The basic table consists of titled rows and columns, with cells at their intersection that contain items pertinent to the row and column title, as in Fig. 37.2. Cells can contain different items such as numbers, single words, sentences or diagrams. Row titles and column titles do not have to be completely homogeneous; it is common to have one dimension containing closely related titles with the second dimension having titles which relate to the first dimension's titles, rather than each other.

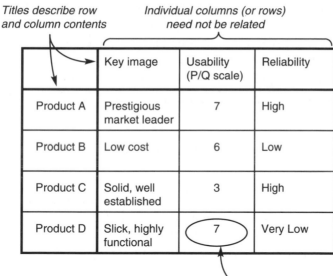

Fig. 37.2 Basic Table

One of the most important aspects of using tables is in selecting the right row and column titles, as incorrect selection can result in the wrong information being collected, the right information being missed or poor interpretation of the information in the table.

Example

In an early project during the quality program, an improvement team in a woolen mill doubled the productivity of the loom shop. They wanted to do something to publicize this, and used Is-Is Not Analysis, as in Fig 37.3, to help them clarify what they wanted to do and to identify actions.

Problem: What shall we do to publicize project success?

	Is	Is Not	Conclusion
What?	Animated overview	Speech day	- Spend time preparing
Why?	Demonstrate success Encourage others	Showing off	- Make purpose clear in introduction
When?	In next company gathering	More than a month out	- Get it scheduled this week
Where?	Main hall	Anywhere else!	- Book the hall - Plan logistics
Who?	To:Whole company By: Project team	Managers only	- Prepare for a big show
How?	Planned, budgeted	Turn up and do it	- Budget from JR - Team meets Mon to plan

Fig. 37.3 Example

Other examples
- A building administrator implements a system for booking rooms, using a table showing rooms against times when they are available. The booker and their charge code are written into a booked slot.
- A team of architects use a table to compare the tensile attributes of a set of proposed structural elements. Elements that are weak in several attributes are rejected.
- A forge team, looking for how to measure their processes, draws a table of key processes against critical success factors for the business.

How to do it

1. Determine the purpose or objective of using the table. Typically this will be one or a combination of:
   - Providing an organizing framework for existing information.

- Prompting for new information that is to be identified.
- Presenting information in a clear and compact format.

Tables are easier to understand if they have a single unifying theme, although they can also be used to combine themes, for example a list of customer needs can have column sets on product features that satisfy those needs and also notes on how well competing products meet the needs.

2. Identify the general categories of what will be in rows and columns. For example, rows are products and columns are details about defects. The table will combine these categories to provide new information and help decision points to be identified.

3. Using the general categories from step 2, determine the exact rows and columns to use. For example, rows are 'products from line 3B' and columns are 'defect category, defect count and fix time'. When selecting rows and columns, beware of the table becoming too large, as this will make it less readable, particularly if it runs over more than one page.

   It is common to put independent items (usually the 'primary' items) in rows and dependent items in columns. For example, the fertilizer to use will depend on the flower being grown, so a table of these would have flowers in rows and fertilizers in columns.

   It is often practical to put the subject with the greatest number of items in rows, as there is usually less space available for columns. This is particularly true when the table contains text (as opposed to numbers or symbols), as this requires a reasonable column width.

4. Design the layout of the table such that the information that it contains will be easily usable. Wide tables may benefit from being drawn in landscape, rather than portrait format.

   If the table is not completely clear, for example when using abbreviations to keep columns narrow, then add a key or instructional text to help its users and readers to understand it.

5. Write the information into the cells of the table. Be clear about the rules of how to select what does and does not go into each cell, and then use them consistently.

6. Interpret the completed table and take appropriate action.

Practical variations

- Write column headings vertically or diagonally, to enable multiple, narrow columns to be used.
- Use multi-level titles on rows and/or columns to effectively produce a multi-dimensional table. This can enable complex conclusions to be drawn, for example in Fig. 37.4, it can be seen that the bronze items generally do better than pewter, and bronze castings of figures are particularly strong in the south. This might lead to an investigation into how pewter items are marketed.

Castings / Region		Figures		Animals		Buildings	
		Pewter	Bronze	Pewter	Bronze	Pewter	Bronze
North	Tot. Sales	100	241	98	221	55	236
	Penetration	12%	75%	32%	66%	16%	71%
South	Tot. Sales	221	332	101	122	144	141
	Penetration	61%	87%	23%	27%	45%	41%
East	Tot. Sales	56	45	21	56	87	33
	Penetration	34%	32%	24%	34%	55%	25%
West	Tot. Sales	32	54	16	55	35	64
	Penetration	10%	25%	6%	26%	12%	36%

Fig. 37.4 Multi-dimensional table

- Use one set of titles, for either rows or columns. In this case, the titles in the other dimension are effectively added as a part of the data in the table, as in Fig. 37.5.

First item in row is effective title, as the rest of the row is related to it

Issue	Priority	Action	Who	When by
Lathe 2x out of spec.	A	Get serviced	JM	12-Jun
New entrants not trained yet on 3B	B	Chase up with training dept.	FA	20-Jun
Hazardous waste left outside in yard	A	Facilities to clean up before inspection next week	FA	11-Jun

Fig. 37.5 One set of titles

- The *Be-Know-Do Grid* is used for selecting people for tasks and positions in a project by separately identifying (a) human qualities ('being') such as creativity, extroversion and tenacity, (b) learned abilities ('knowing') such as experience of specific tools and methods, qualifications, etc., and (c) specific tasks that require doing. These three can form columns, with people or roles as rows, or being and knowing are columns with doing as rows.

Role	Being (human qualities)			Knowing (qualification, skills, experience)			Doing (tasks)	
	Creative	Good judge		Degree	TQ stats.		Running meetings	Data analysis
Team leader	✓	✓		✓			✓	
Statistician		✓		✓	✓			✓

Fig. 37.6 Be-Know-Do Grid

- The *Fact Table* is used to help identify useful data by sorting pieces of information according to how verifiable and useful they are, as in Fig. 37.7.

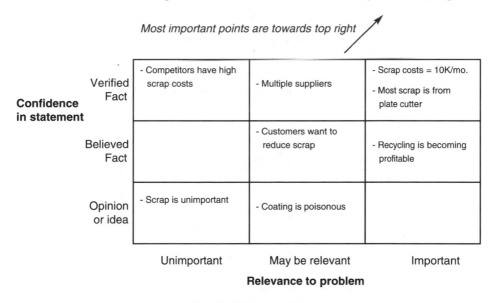

Most important points are towards top right

Confidence in statement			
Verified Fact	- Competitors have high scrap costs	- Multiple suppliers	- Scrap costs = 10K/mo. - Most scrap is from plate cutter
Believed Fact		- Customers want to reduce scrap	- Recycling is becoming profitable
Opinion or idea	- Scrap is unimportant	- Coating is poisonous	
	Unimportant	May be relevant	Important

Relevance to problem

Fig. 37.7 Fact Table

- *Is-Is Not Analysis* is used to help define the boundaries of a problem by identifying what is and what is not relevant in a number of selected areas, as in Fig. 37.8.

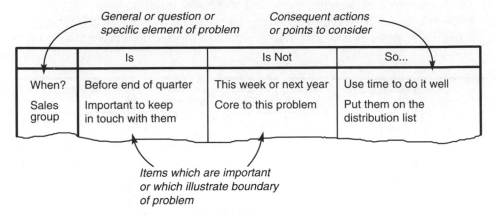

Fig. 37.8 Is-Is Not Analysis

- A *SWOT Analysis* (Strengths, Weaknesses, Opportunities and Threats) uses a simple four-square table, as in Fig. 37.9 to guide investigation of internal/external positives/negatives in any situation, such as when improving the marketing strategy for a new product. This can then lead to specific plans to improve negatives and build on positives.

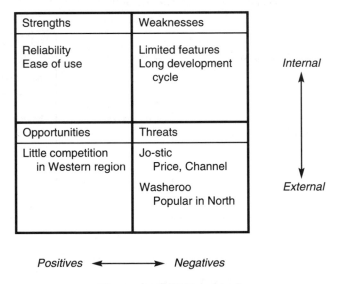

Fig. 37.9 SWOT Analysis

- The *Resource Allocation Matrix,* (or *RAM*) is used in initial planning, to allocate tasks to people. This has tasks in rows and people in columns. The titles can be shown as a hierarchy, for example to show task groups and people's work departments.

Notes

Tables are a general form of Matrices.

See also

Chapters: Tables may help direct and organize results of Brainstorming and Nominal Group Technique. The Prioritization Matrix is a table-based tool. Matrices are a special form of table.

References: A number of books describe table-based tools, including [Kepner 81], [Page-Jones 85], [Scholtes 88] and [Marsh 93].

38 Tree Diagram

What it's for

To break down a topic into successive levels of detail.

When to use it

- Use it when planning, to break down a task into manageable and assignable units.
- Use it when investigating a problem, to discover the detailed component parts of any complex topic.
- Use it only when the problem can be broken down in a hierarchical manner.
- Use it, rather than a Relations Diagram, to break down a problem when the problem is hierarchical in nature.

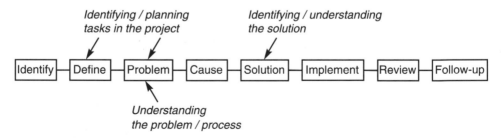

Fig. 38.1 Possible uses in improvement project framework

How to understand it

A common difficulty that occurs when investigating a problem is that it may be understood in broad terms, but the specific detail is not clear. For example, when designing an invoice, it may be known that customer and product details are required, but few people could list every item that should be on the form.

 The Tree Diagram gives a simple method of breaking down a problem, one layer at time, into its component parts, as in Fig. 38.2.

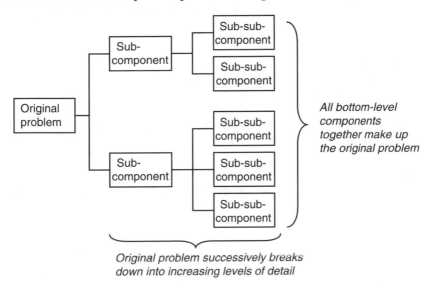

*Original problem successively breaks
down into increasing levels of detail*

Fig. 38.2 Tree Diagram

A key characteristic of the Tree Diagram is that it is a *hierarchy* (as opposed to a network, such as in the Relations Diagram). Each position or *node* on the tree has one predecessor or *parent* and one or more successor nodes, or *children* (this naming probably originates from its use in family trees). There is one initial node (or *root*), which has no parent, and multiple bottom-level nodes (or *leaves*) which have no children.

In many uses of the Tree Diagram, each parent is completely described by its children. Thus the diagram can be reviewed 'bottom-up' to check that the root is satisfied by the combination of all bottom-level leaves.

The method used to build the Tree Diagram is logical and systematic, repeating the same process of analysis and breakdown for each node. This may be contrasted with the more creative and fluid approach used in other methods, such as in building the Affinity Diagram.

Example

A hotel restaurant manager, concerned at low patronage figures and various vague complaints, wanted to find out what affected the satisfaction of her customers in order that areas for improvement might be identified. She decided to use a Tree Diagram to find a basic set of factors to measure that, taken together, would cover all areas. Together with the assistant manager, she defined the method of breaking down the root phrase of 'satisfied customers' as:

- Question to identify children: 'What key factors will directly contribute towards in the parent happening?'.
- Check on children: They should together make up the parent (no key factors missing).
- Break down problem a complete level at a time.
- Stop breaking down when there are about ten leaves on the tree.

   The tree generated is shown in Fig. 38.3. To test the result, a selection of customers were asked to review the diagram, and it was revised accordingly. Measures were then derived from the leaves and a simple process of measurement was set in place. At the end of each month, a project was set up to improve the poorest score of the previous month. Over time, the average score gradually went up, and the restaurant became more popular.

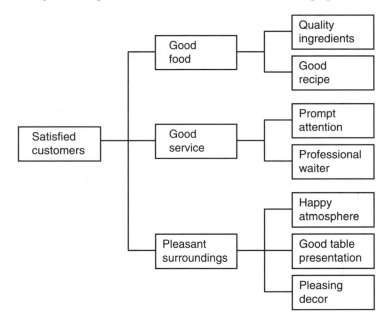

Fig. 38.3 Example

Other examples

- An engine design team used a Tree Diagram to record a break-down of the parts of their own and their competitors' engines. Simpler competitive components were clearly identified.
- An improvement work team of metal formers used a Tree Diagram to break down and share out the tasks involved in doing a presentation to managers of a radical idea for workplace layout.
- A teachers' group, having found key types of truancy with a Relations Diagram then moved on to use a Tree Diagram to identify legal remedial measures for each type.

How to do it

1. Identify the objective of using the Tree Diagram. Examples of this include:
   - Determine the individual tasks that each person on a project team must carry out to achieve a known objective.
   - Describe all sub-assemblies and basic components in a competitor's product.
   - Identify a customer's basic needs of a product.
   - Determining the root causes of a problem.

2. Assemble a small team of people to work on the diagram. These people should be of an analytical (rather than creative) nature, and should have sufficient subject expertise between them to be able to break down the problem to the required level of detail.

3. Define the top-level 'root' statement. This should be a brief phrase which clearly describes the problem at this level, making it easier to identify its individual sub-components. For example, 'Deliver Requirements Proposal'.

   This statement may be derived from the use of another tool. Thus it may be the key cause in a Relations Diagram or the top-level header card in an Affinity Diagram.

   Write this statement on a 3" x 5" card and place it on the middle-left of the work area, visible to all team members.

4. Define the process for breaking down each 'parent' statement into 'child' statements. This can be helped by defining a question to ask of the parent statement, based on the original objective defined in step 1. Possible questions to ask include:
   - What must be done to achieve the parent statement?

- What are the physical parts of the parent?
- Why does the parent happen?

Typically, the child should have a direct (and not distant) relationship with the parent. For example, 'component breakage' may be a direct cause of 'machine failure', rather than 'metal fatigue', which causes the component to break.

This process may also include questions to ask that ensure the child statements together make up a fair representation of the parent statement.

5. Define the criteria to be used to identify when bottom-level 'leaves' have been arrived at, and the problem does not need to be broken down further. For example, 'Tasks that may be allocated to a single person, and will take no more than one week each to complete'.

6. Apply the process defined in step 4 to the top-level statement from step 3, in order to produce the first-level child statements (although if the top-level statement was derived from another tool, then it may be reasonable to also derive the first-level child statements from the same place).

Write these statements on 3" x 5" cards, and arrange them to the right of the top-level statement card, as in Fig. 38.4.

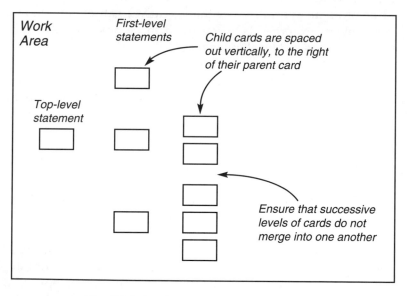

Fig. 38.4 Laying cards in the work area

In many situations, each parent may be expected to have around two to four children. Having one child is often reasonable, but having many children, particularly at the higher levels, can result in an awkward and unmanageable diagram. If this happens, ask whether some of the children should be appearing at a lower level.

7. Repeat this process for each card in the first level, first checking whether the criteria defined in step 5 indicates that further breakdown is required. Arrange the child cards to the right of their parents, ensuring that family groups do not merge.

8. Continue to repeat the process until the criteria defined in step 5 are met and no further breakdown is required. If cards become cramped together, take time to rearrange them such that all parent-child relationships between cards are clear.

9. When the diagram is complete, review the stages, looking for improvements, such as:
   • Statements which are in the wrong place, for example where enthusiasm at early levels has resulted in statements that should be lower down the tree.
   • Levels where the child statements together do not represent their parent very well.
   • General imbalances in the tree, for example where an understood subject is pursued in detail at the expense of other subjects.

   Where improvements are found, rearrange the cards or repeat the process as appropriate.

10. Use the completed tree to help achieve the objective as identified in step 1.

Possible variations

• The diagram may be built vertically, on a flipchart or whiteboard, by using adhesive memo notes.
• Cards may be dispensed with and the diagram drawn directly on a flipchart or whiteboard. This may be quicker, but it can get untidy if the cards need rearranging or a parent has more children than expected, and families crush into one another.

- A *Why-Why Diagram* is a Tree Diagram where each child statement is determined simply by asking 'why' the parent occurs, as in Fig. 38.5. It is thus very similar in use to a Cause-Effect Diagram, and techniques may be borrowed from Cause-Effect Diagram usage. Its simplicity can make it useful in less formal situations.
- *Winner Analysis* uses a Why-Why Diagram to find out why an action either went wrong or went surprisingly right. Lessons learned are used to help improve future situations.

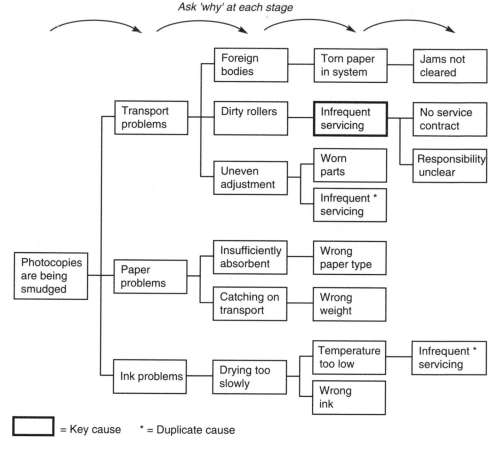

Fig. 38.5 Why-Why Diagram

- A *How-How Diagram* is a Tree Diagram where each child is determined by asking 'how' the parent can be achieved, as in Fig. 38.6. It is thus useful for creating solutions to problems.

    The Why-Why and How-How Diagrams together make a very simple toolset for finding causes of and solutions to problems.

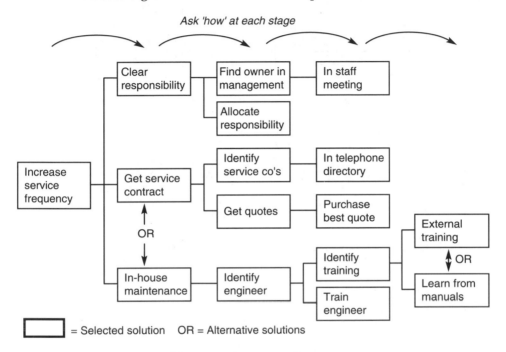

Ask 'how' at each stage

☐ = Selected solution   OR = Alternative solutions

Fig. 38.6 How-how diagram

- Cards containing statements of special note may be marked differently, with asterisks, underlining, etc. Notable cards include key problems, duplicate cards, leaves which are broken down further elsewhere, statements which are explained in more detail elsewhere, etc. Fig. 38.5 shows some examples.
- Although children usually combine to make up their parent, it is also possible that they form a set of alternatives. Where this is done, it should be made clear, for example by writing 'or' between cards. An example can be seen in Fig. 38.6. Where there is a complex combination of 'and's and 'or's, the symbol set used in Fault Tree Analysis may be applied.
- At each level of breakdown, question each bottom-level card and only break down further those cards that look like yielding useful information.

This saves time, but could result in significant areas being missed.

- There are a number of different ways that a Tree Diagram can be displayed, as shown in Fig. 38.7.

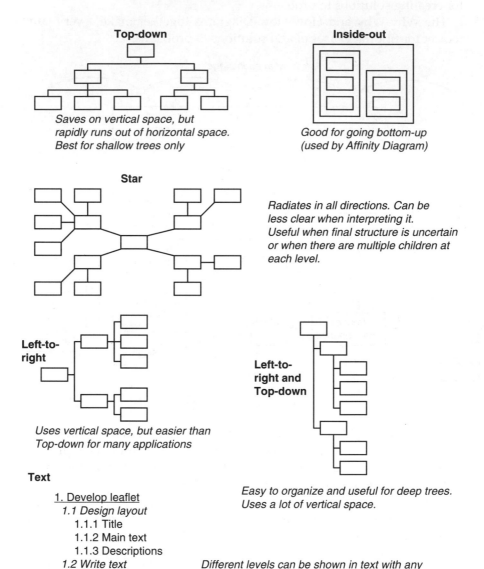

Top-down

Saves on vertical space, but rapidly runs out of horizontal space. Best for shallow trees only

Inside-out

Good for going bottom-up (used by Affinity Diagram)

Star

Radiates in all directions. Can be less clear when interpreting it. Useful when final structure is uncertain or when there are multiple children at each level.

Left-to-right

Uses vertical space, but easier than Top-down for many applications

Left-to-right and Top-down

Easy to organize and useful for deep trees. Uses a lot of vertical space.

Text

1. Develop leaflet
   1.1 Design layout
      1.1.1 Title
      1.1.2 Main text
      1.1.3 Descriptions
   1.2 Write text
      1.2.1 Headings
      1.2.2 Descriptions

Different levels can be shown in text with any combination of font, indenting and numbering. Useful for creating trees with a wordprocessor

Fig. 38.7 Tree shapes

- A *Work Breakdown Structure* (*WBS*) is a Tree Diagram that breaks down a task into allocable units. The bottom-level leaves may thus have individual people and resources allocated to complete these tasks, complete with estimations of effort required. The sum of the effort and resource in all leaves thus gives the total cost of the overall task.

  Computer-based 'project management tools' often combine work breakdown structures with Activity Network-style links to enable complex tasks to be designed and computed such that they may be completed in the shortest possible time.

Notes

The Tree Diagram is one of the second seven tools. It is also called a *Systematic Diagram* or *Dendrogram*.

See also

Chapters: Use Brainstorming, Nominal Group Technique or Surveys to provide input. Several other tools are special forms of Tree Diagram, including the Affinity Diagram, Decision Tree, Cause-Effect Diagram, Process Decision Program Chart. It can be used for breaking down problems for use in the Gantt Chart and Matrix Diagram. The Relations Diagram provides a similar way of breaking down problems, but in a non-hierarchical way.

References: Tree Diagrams are usually discussed by books covering the second seven tools. [Mizuno 88], [Brassard 89] and [Asaka 90] each have a chapter on it. [Oakland 93] and [Gitlow 90] describe it more briefly. Other variations are in [Raybould 71] and [Hamburg 70].

39 Value Analysis

What it's for

To determine and improve the value of a product or process.

When to use it

- Use it when analyzing a product or process, to determine the real value of each component.
- Use it when looking for cost savings, to determine components that may be optimized.
- Use it only when the item to be analyzed can be broken down into sub-components and realistic costs and values allocated to these.

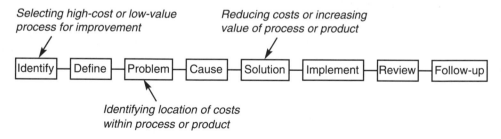

Fig. 39.1 Possible uses in improvement project framework

How to understand it

All commercial activities are performed with the objective of providing value of some kind, where the value is a combination of the benefits gained from the activity and the cost of achieving these benefits. In many situations, both the benefits and the real costs are not understood, for example where they are measured at such a gross level that individual activities cannot be accurately determined. This can cause problems for projects that are aimed at improving these activities, as the real value cannot be found.

Value Analysis is an approach to improving the value of an item or process by first understanding the *functions* of the item and their value, then by identifying its constituent components and their associated costs. It then seeks to find improvements to the components by either reducing their cost or increasing the value of their functions.

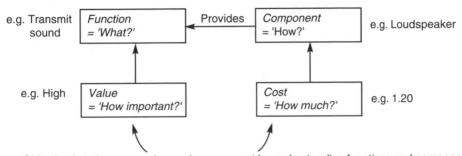

Objective is to increase value or decrease cost by understanding functions and components

Fig. 39.2 Value Analysis

Functions may be broken down into a hierarchy, as in Fig. 39.3, starting with a *basic* function, for which the customer believes they are paying, and then followed by *secondary* functions, which support that basic function.

The purpose of functions may be *aesthetic* or *use*, and basic functions may be either or both of these. For example, a coat may have a use function of 'making you warm' and an aesthetic function of 'looking attractive'. Aesthetic and use functions tend to be separate, and either may be of higher value.

The product or process may be broken down into components, which can be associated with the functions they support. The value of the product or process may then be increased by improving or replacing individual components. This also applies at the whole item being analyzed, which may be completely replaced with a more functional or lower cost solution.

Although this is a simple-sounding technique, it can be quite difficult in practice, as it requires both deep analysis of the product or process to be improved, and also an innovative approach to finding alternatives.

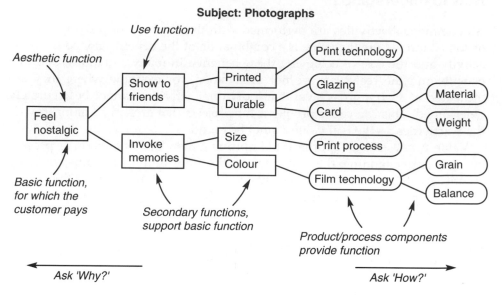

Subject: Photographs

Fig. 39.3 **Function/component hierarchy**

Example

A product manager at a company that produced nails had received several requests from customers for a nail that could not work loose. Identifying this 'improved nail' as a possible new product line, he decided to do a Value Analysis to help identify costs and values.

Working with a major customer in the building industry, he first identified the basic function and measure of an ideal nail as holding two 1cm battens together, such that when the battens were twisted, the wood would break before the nails moved.

With an engineering team, this was broken down into secondary functions, which were evaluated and related to components and costs as in Fig. 39.4. During this process, the concept of how the nail gripped the wood was discussed. They brainstormed alternative ways of gripping wood, and an engineer, who was also an amateur fisherman, came up with the idea of putting barbs on the nails.

The initial prototype was partially successful, but did become a little loose after a period. Spiral barbs helped, and straight barbs on the top of the nail resulted in the nail being locked in place by the final hammer blow.

The solution was produced as a specialist nail, and sold well at twice the price of a normal nail, more than covering the increased production costs.

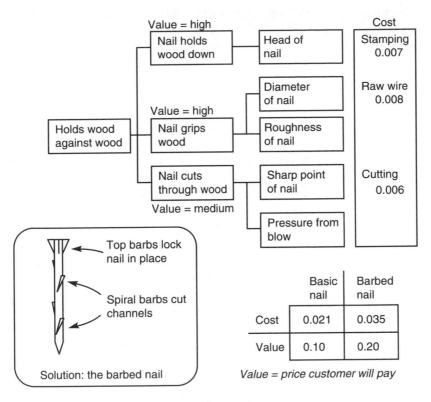

39.4 Example

Other examples

- An engineer in a motor manufacturer does a Value Analysis on the motor casing and the process used to build it. He finds three different sizes of nuts and bolts used, with significant time taken to insert and tighten them. A redesign of the casing changes this to use one size of bolt with threaded bolt holes, which removes the need for nuts. The result is a savings in both material costs and assembly time.
- A marketing manager for a washing-up liquid analyzed the liquid bottle and its use. She discovered that the bottle became slippery when liquid dribbled down the side of the bottle. The shape of the bottle and the spout were both changed to improve grip and reduce dribble. Without any additional advertising, sales of the product subsequently went up by 2%.
- A receptionist, aiming to improve the process of welcoming guests, first determines the basic functions of relaxing guests and finding the objective of their visit. She then identifies her process for achieving these and

brainstorms possible improvements. By experimenting with several approaches over two months, she finds the manner and questioning technique that best achieves her objective.

How to do it

1. Identify what is to be analyzed. This will typically be one of:
   - *A manufactured item.* This can be anything from a screw to an engine, although a more complex item is likely to result in a more complex and time-consuming analysis.
   - *A process or service.* Again, all levels can be analyzed, from a hand assembly process to a complete customer service organization.

2. Identify and prioritize the customers of the item from step 1. This may include external customers, such as 'auto suppliers' and internal customers, such as 'finance manager'.

   Note that external customers are usually more important than internal customers, and that seniority does not necessarily equate with priority. Ask, 'What do they do with it?', 'What would they do without it?'. Thus a customer's preference for a product feature should be more important than the opinion of a senior designer.

3. Identify the basic functions of the item or process from step 1. Basic functions are those things for which the customer believes they are paying. There are usually only one or two basic functions per product or service.

   The best way of finding basic functions is usually to ask the customer. Another possible approach is to observe them in action. Consulting specifications may be appropriate, but is based on the possibly false assumption that these are correct.

   Find the real basic functions by repeatedly asking 'Why?' the item is required until answers can no longer be found. For example, the function of a teenager's dress might be 'to look good'. Asking 'Why?' results in the more basic function of 'attract attention of opposite sex'.

   Differentiate between *aesthetic* functions and *use* functions. Aesthetic functions are associated with feelings, but serve no other practical purpose, for example 'elegant shape' or 'pleasant service manner'. Use functions describe how the item is used, for example 'cutting paper' or 'smoothing wood'. Basic functions may be aesthetic or use functions.

   Describe functions with verb-noun combinations, such as 'cut' and 'wire' in a clear phrase or sentence. Where possible include information that will enable it to be measured, as this will allow improvements to be identified. For example, 'hand-cut mild steel wire of at least 4mm diameter'.

4. Identify the secondary functions of the item by finding other functions that support the basic functions from step 2.

   This may be helped by asking 'How?'. For example, where the basic function of a bottle is to 'contain liquid', a secondary function may be to 'be strong', as this will contribute towards the bottle continuing to contain the liquid, even if it is dropped.

5. Determine the importance, or 'value' of each function to the customers identified in step 1. This will help to prioritize improvements. Assigning a number to this will enable the relative value of different functions to be highlighted. Alternatively a simple rating scale may be used, such as from 'Very Low' to 'Very High'.

   This is not always easy and a degree of estimation is often required. The task can be eased by comparing functions with one another or with value figures that have been used in the past. If possible, use actual customer preferences.

6. Break down the item into its constituent components, for example by using a Tree Diagram for a manufactured item or a Flowchart for a process.

   A manufactured item may benefit from analysis of both materials and process, as this will make costing in step 7 easier, and may also help with determining where value is and is not being added.

   For complex systems, limit the depth to which it is broken down in order to keep the overall analysis to a manageable level. If necessary, separate Value Analyses may be performed on individual sub-components.

7. Measure the cost of each component, as accurately as possible. This may include direct material costs, time costs, labor costs and other resource costs. If they can be measured, additional costs may be included, such as the cost of inspection, testing, scrap, lighting, heating, etc.

   Costs and components may be matched by using a table, such as in Fig. 39.5.

Step 6: Components		Step 7: Costs			Total cost
Basic component	Sub-component	Cost: Material	Labour		
Backing	Wood panel	0.10	0.08		0.52
	Clips	0.15	0.20		1.32
Frame	Moulding	0.22	0.15		1.02

Fig. 39.5 Identifying components and cost

8. Compare the components with the functions, determining which component contributes to which functions. This is often a one-to-one relationship but may also be one-to-many or many-to-many, for example where a book entertains as well as educates.

    Matching functions and components may be done with a table, as in Fig. 39.6.

Step 3: Basic function	Step 4: Secondary function	Step 5: Value to customer	Step 8: Match components to functions Components	Total cost
Support picture	Hold flat	6.2	Panel, glaze, clips	4.22
	Keep clean	3.2	Glaze	1.60
Look attractive	Finish	8.0	Frame, glaze	3.21

Fig. 39.6 Comparing value and cost

9. Identify components that may be improved either to give the same functionality at lower cost or to increase the contribution towards functions. Approaches include:
    - Look for redundant components that do not contribute to any function and which may be eliminated.
    - Look for unsatisfied functions that have no components satisfying them.
    - Identify high cost components, especially those that satisfy low value functions.
    - Identify high value functions and identify components that contribute towards them.

10. Use Brainstorming to create a list of possible improvements to the components identified in step 9.

    Also look for different ways of satisfying the basic functions, even if it means rejecting the current approach and starting again with a clean drawing board. This requires the product or process to be 'mentally destroyed' and then rebuilt anew.

    It may also be worthwhile to investigate new technologies that can be used to increase the value of functions or reduce the cost of components.

11. Evaluate the ideas from step 10 to determine their cost and select those that can be practically implemented. This may include work to develop and refine promising ideas into practical and optimum solutions.

12. Implement selected ideas and measure the costs and values to identify the real benefits gained.

Practical variations

- Abbreviate the method for analyzing simple situations by using the steps of Blast, Create, Refine. 'Blast' means rapidly cutting through existing concepts to expose the bare bones of the problem. In the 'Create' step, alternative solutions are devised. The 'Refine' step is then used to select the best alternative and make it work in practice. This mental model of destruction and thoughtful reconstruction is also useful when doing a more complex analysis.
- Instead of breaking down the item being analyzed, then mapping the components to functions, directly identify components that satisfy identified functions. This is faster, but reduces the chance of spotting redundant components and unsatisfied functions.
- *Zenbara* means 'completely dismantle' and is an approach to understanding an item and inspiring new ideas by slowly and carefully taking it to pieces, discussing the function and design of each piece in turn.
- Use a Matrix Diagram to map complex relationships between functions and components. This can also be used to apportion and evaluate costs and values, as in Fig. 39.7. This may be eased by first converting costs and values to percentages.

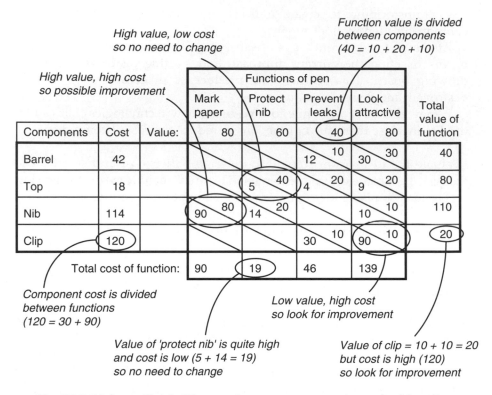

Fig. 39.7 Using a Matrix Diagram to map components against functions

- *Activity Based Costing*, or *ABC*, is an approach to allocating expenses within a workplace, based on actual use of resources. This may be compared with the more normal approach of lumping together all unknown costs into an 'overhead' and allocating a proportion to each department. ABC is thus a form of Value Analysis, taken from the financial viewpoint, and the two tools can be used effectively together.
- In *Function Analysis System Technique* (or *FAST*), functions are written on 3" x 5" cards and arranged in order so that cards to the left answer the question 'Why?' and cards to the right answer the question 'How?'. Separate horizontal chains of cards are then arranged so that functions in different chains that occur at the same time appear above one another, as in Fig. 39.8.

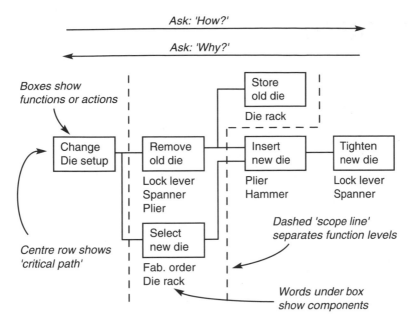

Fig. 39.8 Function Analysis System Technique Diagram

Notes

Value Engineering is the same tool as Value Analysis, but applied during the design phase, to understand and optimize the value of each component of a product or service.

See also

Chapters: Use Nominal Group Technique, Surveys or a Flow Process Chart as appropriate to help identify basic functions. A Tree Diagram may be used to break down the item functions and components. A Flowchart, Flow Process Chart or IDEF0 may be used to find components of a process. Use a Prioritization Matrix to help assign values to functions. Use Brainstorming to identify alternative solutions.

References: [Miles 72] contains a detailed description of Value Analysis from its originator, including many examples.

40 Voting

What it's for

To prioritize and select from a list of items.

When to use it

- Use it as a quick tool when a group must select one or more items from a list, for example as generated by a Brainstorming session.
- Use it when it is important that the group accept the result as fair.
- Use it when the knowledge to enable selection is spread within the group.
- Use it when the opinion of all group members is equally valued.
- It can also be used to 'test the water', to determine opinions without committing to a final selection.
- Use it, rather than a Prioritization Matrix, when the added accuracy of the Prioritization Matrix is not worth the extra effort.

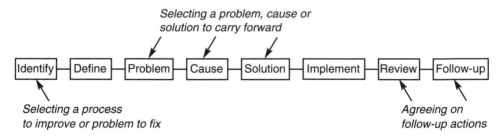

Fig. 40.1 Possible uses in improvement project framework

How to understand it

The situation often arises within projects where a number of items are identified, for example as generated by a Brainstorming session, from which the team must select a limited number for further action. The generation of this list may be an interesting and creative activity, but the selection is not always so convivial, and can be driven by the personal power of an individual in the group, rather than any agreed method.

Voting uses the democratic principle to enable all members of a group to agree on a final selection by giving equal selection power to each person. It is usually an acceptable selection method, as it uses a well-understood and fair principle. By accepting the tool, the group members accept the result.

Voting may be done in secret, preserving the anonymity of each voter, or may be public, for example by a show of hands. Although it is often done as a public activity, this can result in individuals being influenced by others, even within friendly peer groups, where later voters typically follow any emerging trend. With a public voting system, people are also more likely to cling to the items for which they voted, reducing the chances of early consensus.

A good voting session results in a very clear majority for one or two items. If there is either clustering or a wide spread of votes across items, then this may indicate that different criteria are being used, possibly from different points of expertise or different opinions. The advantage of voting within a group situation is that it is easy to discuss and resolve causes of variations in voting.

Although an item selected through voting may be agreeable to the group, this does not always mean that it is correct, and subsequent verification activities may be appropriate if a more confident decision is required.

In addition to selection, voting can also be used for prioritization of a set of items, arranging them in order of importance.

Example

An improvement project team in the shipping department investigated goods that were going missing after despatch. It was believed that a significant proportion went missing some time after they arrived at regional distribution warehouses, but the warehouse managers did not believe this and were unwilling to cooperate. The group Brainstormed ideas for persuading these managers to work with them. They then voted, each person scoring 3, 2 and 1 for their first, second and third suggestions.

The results gave the following prioritized shortlist:

Show them the project results	23 votes
Escalate to higher management	19 votes
Keep talking to them	8 votes
Bypass through personal contacts	6 votes
Get aggressive	2 votes

Further discussion revealed that higher management was currently embroiled in an annual planning cycle and would be unlikely to be much help at the moment. It was thus agreed to first present the results of the project so far to the warehouse managers, to show the how clearly the data pointed to this cause.

Other examples

- A marketing team used a Cause-Effect Diagram to identify possible causes of consumer rejection of a product. They voted on what were believed to be key causes. Later verification confirmed all but one key cause.
- A number of possible improvement projects were identified by managers of a small company. They identified selection criteria of, 'easy to do with a good chance of success' and voted on the projects to start up.
- A production team identified several possible solutions to address an overheating problem, caused by lack of localized ventilation. There was no clear best method, so they voted on which to test first.

How to do it

1. Identify the objective of selecting items from a given list. This may be for further investigation or for specific action.

2. Decide on the level of secrecy or anonymity that will be best for the voting session. Anonymity is important in groups where some individuals may be influenced by the actual or perceived power of others in the group.

   Consider recruiting a facilitator to help run the voting session. This person will ensure voting is fair and will preserve any confidences and secrecy of votes, enabling each person in the group to have equal voting power.

3. Decide on how many items to select from the list. This may be just one item, the top three or a more vague 'top few', to be guided by the eventual distribution of votes.

4. Identify the criteria to be used when voting. These form the guidelines that everyone should use to judge the items when casting their votes and often contain considerations of both benefits and costs. For example, an item that achieves objectives very well may be judged to be less desirable if it is expensive and difficult to implement.

    Where more than one criterion is identified, be clear about the relative importance of each. For example, 'Equal highest priority: Effect on revenue this year and time to implement. Of secondary importance: cost and people required'.

    Display the criteria prominently, alongside the list of items for which votes are to be cast.

5. Agree on the method of voting to use. There are several common methods:
    - *One person one vote.* This is simple, but does not allow a spread of opinion to be shown, especially in situations where the aim is to identify the top few items (not just the top one).
    - *Several votes each.* This allows opinion to be spread, but makes a second choice equally as important as a first choice.
    - *Several weighted votes each.* This gives several votes, each of different value, for example three votes of value 3, 2 and 1. Use the number of items being voted for to help decide on the number of votes to give each person.

    A larger number of votes per person will result in an increase in the time spent in the process, both in deciding what to vote for and in interpreting the results afterwards.

6. Vote. There are three basic approaches that can be taken to this:
    - *Total anonymity.* Write the choices, in order, on a slip of paper and hand it to the facilitator, who, when all votes are handed in, totals them up and writes them next to the items for which votes have been cast.
    - *Partial anonymity.* People come out and write their own votes next to the appropriate items. This is okay for groups who work comfortably together and can be done where there is no neutral facilitator.
    - *Public voting.* Use a show of hands or calling out votes one person at a time. This is quickest, but is also most likely to result in people being influenced by the votes of other people, rather than their own judgment against criteria.

7. Add up the votes and write these totals on the displayed list, next to the appropriate items.

8. Look at the distribution of votes. If there is not a Pareto distribution (most votes on a few items), then discuss why, bringing out different points of view that led to this diversity. If the spread is wide and viewpoints are changed by this discussion, repeat the vote.

9. Discuss each item which has received a significant number of votes, enabling everyone to agree with or accept the reasons for selecting it.

10. Verify the selected items. For example, if a solution was selected on its perceived low cost of implementation, work out the actual costs.

Practical variations

- When adding up votes, display them in a Pareto Chart to emphasize the distribution and weight of voting.
- Discuss all items which have votes cast against them, even those with only one vote. This helps the team to be more comfortable that all of their selected items have been considered and enables key points to be identified that perhaps only one person has spotted.
- Discuss all items before voting begins. This slows down the process, but ensures clear agreement of what is being voted for. Beware of this becoming a canvassing session.
- Reduce the list before voting by combining similar items. This prevents a big vote being hidden, as several people vote for the same thing in different places.
- *Multivoting* involves reducing the list in several steps, where:
    - Each person gives one vote each to one third of the items on the list.
    - Only items for which at least half the group voted are carried forward.
    - This is repeated until a manageable number of items is left.
- Have separate sets of people generating the list and voting on it. This ensures voting will be a more objective exercise.

Notes

Voting is a common route to a 'quick' solution. A danger with this is where an unconsidered vote becomes 'cast in stone' and cannot easily be changed.

See also

Chapters: Use Voting to select from the results of Brainstorming or key causes in a Cause-Effect Diagram or Relations Diagram. It is an integral part of Nominal Group Technique. The Prioritization Matrix gives a more rigorous but more time-consuming method of prioritizing a list of items.

References: Few books discuss voting in any detail. [Scholtes 88], as a team-focused book, discusses it to some extent.

Appendix A: Tool Finder

Objective of chapter
To help in the selection of tools for specific applications.

Although it is useful to have a broad toolkit available, it can still be difficult to select the appropriate tool for a given situation. This appendix aims to help you with this task by giving two approaches to choosing the right tool:

1. Starting from the project framework.
2. Starting from the task.

First, tools may be used in an organized project, typically using a framework as described in Chapter 1. This has a number of phases where specific actions may be performed. A smaller toolkit may be thus defined for each phase and sub-phase, making selection easier.

In addition to use in a defined framework, tools may also be used in any appropriate situation, for example as an ongoing process measurement or in a meeting where there is a need to organize some confused information. In such cases, the project framework is irrelevant, and the starting point for identifying the tool is the task in hand.

In either case, review the possible tools and decide first whether using a tool would be of benefit (for example, some situations may be too simple to merit their use), then select the most appropriate tool. In this decision, include consideration of what tools are already understood and the effort required to learn and use the tool.

Starting from the project framework

This section identifies tools which may be used in each of the phases of the process improvement framework outlined in Chapter 1. Tools are identified under each of the 'possible activity' bullet points from the original description.

1. Identify

- Reviewing existing measurements, looking for poorly performing processes.
  Track continuous process performance with a *Control Chart* or *Line Chart*. Use a *Check Sheet* to collect measurements. Processes performing out of specification may be identified by using a *Histogram* or by measuring *Process Capability*.

- Identifying customers, their needs, expectations and satisfaction with current processes.
  Find actual customer needs and expectations with a *Survey*. Use a *Brainstorm* or *Tree Diagram* to help identify questions to ask them.

- Defining criteria for selecting candidate projects.
  Use the *Nominal Group Technique* or *Brainstorming* to identify criteria.

- Describing candidate projects in a format that will ease selection.
  The *Pareto Chart* will show measurements in priority order. The *Bar Chart* can also be used to compare measurements. Use *Failure Mode and Effects Analysis* to identify products or processes carrying significant risks.

- Selecting a process to improve.
  In a group, use *Voting* for a quick selection or a *Prioritization Matrix* for a more rigorous approach. Use the *Force-Field Diagram* for resolving for-and-against arguments. Use a *Decision Tree* to select from alternative possible outcomes.

2. Define

- Identifying resources needed, such as team members, expertise, training and facilitation.
  Use a *Tree Diagram* to break down tasks into specific detail. Use the *Gantt Chart* to make outline and detailed plans. Use the *Activity Network* to

calculate overall timescales. Use the *Process Decision Program Chart* to find potential problems and contingencies.

- Gaining commitment from management to support project.
  Use the output of tools to present details of the problem and the estimated cost of resolution.

- Recruiting and training the project team.
  Identify the subset of tools that may be used in the project. Either select people who are experienced in their use or train them in their use (preferably just before they use them).

- Gaining a basic understanding of the problem to be addressed.
  Use *Brainstorming* to help find areas to investigate. Use *Nominal Group Technique* to collect information from within the group. Use a *Survey* to gather information from larger groups.
  Organize available numeric data in a *Control Chart, Line Graph* or *Bar Chart* to help understand past trends. Organize available textual data with an *Affinity Diagram* or *Relations Diagram*.

- Understanding the context and purpose of the process to be improved.
  Produce an outline of the process using the *Relations Diagram, Flowchart, Flow Process Chart* or *IDEF0*. In particular, look at the outputs and inputs of the process. Use a *Survey* to identify customer requirements and identify how well these are met by process outputs.

- Defining specific objectives for the project.
  Use the measurements and investigation so far to help identify the key problem to be solved or improved. Use the *Nominal Group Technique* or *Brainstorming* to identify possible objectives. Use the *Prioritization Matrix* or *Voting* to select which to use.

- Identifying measures to determine how well the objectives are met.
  Use the process outline to identify where to measure. Use the defined objective to help identify specific measures (it will be clear what must be measured if a good objective statement has been used). If necessary, use the *Nominal Group Technique* or *Brainstorming,* coupled with the *Prioritization Matrix* or *Voting*.

- Deciding what data to collect and how it will be collected.
  Use the measures to identify specific data to collect. Design a *Check Sheet* or *Tables* to contain the data.

- Making initial plans for future stages.
  Break down tasks with a *Tree Diagram*. Use a *Gantt Chart* to make outline plans. Use the *Activity Network* to calculate actual timescales. Use the *Process Decision Program Chart* to identify risks and contingencies.

3. Problem

- Mapping out the process or problem to understand it in detail and identify potential problem areas.
  Map the process detail with *IDEF0* or *Flowchart*. Use the *Flow Process Chart* for manual processes and the *String Diagram* for processes that involve significant movement.
     Break down products or problems with *Value Analysis*. Use a *Matrix Diagram* to investigate how requirements are met.

- Measuring the process to identify and verify problems.
  Plot measurements in a *Control Chart, Line Graph* or *Bar Chart*. Investigate process distributions with a *Histogram* or *Scatter Diagram* and by measuring *Process Capability*. Use *Design of Experiments* or a *Matrix Data Analysis Chart* for deeper investigation.
     Find more information about the process with a *Survey, Brainstorming* or the *Nominal Group Technique*. Collect data in a *Check Sheet* or *Tables*. Organize the information with the *Tree Diagram, Affinity Diagram* or *Relations Diagram*.
     Use the *Process Decision Program Chart, Failure Mode and Effects Analysis* or *Fault Tree Analysis* to identify potential problem areas.

- Prioritization and selection of specific problems that are to be addressed.
  Organize measurements into priority order using the *Pareto Chart*. Agree on priorities in a group using the *Prioritization Matrix* or *Voting*. Use the *Force-Field Diagram* to resolve for-and-against decisions.

- Revising plans to reflect new knowledge.
  Update plans using the same tools as in the previous phase.

4. Cause

- Identifying possible causes of the problem.
  Use the *Cause-Effect Diagram* to identify possible causes of a known effect. Use a *Relations Diagram* where there are complex relationships.

Use *Failure Mode and Effects Analysis* to help find why systems have failed.

- Selection of key causes to address.
  Use a *Prioritization Matrix* or *Voting* to select key causes for further investigation. Use the *Force-Field Diagram* to resolve for-and-against decisions.

- Determining measures to verify identified key causes.
  If measures are not clear, use *Brainstorming* or *Nominal Group Technique* to help identify them.

- Designing experiments to verify key causes.
  Use a *Scatter Diagram* to investigate uncertain relationships. Use *Survey* or *Nominal Group Technique* to gather information from people. Use *Design of Experiments* for deeper investigations.

- Measuring the process to verify that causes are key, as suspected.
  Use a *Check Sheet* or *Tables* to gather numerical data. Use a *Survey* to gather data from groups of people. Display results in a *Line Graph, Pareto Chart* or *Bar Chart.*

5. Solution

- Identifying a number of possible solutions to fix the identified key causes.
  Create new ideas with *Brainstorming,* or use a *Cause-Effect Diagram* to find how to cause desired results. Break down detail of solutions with a *Tree Diagram* or *Relations Diagram.* Use *Value Analysis* to help find specific solutions. Show process changes with *IDEF0, Flowchart, Flow Process Diagram, String Diagram* or *Relations Diagram.*

- Selection of a subset of possible solutions.
  Use *Failure Mode and Effects Analysis* to identify how solutions may fail. Use *Voting* or *Prioritization Matrix* to help select possible solutions. Use the *Force-Field Diagram* to resolve for-and-against decisions.

- Identifying feasibility, cost and benefit of selected solutions.
  Use a *Tree Diagram* to break down actions. Use the *Process Decision Program Chart , Fault Tree Analysis* or a *Decision Tree* to identify possible risks, payoffs and contingencies. Use *Tables* to organize other information.

- Examining related processes, to ensure the solution will not adversely affect them.
  Survey the process owners and users, to check that changes are acceptable. If appropriate, draw a *Flowchart* or *IDEF0* diagram.

- Designing experiments to verify selected solutions.
  Use *Design of Experiments* to verify solutions. Use *Brainstorming* or *Nominal Group Technique* to identify other ways of testing the solution. Use a *Matrix Diagram* to compare requirements against implementation details.

- Testing of final solution, preferably using measures identified in stage 2.
  Use a *Control Chart, Line Graph, Histogram* or *Bar Chart* or other previously used tools to show differences from previous measurements.

6. Implement

- Obtaining authority to implement the solution.
  Use measurements and plans from using tools in previous phases to demonstrate potential benefits of implementing solution.

- Training people on the changes made.
  Use results of using tools in previous phases to demonstrate reasons for change.

- Changing documentation.
  Use results of using tools in documents as appropriate. Use *Tree Diagram* to break down structure of document.

- Ensuring that the solution implemented is as planned.
  Track implementation using *Gantt Chart*. Use *Check Sheet* to check off actions completed.

- Using measurements (as identified in stage 2) to identify the real improvements.
  Measure the process as planned, collecting information with a *Check Sheet, Tables* or *Survey* and showing numerical results in a *Control Chart, Line Graph* or *Bar Chart, Histogram,* or the same tool that was used to measure the process in earlier stages.

- Measuring related processes to ensure that they are not adversely affected.
Use a *Survey* of process owners and users plus any charts they use to identify changes. Use a *Scatter Diagram* to identify correlations.

7. Review

- Reviewing measures made, to determine the actual improvement in the process against goals or expectations.
Compare 'before and after' measurements, using the *Histogram, Scatter Diagram, Bar Chart* or *Pareto Chart.* Identify trend changes in a *Control Chart* or *Line Graph.* Identify opinion changes in a follow-up *Survey.* Use *Tables* to summarize information.

- Determining why improvements did not occur as expected.
Review output of tools used previously to check decisions made, including those used for problem analysis, cause analysis, solution creation and planning. Use *Failure Mode and Effects Analysis, Fault Tree Analysis* or *Cause-Effect Diagram* to identify why problems occurred. Use *Brainstorming* to help discover unidentified problems. Use an *Affinity Diagram* or *Relations Diagram* to help understand unclear opinions and issues.

- Reviewing the use of the tools and framework, to find how well they were applied and how their use may be improved.
Use a *Survey* of the project team and other appropriate people. Use the *Nominal Group Technique* to quickly collect thoughts within the group.

- Deciding whether to continue the project by looping back to previous stages for further process improvement or to draw it to a close.
Review measurements and determine possible costs and benefits of options. Use a *Force-Field Diagram* to balance the two options.

- Holding a general project review of the success of the overall project to determine 'best practices' and other learning points.
Use a *Survey* of the team and other affected people or the *Nominal Group Technique* in a single meeting. Use *Voting* or a *Prioritization Matrix* to select action points and display results in a *Pareto Diagram.*

8. Follow-up

If the implementation was successful:
- Standardizing the solution, writing it up as a normal operating procedure and spreading it to other areas.
  Document the changed process with *IDEF0, Flowchart, Flow Process Diagram, String Diagram* or *Relations Diagram*. Use outputs from other tools to help demonstrate benefits of change. Implement ongoing monitoring measurements with a *Control Chart* or *Line Graph*.

- Looping back to previous stages for further improvements.
  Use a *Decision Tree* or *Force-Field Diagram* to help identify the best course of action to take.

- Closing down the project, as below.

If the implementation was unsuccessful:
- Addressing the cause of the lack of success, to prevent it recurring.
  Use new measurements from tools to ensure correct causes are identified.

- Looping back to previous stages to correct and repeat actions.
  Review use of tools and change as appropriate.

If the project is being closed down:
- Writing up the project as a 'success story'.
  Use the output of the tools as actually used in the project, rather than creating them specifically for the write-up (this makes the report much more credible).

- Presenting results to managers and other groups.
  As with the write-up, use the graphical output from tools that was actually used. Select a few key ones to illustrate specific points, rather than trying to show every graph and list that was used.

- Using the lessons learned to improve the improvement process itself.
  Use the *Pareto Chart, Prioritization Matrix* or *Voting* to help select the most important changes to make.

- Celebrating the success.
  Post large versions of key tool outputs on the walls. Combine celebration with presentation of results to other people.

- Planning for future projects.
  Measure processes as in the Identify phase. Use the *Gantt Chart* to plan broad timescales for actions.

Starting from the task

This section assumes you are not using the process improvement framework from Chapter 1, and thus starts from the basic task that you may be aiming to perform. This will probably be more useful if you are using a different framework or want to use a single tool in a more general problem-solving situation.

It is divided into the following three main sections, as discussed in more detail in Chapter 1:

1. Collecting information.
2. Structuring information.
3. Using information.

1. Collecting information

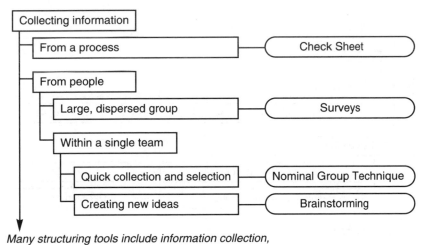

Many structuring tools include information collection, often using elements of Brainstorming

Fig. A.1 Collecting information

2. Structuring information

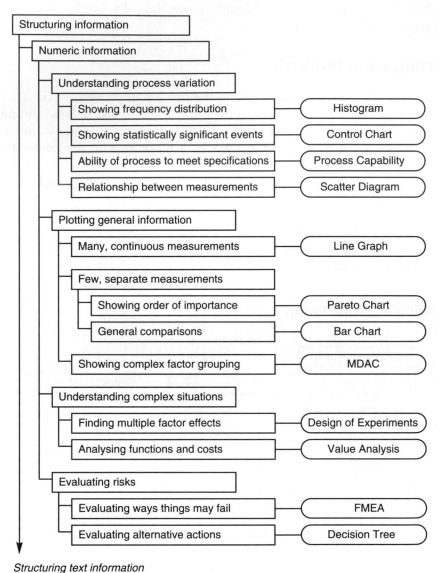

Structuring text information

Fig. A.1 Structuring numeric information

Structuring information (continued)

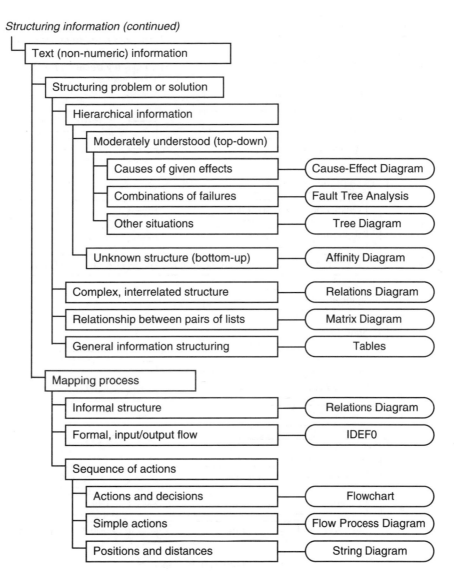

Fig. A.2 Structuring problems and processes

3. Using information

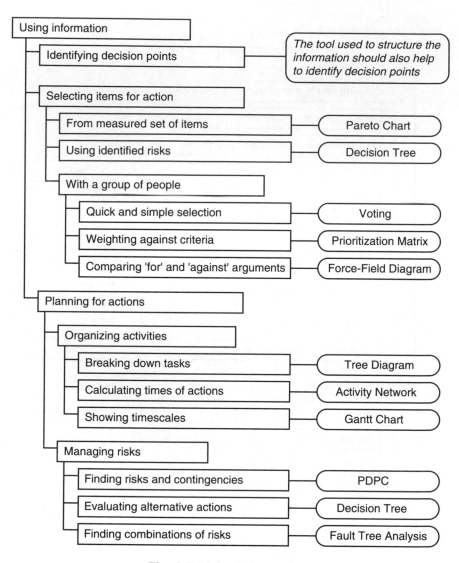

Fig. A.3 Using Information

Bibliography

Books can be viewed as tools, as their knowledge can be learned and applied to the work environment. The problem in choosing books is sometimes in knowing which books to read. In order to make this bibliography more of a toolkit, the titles are briefly annotated with a bias towards their 'tool' content.

There is a deliberate bias towards books, rather than papers, as these tend to be more accessible. The few papers referenced occurs where no book on the tool was known. The books are a mixture of UK and USA publications.

[Ackerman 87]
Roger B. Ackerman, Roberta J. Coleman, Elias Leger and John C. MacDorman, *Process Quality, Management and Improvement Guidelines*, AT&T, 1987
The AT&T book on quality improvement, giving details of their improvement process, plus descriptions of a number of tools.

[Adair 86]
John Adair, *Effective Teambuilding*, Pan, London, 1986
A clear book about making teams work, including discussion of various role types found in groups.

[Adams 74]
James L. Adams, *Conceptual Blockbusting, A Guide to Better Ideas*, W. H. Freeman and Co., San Francisco, 1974
An original book, describing various approaches to creating new ideas.

[Argyle 83]
Michael Argyle, *The Psychology of Interpersonal Behaviour*, Penguin, London, 1983
An academic but readable book on the basics of how people and groups interrelate.

[Asaka 90]
Tetsuichi Asaka and Kazuo Ozeki (eds), *Handbook of Quality Tools*, Productivity Press, Cambridge, MA, 1990

Detailed descriptions of how to use the first seven and five of the second seven tools, plus examples and discussions on general quality improvement.

[Barra 83]
Ralph Barra, Putting Quality Circles to Work, McGraw-Hill, NY, 1983

A broad description of quality circles, including an appendix with brief descriptions of a number of tools.

[Basili 88]
Victor R. Basili and H. Dieter Rombach, *The TAME Project*, IEEE Transactions on Software Engineering, Vol. 14, No. 6, June 1988, pp. 758-753.

Discusses an approach to improvement that includes the 'goal-question-metric paradigm' as a method of determining measures through questioning objectives.

[Belbin 81]
R. Meredith Belbin, *Management Teams, Why They Succeed or Fail*, Butterworth-Heinemann, Oxford, 1981

A classic study, identifying different personality types how they afffect a team's performance.

[Boehm 90]
Barry Boehm, *Software Risk Management*, IEEE Computer Society Press, 1990

A comprehensive collection of papers on risk management put together into an overall framework. Although aimed at software projects, much is applicable in many other situations.

[Brassard 89]
Michael Brassard, *The Memory Jogger Plus+*, Goal/QPC, Methuen MA, 1989

A very practical book on how to use the second seven tools, including several worked examples per tool. Includes the original *Memory Jogger* as an appendix, which summarises the first seven and some other tools.

[Buzan 89]
Tony Buzan, *Use Your Head (third edition)*, BBC, London, 1989

Describes some learning and problem solving tools, with a good description of mind-maps.

[Clark 52]
Wallace Clark, *The Gantt Chart (third edition)*, Pitman, London, 1952
   Contains a wealth of detail on the Gantt Chart, including many variations on its use.

[Dale 94]
Barrie G. Dale (ed.), *Managing Quality*, Prentice Hall, Hemel Hempstead, 1994
   A large book covering many areas of quality, including summaries of many tools and a chapter on FMEA.

[DeBono 67]
Edward DeBono, *The Use of Lateral Thinking*, Pelican, Harmondsworth, UK, 1967
   One of the classic books on creative thinking, it describes a 'sideways' approach to problem solving.

[DeBono 71]
Edward DeBono, *Lateral Thinking for Management*, Pelican, Harmondsworth, UK, 1971
   An update of his ideas on lateral thinking, with a range of techniques for using it. Includes a detailed description of brainstorming.

[Deming 82]
W. Edwards Deming, *Out of the Crisis*, Cambridge University Press, UK, 1982
   The classic book from 'the father of modern quality' covers his 14 points for management, and includes numerous examples of his statistical approach.

[Doyle 76]
Michael Doyle and David Straus, *How to Make Meetings Work*, Jove, NY, 1976
   A detailed book on running meetings, including the use of a faciliatator.

[Enrick 85]
Norbert L. Enrick, *Quality, Reliability and Process Improvement (eighth edition)*, Industrial Press, NY, 1985
   Has a strong manufacturing and statistical bias, but also briefly discusses some other 'group' tools, including process flow diagrams and fault tree analysis.

[Feigenbaum 86]
Armand Feigenbaum, *Total Quality Control (third edition)*, McGraw Hill, NY, 1986

One of the very original books on total quality, first published in 1951. It describes the use of many tools in its 800+ pages,.

[Fink 85]
Arlene Fink and Josephine Kosecoff, *How to Conduct Surveys*, Sage Publications, Beverley Hills, 1985

A readable book on surveys, covering measurement and analysis in detail, but without using complex mathematics.

[Fisher 81]
Roger Fisher and William Ury, *Getting to Yes*, Business Books, London, 1981

An excellent book on collaborative negotiation which includes a good description of brainstorming.

[Foster 91]
Timothy R. V. Foster, *101 Ways to Generate Great Ideas*, Kogan Page, London, 1991

Full of simple tricks and tips to keep the mind out of the rut and focused on different and divergent thinking.

[Francis 90]
Dave Francis, *Effective Problem Solving*, Routledge, London, 1990

A book on solving general management-type problems. Has a chapter each on setting objectives and setting measures.

[Frank 90]
Milo Frank, *How to Run a Successful Meeting in Half the Time,* Corgi, London, 1990

A terse book full of tips on how to make meetings work. The title implies a common complaint - that our meetings tend to be very unproductive.

[Gitlow 90]
Howard S. Gitlow, *Planning for Quality, Productivity and Competitive Position*, Dow Jones-Irwin, Homewood, IL, 1990

Describes the second seven tools, plus a few others, especially within the context of the Deming approach to quality. Includes a chapter on teaching them to others.

[Gordon 61]
William J. J. Gordon, *Synectics*, Harper and Row, NY, 1961
  The original book on synectics, an alternative to Brainstorming.

[Grant 80]
Eugene L. Grant and Richard S. Leavenworth, *Statistical Quality Control (fifth edition)*, McGraw Hill, NY, 1980
  A classic book, first published in 1946, which covers Control Charts and sampling in great detail.

[Hamburg 70]
Morris Hamburg, *Statistical Analysis for Decision Making*, Harcourt, Brace and World, NY, 1970
  Describes the mathematics behind a number of tools, including Decision Trees, Scatter Diagram and variation.

[Hoinville 78]
Gerald Hoinville, Roger Jowell and Associates, *Survey Research and Practice*, Heinemann, 1978
  A practical book on conducting Surveys, including details on building questionnaires, conducting interviews and postal surveys.

[ILO 79]
International Labor Organization, *Introduction to Work Study (Third Edition)*, International Labor Organization, Geneva, 1979
  A detailed book on Work Study, first published in 1957. Includes many examples and variations on String Diagrams and Flow Process Charts.

[Ireson 88]
W. Grant Ireson and Clyde F. Coombs, Jr, *Handbook of Reliability Engineering and Management*, McGraw Hill, NY, 1988
  A comprehensive book on reliability, including a chapter on failure analysis which gives detailed descriptions of FMEA and FTA.

[Ishikawa 76]
Kaoru Ishikawa, *Guide to Quality Control*, Asian Productivity Organisation, Tokyo, 1976
  A classic book on the first seven tools, it discusses many variations not seen elsewhere.

[Juniper 89]
Dean Juniper, *Successful Problem Solving*, Foulsham, Slough, 1989
   A comprehensive collection of tools for creative problem-solving, including unusual-sounding methods such as 'Zwicky's Morphological Method' and 'Simberg's Transformation'.

[Juran 79]
Joseph Juran, Frank Gryna and R. S. Bingham (eds), *Quality Control Handbook (third edition)*, McGraw Hill, NY, 1979
   One of the classics of quality, originally published in 1951. Contains clear and detailed descriptions of statistical tools, from Control Charts to Response Surfaces.

[Juran 88]
Joseph Juran, *Juran on Planning for Quality*, The Free Press, 1988
   An important book from one of the key quality masters, describing a number of tools and including the development of a 'spreadsheet' which is very similar to QFD.

[Kepner 81]
Charles Kepner and Benjamin Tregoe, *The New Rational Manager*, John Martin, London, 1981
   Describes the Kepner-Tregoe method of problem solving, which includes the use of several table-based tools, including variations on the Matrix Diagram and the Prioritization Matrix.

[King 89]
Bob King, *Better Designs in Half the Time (third edition)*, GOAL/QPC, Methuen, 1989
   A book on the details of Quality Function Deployment, including descriptions of other tools that may be used in the overall QFD process, such as Force-Field Diagrams.

[Kotler 88]
Philip Kotler, *Marketing Management, Analysis, Planning and Control (sixth edition)*, Prentice Hall, Englewood Cliffs, NJ, 1988
   A popular marketing textbook, describing many of the classic marketing techniques, including surveys and creative methods for identifying new products.

[Logothetis 92]
N. Logothetis, *Managing for Total Quality*, Prentice Hall, 1992
Describes a number statistical methods, including Control Charts and Design of Experiements (including Taguchi's approach).

[Lyonnet 91]
P. Lyonnet (Trans. Jack Howlett), *Tools of Total Quality*, Chapman Hall, 1991
Describes statistical methods for use in quality, with a fairly strong mathematical bias.

[Marsh 93]
John Marsh, *The Quality Toolkit*, IFS, Bedford, UK, 1993
A book describing a quality improvement framework, along with brief descriptions of many tools.

[Martin 85]
James Martin and Carma McClure, *Diagramming Techniques for Analysts and Programmers*, Prentice Hall, Englewood Cliffs, NY, 1985
A broad collection of tools used in computing for graphically describing processes.

[Miles 72]
Laurence D. Miles, *Techniquse of Value Analysis and Engineering*, McGraw Hill, NY, 1972
A detailed book on Value Analysis and Value Engineering from the originator of the techniques.

[Mizuno 88]
Shigeru Mizuno (ed), *Management for Quality Improvement (the 7 new QC tools)*, Productivity Press, Cambridge, MA, 1988 (Original Japanese publication in 1979)
A definitive description of the second seven tools, translated from the Japanese.

[Moore 88]
P. G. Moore and H. Thomas, *The Anatomy of Decisions*, Penguin, London, 1988
Discusses decision trees in detail, without using too much mathematics.

[Morris 77]
Desmon Morris, *Manwatching*, Triad Panther, St. Albans, 1977
   A classic book on body language, showing how observation can help communication. Includes discussion of differences in international signals.

[Oakland 90]
John Oakland and Roy Followell, *Statistical Process Control (second edition)*, Butterworth-Heinmann, Oxford, 1990
   A clear description of statistical tools, readable by non-mathematicians too.

[Oakland 93]
John Oakland, *Total Quality Management (second edition)*, Butterworth-Heinmann, Oxford, 1993
   A practical and wide-ranging book on TQM which includes brief descriptions of a large number of quality tools, including the second seven tools.

[O'Connor 91]
Patrick D. T. O'Connor, *Practical Reliability Engineering (third edition)*, Wiley, Chichester, 1991
   A handbook for reliability engineering, including descriptions of FTA and FMEA.

[Oppenheim 92]
A. N. Oppenheim, *Questionnaire Design and Attitude Measurement (second edition)*, Pinter, London, 1992
   A wide-ranging and readable book on questionnaires and surveys, with a focus on finding people's views and analysis of the results.

[Osborn 57]
Alex Osborn, *Applied Imagination*, Charles Scribner and Sons, NY, 1957
   The orginal book on brainstorming.

[Owen 93]
Mal Owen, *SPC and Business Improvement*, IFS, Kempston, 1993
   A readable book on the use of SPC in service industries, including many actual examples of use. Covers the first seven tools, but with a strong focus on Control Charts.

[Page-Jones 80]
Meilir Page-Jones, *The Practical Guide to Structured Systems Design*, Yourdon Press, NY, 1980
A book on software systems design, describing Data Flow diagrams in detail.

[Page-Jones 85]
Meilir Page-Jones, *Practical Project Management*, Dorset House, NY, 1985
A readable book about software project management, including descriptions of Gantt Chart, Activity Network and some Table-based tools.

[Parnes 62]
Sidney J. Parnes and Harold F. Harding (eds), *A Source Book for Creative Problem Solving*, Charles Scribner and Sons, NY, 1962
A collection of methods for idea generation, including brainstorming and others.

[Pease 81]
Allan Pease, *Body Language*, Sheldon Press, London, 1981
A well-illustrated book on the unspoken language of the body. Useful for better understanding when verbal communication is not enough.

[Pease 85]
Allan Pease and Alan Garner, *Talk Language*, Simon and Schuster, London, 1985
Describes the 'inner meaning' of verbal communication which may be useful in Surveys and other interpersonal situations.

[Radice 85]
R. A. Radice, N. K. Roth, A. C. O'Hara Jr. and W. A. Ciarfella, A *Programming Process Architecture*, IBM Systems Journal, Vol. 24, No. 2, 1985, pp. 79-90
Describes an approach to programming, including use of the ETVX paradigm.

[Rawlinson 81]
J. Geoffrey Rawlinson, *Creative Thinking and Brainstorming*, Gower, Farnborough, 1981
A detailed book on brainstorming, including 'tricks of the trade' and several variations such as Attribute Listing and Morphological Analysis.

[Ray 89]
Michael Ray and Rochelle Myers, *Creativity in Business*, Doubleday, NY, 1989

Based on a dramatic university course, this book includes many techniques for promoting creative thinking, from 'destroying judgement' to yoga and zen.

[Raybould 71]
E. B. Raybould and A. L. Minter, *Problem Solving for Management*, Management Publications, London, 1971

A book about problem solving within a method study framework. It discusses many tools and techniques of the work study discipline, including chapters on analytical and creative approaches.

[Robson 93]
Mike Robson, *Problem Solving in Groups,* Gower, Aldershot, 1993

A book focused primarily on group problem solving, with a problem-solving framework and descriptions of several tools, including Brainstorming and several of the first seven tools.

[Rose 57]
T. G. Rose, *Business Charts*, Pitman, London, 1957

Not a recent book, but contains a wealth of detail on various Bar Charts and Line Graphs.

[Roy 90]
Ranjit Roy, *A Primer on the Taguchi Method*, Van Nostrand Reinhold, NY, 1990

Describes Design of Experiments, particularly from the Taguchi viewpoint, in careful detail.

[Scholtes 88]
Peter R. Scholtes, *The Team Handbook*, Joiner, Madison WI, 1988

A practical and readable book on using teams in quality improvement, based on Deming's approach to quality. It contains a chapter covering the first seven tools.

[Shaw 81]
Marvin E. Shaw, *Group Dynamics (third edition)*, McGraw Hill, NY, 1981

A detailed and academic book about how people work together in small groups, including sections on personalities, group goals and problem-solving groups.

[Shingo 86]

Shigeo Shingo, *Zero Quality Control: Source Inspection and the Poka-yoke System*, Productivity Press, Stamford, 1986

A classic book which covers mistake-proofing, from the modern originator.

[Sinha 85]

Madhav Sinha and Walter Willborn, *The Management of Quality Assurance*, Wiley, NY, 1985

An extensive textbook on quality. It has a management bias, but also covers lower level detail, such as the use of statistics, and discusses basic tools.

[Suzaki 87]

Kiyoshi Suzaki, *The New Manufacturing Challenge*, Free Press, NY, 1987

Describes a number of tools and techniques aimed at the manufacturing environment, including Poka-Yoke, Kanban and Process Analysis.

[Vorley 91]

Geoff Vorley, *Quality Assurance Management*, Whitehall Communications, Mainstone, UK, 1991

The book of the UK Institute of Quality Assurance's Quality Management examination, including descriptions of many different tools.

[Wadsworth 86]

Harrison M. Wadsworth Jr., Kenneth S. Stephens and A. Blanton Godfrey, *Modern Methods for Quality Control and Improvement*, Wiley, NY, 1986

A detailed textbook including descriptions and variations of many statistical and graphical tools. It also includes a section describing basic statistics.

Index